LONDON UNDERGROUND STATIONS

David Leboff

IAN ALLAN
Publishing

Contents

Front cover: **Park Royal station showing clearly the 1930s circular booking hall and square tower of this Piccadilly Line station.** *High Madgin*

Back cover top: **The original signalbox at Chesham.** *LUL*

Back cover bottom: **The recently restored booking hall at Kilburn Park showing the pendant lighting and replacement tiles.** *LUL*

Note:
Under each station is a bar giving detailed information. This is as follows:

- ● Line(s) served
- ● 1993 passenger usage
- ● 1993 interchange usage (if applicable)
- ● station type
- ● Listing status (if any)

First published 1994

ISBN 0 7110 2226 7

Designed by Ian Allan Studio

Published by Ian Allan Publishing: an imprint of Ian Allan Ltd, Terminal House, Station Approach, Shepperton, Surrey TW17 8AS; and printed by Ian Allan Printing Ltd, Coombelands House, Coombelands Lane, Addlestone, Surrey KT15 1HY.

Bibliography

N. M. Bailey, [miscellaneous] *Station Design Audit Booklets;* London Underground, 1993

T. C. Barker, *Moving Millions – A Pictorial History of London Transport;* George Allen & Unwin, 1963/1974

T. C. Barker & R. M. Robbins, A *History of London Transport; volumes 1 and 2*

C. Barman, *The Man Who Built London Transport*; David & Charles, 1979

M. Binney & D. Pearce (eds), *Railway Architecture*; Orbis, 1979

J. Blake & J. James, *Northern Wastes*; North London Transport Society, 1993

H. V. Borley, *Chronology of London Railways*; RCHS, 1982

J. G. Bruce, *The Big Tube – A Short History of London's Great Northern & City Railway*; London Transport, 1976

B. Carpenter; *Piccadilly Line Extension – The Diamond Jubilee*; London Transport, 1992

P. Connor, *Underground Official Handbook*; Capital Transport, 1990

P. Connor, *Going Green – The Story of the District Line*; Capital Transport, 1993

D. F. Croome & A. A. Jackson, *Rails Through The Clay*; Capital Transport/London Transport Museum, 1993

Davis & Bayne architects, [miscellaneous] *Station Design Audit Booklets*; London Underground, 1993

J. R. Day, *The Story of London's Underground*; London Transport, 1978

H. Douglas, *The Underground Story*; Robert Hale, 1963

D. F. Edwards & R. Pigram, *The Romance of Metro-Land*; Midas Books, 1983

D. F. Edwards & R. Pigram, *Metro Memories*; Baton Transport, 1983

D. F. Edwards & R. Pigram, *London's Underground Suburbs*; Bloomsbury Books, 1986

H. G. Follenfant, *Underground Railway Construction*; London Transport, 1969

Fry Drew Knight & Creamer architects, [miscellaneous] *Station Design Audit Booklets*; London Underground, 1993

J. & L. Gibbons architects, [miscellaneous] *Station Design Audit Booklets*; London Underground 1993

J. Glover, *London's Underground*; Ian Allan, 1991

F. W. Goudie, *Wembley Park to Stanmore*; Forge Books, 1986

C. Graves, *London Transport at War 1939-1945*; Oldcastle Books, 1989

O. Green, *The London Underground – An Illustrated History*; Ian Allan, 1990

C. M. Harris, *What's in a Name*; Midas Books, 1979

P. P. Holman, *The Amazing Electric Tube – A History of The City & South London Railway*; London Transport Museum, 1990

M. A. C. Horne, *The Bakerloo Line – A Short History*; Nebulous Books, 1990

M. A. C. Horne, *The Central Line – A Short History*; Nebulous Books, 1987

M. A. C. Horne, *The Northern Line – A Short History*; Nebulous Books, 1987

M. A. C. Horne, *The Victoria Line – A Short History*; Nebulous Books, 1988

M. A. C. Horne & R. E. Bayman*, The First Tube – The Story of the Northern Line*; Capital Transport, 1990

H. F. Howson, *London's Underground*; Ian Allan, 1962

A. A. Jackson, *London's Local Railways*; David & Charles, 1978

A. A. Jackson, *London's Metropolitan Railway*; David & Charles, 1986

A. A. Jackson, *Semi-detached London*; Wild Swan, 1991

A. M. S. John architects, [miscellaneous] *Station Design Audit Booklets*; London Underground, 1993

C. Klapper, *London's Lost Railways*; Routledge & Kegan Paul, 1976

T. S. Lascelles, *The City & South London Railway;* Oakwood Press, 1987

C. F. Lee, *The Bakerloo Line*; London Transport, 1973

C. F. Lee, *The Central Line*; London Transport, 1974

C. F. Lee, *The District Line*; London Transport, 1973

C. F. Lee, *The East London Line & the Thames Tunnel*; London Transport, 1976

C. F. Lee, *The Bakerloo Line*; London Transport, 1973

C. F. Lee, *The Metropolitan Line*; London Transport, 1973

C. F. Lee, *The Metropolitan District Railway*; Oakwood, 1988

C. F. Lee, *The Northern Line*; London Transport, 1973

C. F. Lee, *The Piccadilly Line*; London Transport, 1973

Keith F. Leicester architects, [miscellaneous] *Station Design Audit Booklets*; London Underground, 1993

L. Menear, *London's Underground Stations*; Baton Transport, 1985

Perry architects, *Changing Stations: A Review of Recent London Underground Station Design*; London Underground Architectural Services, 1993

D. Rose, *The London Underground: A Diagrammatic History*; Douglas Rose, 1990

R. Symes & D. Cole, *Railway Architecture of Greater London*; Osprey, 1973

S. Taylor, *A Journey Through Time*; Laurence King, 1992

R. Trench & E. Hillman, *London Under London*; John Murray, 1993

C. F. A. Wilmot, *The Railway in Finchley*; Finchley Public Libraries Committee, 1962

Introduction

There have been many books written over the years about the London Underground network and the railway companies from which it developed. They have covered a wide variety of topics, from rolling stock to signalling and from maps to engineering. Yet very few refer to the system's stations other than as historical reference points and it was with this in mind that I undertook to prepare this handbook.

Why do we need a book about Underground stations, I hear you ask? Surely they simply act as a means of access to the trains? Although this is largely true, they include some of the best examples of municipal architecture in London, especially in the interwar years. Many reflect not only the continual evolution of the railways to which they belong but also the history of the local communities they serve. This is particularly true of suburban areas where the railway was the life-line to the city proper. The wide variety of designs and styles, dating from the 1860s through to the 1990s, reflect the long (and sometimes glorious!) history of the world's oldest metro system and compare favourably with the often monotonous buildings found elsewhere.

Before outlining the purpose behind the book, perhaps I can say what it is not. It is not, for instance, a history of the Underground or London Transport – there are several well-known volumes which act as authorities on these subjects. Nor is it a study of certain eminent architects, such as Charles Holden and Frank Sherrin, whose work is extensively represented around the city, although much reference will be made to these men.

Instead this publication aims to provide a simple yet comprehensive guide to all of the stations owned (as against served) by London Underground, with the details including those relating to layout, design, history and other noteworthy features. Disused and non-Underground owned stations have not been included, although some information on these buildings is included at the end of the book.

A book of this type can never be absolutely comprehensive or up-to-date, largely owing to restrictions on space and the continuing development of the system. In addition, it is often difficult to ascertain the true history of a particular building, especially when different sources of information conflict. Nevertheless, I hope the book will prove useful to railway enthusiasts and casual travellers alike. If the interest of any readers is excited into looking around them as they use the system, then it will have served its purpose.

1 November 1993   *David Leboff*, Hendon

Abbreviations

BS&WR	Baker Street & Waterloo Railway
C&SLR	City & South London Railway
CCE&HR	Charing Cross, Edgware & Hampstead Railway
CLR	Central London Railway
DR	District Railway
ECR	Eastern Counties Railway
GCR	Great Central Railway
GER	Great Eastern Railway
GN&CR	Great Northern & City Railway
GNP&BR	Great Northern, Piccadilly & Brompton Railway
GNR	Great Northern Railway
GWR	Great Western Railway
H&CR	Hammersmith & City Railway
L&BR	London & Birmingham Railway
L&CDR	London, Chatham & Dover Railway
LNER	London & North Eastern Railway
LNWR	London & North Western Railway
L&SR	London & Southampton Railway
LSWR	London & South Western Railway
LB&SCR	London Brighton & South Coast Railway
LER	London Electric Railways
LMS	London Midland & Scottish Railway
LPTB	London Passenger Transport Board
LT&SR	London Tilbury & Southend Railway
LTB	London Transport Board
LTE	London Transport Executive
M&SWJR	Metropolitan & St John's Wood Railway
MDR	Metropolitan District Railway
MR	Metropolitan Railway
NSE	Network SouthEast
SER	South Eastern Railway
UERL	Underground Electric Railways Co of London Ltd
UTS	Underground Ticketing System
W&CR	Waterloo & City Railway
WLR	West London Railway

Acton Town

Dist/Picc   3.8m   2.5m   Surface

Layout: Street level ticket hall leading down to two island platforms via two over-bridges and four staircases.

History: Opened as 'Mill Hill Park' on 1 July 1879 on the DR extension from Turnham Green to Ealing Broadway. The station was rebuilt around 1910 to allow for the segregation of Ealing Broadway and Hounslow services, including the provision of island platforms to serve three tracks. Its name changed to 'Acton Town' at this time (from 1 March 1910). Further reconstruction took place for the inauguration of Piccadilly Line services beyond Hammersmith, which commenced on 4 July 1932, although this work was not completed until the following year. A short platform to serve District Line's shuttle trains to South Acton was in use until this service was stopped on 28 February 1959. The platform remains intact, partially hidden behind advertising hoardings, opposite platform 4.

Design: Nothing remains of the 1879 and 1910 vintage buildings which originally stood on this site. The existing structure is typical of the style developed by Charles Holden in the early 1930s and is similar to several other stations, such as Northfields and Oakwood, built for the Piccadilly Line extensions. The broad ticket hall has been constricted by the installation of an intrusive ticket office but otherwise retains its spacious feel. Original bronze-framed light fittings survive around the perimeter walls. It is characterised by a complex network of overbridges and staircases leading to the two island platforms. Platform areas lack the elegance of those designed later in the decade and most of the concrete finishes are now showing their age. Nevertheless, they display the simple, functional style that typifies work of this vintage.

History: Opened on 18 November 1876 on the MR extension from Liverpool Street. The station served as the terminus for less than six years, when the line was extended further to Tower of London station (now the site of Tower Hill station). Alterations to the track layout were carried out around 1909, while reconstruction of the station was completed around 1926.

Design: Designed by the MR's chief architect, Charles Walter Clark, the existing building is similar to several other stations built for the line in the mid-1920s, such as Edgware Road and Willesden Green. The white terracotta tiling, with embossed station name lettering, remains much as it was when first built, although the ticket hall was extensively modified in the 1980s for the installation of a new ticket office. It has subsequently been refinished in a most attractive manner, making use of textured tiling similar in style to the original design. A wide overbridge concourse – installed during the 1926 reconstruction – is linked to both ticket hall and platforms by staircases with open balustrades, although the view is spoilt by a plethora of advertising panels and information displays. The rear elevation of the main building retains the green glass-block tiles that once faced the ticket hall interior. At platform level, the station is characterised by a splendid train shed and the remains of the original brick retaining walls, which have recently been restored. Bland low level canopies cover the northern end of the platforms, replacing the more decorative versions which existed originally. The rafting-over of the tracks at the St Botolph Street end has also substantially diminished the platforms' appearance.

Features: The massive iron brackets holding up the main roof are quite distinctive and indicate how many of the original MR and DR stations would have looked when first constructed. Platform number signs, dating from the 1926 reconstruction, are still to be found on both sets of platforms.

Aldgate

Circ/Met   3.8m   Sub-Surface   Grade II (prop.)

Layout: Street level ticket hall leading down to two island platforms via an over-bridge and four staircases

Aldgate East

Dist/H&C   7.4m   0.4m   Sub-Surface

Layout: Access from numerous staircases at street level to two sub-surface ticket

Above:
The frontage of Aldgate station.
All uncredited photographs are by courtesy of London Underground Ltd

Below:
A Hammersmith & City train bound for Whitechapel arrives at Aldgate East.
Hugh Madgin

halls, with further staircases down to two single platforms.

History: Opened on 6 October 1884 on the DR extension from Mansion House to New Cross (now known as New Cross Gate). The station was also served from the same date by MR services, when extended from north of Aldgate to New Cross. It was resited several hundred metres to the east on 31 October 1938 to allow for the enlargement of the nearby triangular junction at Aldgate. The station was known as 'Commercial Road' prior to opening.

Design: Reconstruction has taken place several times during the station's history – in the late 1900s, around 1927 and most recently in 1938. The existing entrances are located in the base of non-Underground owned buildings and are fairly nondescript, with the exception of that housing the Whitechapel Library. Staircases, passageways and ticket halls are clad with cream faience wall tiling typical of the late 1930s. The platforms are amongst the longest on the entire system and are faced with small square cream tiles, similar to other stations of the same vintage, such as St John's Wood and King's Cross (Metropolitan). The high nature of the ceiling (a consequence of track lowering during the 1938 reconstruction) and the prominent columns give an atmosphere of spaciousness unique to this station.

Features: The platform walls contain many decorative tiles by Harold Stabler, portraying motifs such as the Palace of Westminster, St Paul's and the London Transport roundel. Extremely rare 1930s silhouette roundels with their original infill lettering intact have survived in good condition above two of the entrance staircases.

Aldwych

Piccadilly 0.3m Tube

Layout: Street level ticket hall leading to a single platform via lifts and passageways.

History: Opened as 'Strand' on 30 November 1907, just under a year after the remainder of the original section of the GNP&BR. It was originally planned that the station would form the southern terminus of the Great Northern & Strand Railway. However, this company merged with the Brompton & Piccadilly Circus Railway in 1901 to create the GNP&BR – later to become the Piccadilly Line – leaving the Holborn-Aldwych section as an historical oddity. Only a restricted shuttle service from Holborn has been run for much of its history, making use of the northbound platform tunnel, although a late night through service for theatre traffic existed until at least October 1908. The station was given its current name on 9 May 1915 to avoid confusion with the Northern Line station at Charing Cross, which changed its name to Strand on the same day. Aldwych was closed between 22 September 1940 and 30 June 1946 for use by Westminster City Council as a public air raid shelter.

Design: The station building was designed by the main architect for the Underground group, Leslie W. Green, and is unusual in that it has two elevations (facing Surrey Street and the Strand) which are not directly connected. Only Camden Town of surviving Green stations also has this distinction. It occupies the site of the Strand Theatre which had stood in this location since 1832. The blood red terracotta tiling is in good condition and retains early lettering on the white tiled bands, although the previously arched windows at first floor level of the Surrey Street facade have been replaced by square versions at some point. In many ways, Aldwych is the best preserved of all Green's stations, especially within the ticket hall. It retains its original floor finish and timber panelled lifts, although the latter will need to be replaced if the station is to remain in passenger service. The original ticket office also still exists despite the installation of the UTS suite (on the site of an old lift shaft), although it has not been operational since 16 October 1922 because of the station's low usage. The lower levels feature cream and dark green banded tiling, although this is incomplete at the platform ends. This platform is notable for being substantially shorter than any other elsewhere on the system.

Features: The word 'Strand' can still be seen embossed on the platform tiling and behind the external canopy, which had been installed by the mid-1920s. Some superb tiled lettering can also be seen on the wall just inside the main entrance, along with a fine 1920s roundel on the headwall.

The southbound platform and tunnel, which had been little utilised since 1912, were officially made surplus to operational requirements on 15 August 1917 and the former is now used by London Underground as a testing area for new equipment and finishes. The lift is the only 1906/07 vintage machine to survive in operational use and contains an inbuilt ticket office – again, a unique feature.

Alperton

Layout: Street level ticket hall leading up to two single platforms via a subway and staircases.

History: Opened as 'Perivale-Alperton' on 28 June 1903 on the DR extension from Ealing Common to South Harrow. The station was renamed Alperton on 7 October 1910 and was completely rebuilt for the transfer of services to the Piccadilly Line, which took place on 4 July 1932, although work was not completed until the following year.

Design: The existing building was designed by Stanley Heaps but incorporated many features distinctive of Charles Holden's stations of the early 1930s. An early example of the concrete-capped, brick box style first used at Sudbury Town, it fails to reach the high standards of many of its contemporaries, partly because of its awkward location next to the bridge carrying the railway. The ticket office has been carefully incorporated into the fabric of the station, unlike at so many other locations. At platform level, the matching concrete canopies are perhaps the most attractive features of the station, being both elegant and functional.

Features: This station was one of only two locations (the other being Greenford) where escalators were installed to take passengers *up* to platform level. The single escalator was originally used in the Dome of Discovery at the Festival of Britain in 1951 and was then relocated to serve Alperton's eastbound platform, starting service on 27 November 1955. It was taken out of operational use on 23 September 1988 (although not officially abandoned until 8 December 1990) and the bricked up access points may be observed at the top and bottom of the adjacent staircase. The timber barrier in the ticket hall features an odd raised section resembling a

hangman's scaffold, which originally housed a gate giving access to the escalator.

Amersham

Layout: Street level ticket hall leading to one single and one island platform linked by a footbridge.

History: Opened on 1 September 1892 on the MR extension from Chalfont Road (now Chalfont & Latimer) to Aylesbury. The station was renamed 'Amersham & Chesham Bois' between 12 March 1922 and around 1934, when the original title was restored. It became the terminus of the line for regular Underground services on 11 September 1961 when the stations north of this point were transferred to British Railways' control.

Design: The exterior consists of an uninteresting, dark brick building. Its only notable feature is a prominent timber canopy which sits uncomfortably above the entrance. The small ticket hall was refurbished during the installation of UTS equipment and retains few of its original features. In contrast, the main platform buildings and canopies survive largely unchanged, although they are spoilt by the high degree of visual clutter. The canopies are supported by the standard decorative brackets used by the MR and are notable for the distinctive gable form above the serrated valance; the extensive use of glazing creating a bright and attractive environment beneath. An original latticed footbridge also survives, although a second bridge, built to provide direct access across the railway tracks, was replaced as recently as 1989.

Features: Amersham is located in the Chiltern hills and is the highest station on the Underground network (at 490ft/ 149.35m above mean sea level).

Angel

Layout: Street level ticket hall leading down to two single platforms via two flights of escalators and a mid-level concourse.

History: Opened on 17 November 1901 on the C&SLR extension from Moorgate. The station acted as the terminus until the line was extended further (to Euston) in May 1907. It was closed temporarily between 9 August 1922 and 20 April 1924 to allow for the enlargement of the running tunnels to match the diameter found on most other tube lines and for general station modernisation, including the replacement of the original lifts.

With the advent of new office developments in the mid-1980s, passenger usage increased dramatically and the narrow island platform presented considerable safety difficulties. Work commenced in 1989 to rebuild the entire station, the scheme allowing for the provision of a completely new northbound platform, two banks of escalators (the upper set being the longest in western Europe) and a new ticket hall built into an office development in Islington High Street. The new ticket hall and northbound platform were opened on 10 August 1992, although teething problems with the escalators led to the station not being fully operational until 17 September. The rebuilt southbound platform was reopened on 19 October 1992, with all finishes completed by early 1993.

Design: The original C&SLR building designed by Sidney Smith still exists on City Road at its junction with Torrens Street, although it is almost unrecognisable under large expanses of corrugated metal sheeting, installed following lift replacement and UTS installation in the mid-1980s. The red brick side elevation dates from 1901 but the main facade was reclad with cream terracotta in the 1920s during the station's temporary closure and small sections of this may still be observed.

The new ticket hall is located in the base of a large office development facing Islington High Street and its wide concourse is in stark contrast to the cramped hall it replaces. Cream wall panels, two-tone brown tiling and granite flooring feature throughout the station, along with fully integrated passenger security, seating and vending facilities. The southbound platform is noticeably wider than its counterpart, for it occupies the space previously occupied by the northbound tracks prior to reconstruction.

Archway

Northerrn 5.0m Tube

Layout: Street level ticket hall leading down to two single platforms via escalators and low level concourses, passageways and staircases.

History: Opened as 'Highgate' on 22 June 1907 as the terminus of the north-eastern branch of the CCE&HR. The station was known as 'Archway Tavern' at an early stage of planning. An additional entrance from Highgate Hill was opened in 1912. Access to the platforms was completely altered through the installation of escalators, which were brought into service on 15 June 1931. The station acted as a terminus until the line was extended to East Finchley on 3 July 1939. In order to differentiate it from the new Highgate station being built on the extension, the station's name changed first to 'Archway (Highgate)' on 11 June 1939 and then to 'Highgate (Archway)' on 19 January 1941. The station finally gained its current title in December 1947. A new ticket hall was opened in October 1977 within the base of a large tower block on the site of the earlier entrance buildings.

Design: The original station building had a typical Green facade, similar in scale and style to the one which survives at Goodge Street. The Highgate Hill entrance was rebuilt around 1930 in 'Holdenesque' style and featured a tall, heavily glazed frontage leading on to a new ticket hall. Both were demolished to be replaced by drab and undistinguished facades as part of the redevelopment. Finishes range from standard UTS in the ticket hall, through 1930s vitreous enamel tiles in the lower concourse to a tastefully styled green and white tile scheme installed in the late 1970s. Some original 1907 tiling also survives in the passageway from the spiral staircase to the northbound platform.

Features: Few of the station's original features are in public areas. However, the lift shafts and their access passageways remain and can be glimpsed through grilles at the base of the spiral staircase.

Above:
The large brick drum of Holden's Arnos Grove station looms over Bowes Road.
Hugh Madgin

Below:
The original 1863-vintage platforms of the Metropolitan station at Baker Street.
Hugh Madgin

Arnos Grove

Piccadilly 2.7m Surface Grade II

Layout: Street level ticket hall leading down to two island platforms via an overbridge and four staircases.

History: Opened on 19 September 1932 on the Piccadilly Line extension from Finsbury Park to Cockfosters. The station acted as a temporary terminus until 13 March 1933, when the line to Enfield West (now Oakwood) was opened.

Design: The building was designed by Charles Holden and is widely regarded as an outstanding example of 1930s railway architecture. Reputedly modelled on Erik Asplund's public library building in Stockholm, it consists of a large brick drum above a single-storey block at ground level. The ticket hall features a high ceiling supported by a concrete column, around which the original passimeter is still located. The UTS ticket office has been tastefully incorporated into the wall finishes without spoiling the overall design. Other areas of the station are less interesting, although the rectilinear concrete platform canopies and five wooden seating/signing units have survived in good condition.

Features: The passimeter, which had remained in a derelict state since its closure in 1988, was refurbished in January 1990 and is now used as a miniature museum and art gallery. A tubular bronzed barrier line was installed at around the same time.

Arsenal

Piccadilly 1.6m Tube

Layout: Street level ticket hall leading down to two single platforms via ramped passageways.

History: Opened as 'Gillespie Road' on 15 December 1906 on the GNP&BR. The station was renamed 'Arsenal (Highbury Hill)' on 31 October 1932 (to coincide with the arrival of the football club of the same name at the nearby Highbury stadium); the surface building being rebuilt and enlarged by February 1934. The 'Highbury Hill' suffix was lost over time.

Design: The original surface building was designed by Leslie Green and was similar in scale and style to the Strand frontage of Aldwych station. In contrast, the existing building consists of a plain, white painted facade dominated by a huge mosaic roundel at high level – a most unlikely scene to find in this essentially residential road. This feature was completely renewed to its original specification in early 1993, along with the installation of floodlighting and grey faience tiles at low level. The ticket hall was largely retiled in 1988 for the installation of UTS equipment, while the long access passageways and platforms remain largely as they were when first built and feature a mauve, white and green tiling scheme throughout. The main corridor is divided by an ugly set of railings which segregates the general public from football supporters on match days.

Features: The platform walls still retain the original 'Gillespie Road' tiled lettering, although all but one of these is currently obscured behind advertising. Other directional signing, embossed on the tiling on both sides of the platforms, may also be seen.

Baker Street

Bak/Circ/H&C/Jub/Met 19.6m 29.1m

Misc Grade II

Layout: Staircase access from two subsurface ticket halls down to two island surface platforms (Metropolitan) and two single sub-surface platforms (Circle and Hammersmith & City). Also, an adjacent street level ticket hall leading down to four single tube platforms via two banks of escalators, an intermediate level concourse and numerous low level passageways.

Listing pertains primarily to Circle Line platforms and ticket hall.

History: The station's current Circle Line platforms were opened on 10 January 1863 to serve the original section of the MR, between Farringdon Street and Paddington (Bishop's Road). Italianate entrance pavilions, which originally occupied the eastern corners of the adjacent road junction, were replaced around 1911 by a single sub-surface ticket hall and surface building facing on the north side of Marylebone Road, along with metal footbridges at each end of the platforms. At around the same time, a small sub-surface ticket hall was built, along with an iron footbridge, over the top of the western end of the Circle Line platforms, with access gained from a small entrance on the northeastern corner of the enlarged road junction. A sub-surface ticket hall was provided on the south side of Marylebone Road in April 1923 in anticipation of increased traffic for the British Empire Exhibition at Wembley (this hall was subsequently modernised as part of a major road widening scheme around 1967). A large block of flats (known as Chiltern Court) was constructed over, and on either side of, the 1911 building between 1927 and 1930.

Services on the single line spur to Swiss Cottage (adjacent to the current Jubilee Line station), opened by the M&SJWR, commenced on 13 April 1868, with through trains to Moorgate Street using a junction to the east of the main station. A small ticket hall and iron footbridge, providing interchange between the two services, was built on the north side of Marylebone Road in 1869, with a new building constructed next to Madame Tussaud's in 1888. Platform level interchange between the two stations was not opened until 10 years later. The branch line station (known initially as 'Baker Street East') originally had two side platforms beneath an overall roof. The latter was replaced in the early 1890s when the track layout was substantially altered to create an additional island platform, with a standard umbrella canopy over each. These facilities were in service from 14 November 1892, although they failed to solve the serious congestion and interchange problems that existed previously. The track and platform layouts were redesigned again prior to World War 1 and by 1925 they had, with minor alterations, attained the arrangement that exists today. Two small passageways linking the enlarged platforms 1 and 2 (the westernmost main line platforms) with the eastbound Circle Line platform were first used on 23 September 1929. Extensive staff accommodation facilities were provided in the space between platforms 2 and 5 around 1977.

Services on the BS&WR commenced on 10 March 1906, with the station acting as a terminus until 27 March when the line was extended to Great Central (now Marylebone). A footbridge, connecting the ticket hall with the northern end of M&SJWR platforms, was constructed soon after, funded by the BS&WR. A branch of the original section of the Bakerloo Line through new tube tunnels to Finchley Road opened on 20 November 1939, necessitating the building of an additional southbound platform. Cross-platform interchange at low level between the two southbound tracks was not possible until December 1940. The Stanmore branch was subsequently taken over by the Jubilee Line when the latter was opened on 1 May 1979, with northbound services using a new platform, thereby allowing cross-platform interchange between the lines in both directions. Escalators from the Bakerloo Line platform to the new concourse under the Metropolitan Line platforms and from there up to street level were brought into service on 15 October 1914 and 24 November 1940 respectively.

Design: The nine-storey block containing the station entrances and Chiltern Court dominates the whole area to the north-east of the adjacent road junction. Faced with Portland stone, it features massive arched recesses around its perimeter to first floor level, now dominated by shop units and a cinema. The three arched bays in the centre of the Marylebone Road elevation formed the original entrance to C. W. Clark's 1911 combined ticket hall and therefore pre-date the rest of the building by almost 20 years. The retaining wall to the cab ramp also dates from this time and is constructed in the same style, as is the small entrance on the corner of the road junction, which now acts as a subway entrance. Two cantilevered canopies above the outer bays, which housed the ticket hall access staircases, were replaced on 17 March 1924 by a colonnaded porch which extended out across the full extent of the cab ramp. Unfortunately, this was demolished following bomb damage during World War 2.

The main ticket hall was modernised in the mid-1980s and reflects well its MR history. Pastel shades are prominent and many of the original features are retained, although the relatively low level of illumination diminishes their effectiveness. This area has been modified several times, most extensively around 1930 for the installation of the broad flight of steps leading down to the eastbound Circle Line platform via an ornate metal portal. A memorial to MR workers killed during World War 1 is located on the right-hand wall at the base of this staircase. One of the two 1911 staircase entrances to the ticket hall has been taken over by the new ticket office and now contains the excess fare window, with a pastiche embossed sign above declaring 'Restored 1987'.

The Circle Line platforms were also restored in the early 1980s through the removal of timber panelling and paintwork which had been in place since the late 1920s. They retain many of the features of the original 1863 station, with the brick overall ceiling and recesses dating from this time, although the shafts which originally allowed natural daylight through are now lit artificially and the dull yellow lighting creates an atmosphere unique to this station. Glazing which originally existed within the recesses, along with those at Great Portland Street and Euston Square, was removed in the late 1860s in order to address the severe ventilation problems faced by this section of line during the days of steam operation. The original timber floor surfaces were replaced as a safety measure by an artificial stone finish around 1906. Similar work was also carried out at all stations between Euston Square and Swiss Cottage (Metropolitan).

The current Metropolitan Line platforms feature cream faience-clad columns, umbrella canopies and timber-lined staircases from the main ticket hall, all dating from the 1911-13 reconstruction. These areas have subsequently been marred by the installation of a slatted false ceiling beneath the canopies, although they have been enhanced in recent years by train information screens and a tiled floor finish throughout. A single fluted lamp standard, probably dating from the mid-1920s, survives at the northern end of platforms 3 & 4. Nearby, a timber-lined footbridge and associated staircases, which originally linked these platforms with the old Bakerloo Line ticket hall, survive in good condition and feature a fine 1920s directional sign.

The surface level ticket hall was refurbished for the opening of the Jubilee Line in 1979 and it, along with the middle concourse and Bakerloo Line platforms, is clad in a two-tone tiling scheme featuring Sherlock Holmes silhouettes of various sizes as a recurring theme. The low level concourses, passageways and Jubilee Line platforms have been clad with orangy-red wall tiling and white panelled ceilings. Yellow bands over the tracks have been provided to indicate the exits from each platform, while speckled terrazzo floor tiles have been installed throughout. These deep-level areas represent some of the most modern and attractive on the network.

Features: Shallow recessed bays and overbridge openings at the western end of each Circle Line platform indicate the entrances from the original 1863 pavilions located at street level.

The original red terracotta Bakerloo Line ticket hall building, designed by Leslie Green and redundant from 1940, was located in Baker Street itself, directly to the north of the main Chiltern Court complex. It was demolished as recently as 1964. The lifts, which gave access to low level until the advent of escalators, were not removed immediately and were reactivated briefly in 1945 during the VE-Day celebrations.

A plaque within the road side of the taxi ramp retaining wall commemorates the commencement of the building's major reconstruction.

The original 1911 building allowed for the inclusion of a luggage lift between street, ticket hall and platform levels. The metal shutters containing this equipment may still be observed, most noticeably on the main elevation where raised lettering in the bay to the right of the entrance staircase identifies the location.

As well as Chiltern Court, two other significant buildings occupy part of the block bounded by Baker Street, Marylebone Road and Allsop Place. The more notable is Selbie House facing on to Allsop Place. Designed by Clark as the headquarters of the MR, it is still a major office complex used by London Underground. It was opened in January 1914 and is faced with white terracotta in typical Clark fashion, which incorporates railway motifs such as the entwined MR lettering on either side of each entrance porch. The other building is Chalfont Court at the northern apex of the site. Although having no direct connection to the railway, it could not be built until the quadrupling of the tracks north of the station had been completed in 1913. Although not similar to Chiltern Court in terms of design, Clark was once again the architect in charge.

Above:
An Edgware-bound working of 1972 Stock arrives at Balham station. *Hugh Madgin*

Below:
The Holden exterior to Balham station.

Balham

Northern 6.9m Tube Grade II

Layout: Sub-surface ticket hall leading down to two single platforms via escalators and a low level concourse.

History: Opened on 6 December 1926 on the Northern Line extension from Clapham Common to Morden, which had commenced in operation three months earlier. Severe damage was caused on 14 October 1940 when a bomb scored a direct hit on the road junction, causing extensive damage to the platforms and killing 64 people sheltering from the air raid.

Design: The two surface buildings, located on corner sites on opposite sides of Balham High Road, are typical of the style devised by Charles Holden for the stations on the Northern Line extension. They are faced with Portland stone and incorporate substantial areas of glazing, which feature large roundels as part of their design. A large cast iron chandelier is fitted within each of the access buildings. The station's walls are clad with original white tiles with green trim throughout, except on the ticket office frontage which has been treated most unsympathetically. A black glazed 'help point' occupies a prominent position in the ticket hall, installed around 1987 as part of a major package of passenger security measures for this part of the Northern Line. The platforms remain much as they were when they first opened, although the areas of wall without tiling at their northern end are a reminder of the damage caused by the wartime bomb blast.

Bank

Cent/North 14.3m 13.4m Grade I

Layout: Two sub-surface ticket halls leading down to four single platforms via escalators (to Central Line), lifts (to Northern Line) and numerous low level passageways. Also, a moving walkway link to British Rail's Waterloo & City Line and escalators to Monument station and the terminus of the Docklands Light Railway.

Listing pertains to Threadneedle Street/ Princes Street entrance only.

History: The W&CR opened a station known as 'City' on 8 August 1898, although this was sometimes referred to as 'Mansion House'. The main Underground station was opened as 'Bank' on 25 February 1900 on the C&SLR extension to Moorgate. It became the terminus for the CLR when services commenced on 30 July of the same year. Low level interchange was possible from this time, although a subway link between the two ticket halls was not opened until 3 May 1911. Northern Line areas were closed between 29 November 1923 and 30 November 1924 to allow for the enlargement of the running tunnels. The Central Line ticket hall was reconstructed around this time, resulting in the provision of several new entrances at street level and new escalators, brought into service on 7 May 1924, with all works being completed on 5 May 1925. The entrance from Cornhill Exchange is particularly notable, retaining as it does original railings and lamps on plinths at the head of the staircase. Installation of flood alleviation measures, because of the danger of bomb damage to the nearby tunnels under the Thames, led to the Northern Line platforms being closed again between 7 September 1939 and 18 May 1940. The Central Line areas suffered severe damage on 11 January 1941 when a bomb destroyed the roadway and the blast carried down the escalator shaft, killing a total of 56 people, with a further 69 seriously injured. The escalator link to Monument was introduced on 18 September 1933, while the Waterloo & City Line station was renamed 'Bank' on 26 October 1940. The 'Travelator' link between the Waterloo & City platforms and the main Underground ticket hall was opened on 27 September 1960.

Design: Northern Line areas retain the green and white vitreous tiling installed in the 1920s, while some of the white C&SLR tiling is still evident at the base of the platforms' trackside walls and on the vaulted soffits. The Central Line platforms are still faced with the original CLR white tiling, although this is now in very poor condition and is currently painted over. All of the original CLR and Northern Line finishes are to be replaced as a part of a major station upgrading scheme which will integrate Monument and related station areas with a common design theme, utilising off-white faience tiling and brown flooring throughout. Some of this work has already been

Above:
The entrance to Bank station at the corner of Princes and Threadneedle Streets is incorporated into the structure of the Bank of England. *Hugh Madgin*

implemented at low level, especially in connection with the DLR extension, but it is not likely to be completed before 1998.

Features: The entrance built within the Bank of England building at the end of Threadneedle Street is the only Grade I listed feature on the Underground system. Distinctive roundel-cum-name signs above the entrance staircases are also unique to this station and date from the mid-1920s. The original C&SLR ticket hall occupies the crypt of St Mary Woolnoth church, with access originally by means of two stations in the forecourt. Bank was the only station on the original section of the CLR which was not accessed by means of a street level building.

Barbican

Circ/H&C/Met 8.1m Sub-Surface

Layout: Sub-surface level ticket hall leading down to one island and two single platforms via staircases. Two of the four sets of tracks are used for British Rail Thameslink services.

History: Opened as 'Aldersgate Street' on 23 December 1865 on the eastern extension of the MR from Farringdon Street to Moorgate Street. The GNR commenced use of the set of tracks to the south of the Metropolitan from 1 March 1866. The station's title was changed to 'Aldersgate' on 1 November 1910 and later to 'Aldersgate & Barbican' in 1923. Its current name was adopted on 1 December 1968.

Design: The original station building was a single-storey, light-coloured brick structure which was rather plain compared with many of the stations constructed at around that time. It was severely damaged during World War 2 and finally demolished around 1955, along with the standard overall roof which extended over the platforms and tracks. During the early 1960s, the entrance and a new sub-surface ticket hall were incorporated into an office development, which was subsequently rebuilt around 1990. At platform level, the station has kept its high brick retaining walls, which have been cleaned in recent years. Plain metal canopies, installed in the 1960s, have adversely affected the atmosphere of the station, which can be contrasted with adjacent Farringdon. However, the decorative brackets which supported the original roof still exist at high level above the two side canopies.

Barkingside

Central 0.5m Surface Grade II

Layout: Street level ticket hall leading to two single platforms linked by a footbridge.

History: Opened on 1 May 1903 by the GER on its branch line between Woodford and Ilford. The station was temporarily closed between 22 May 1916 and 30 June 1919. The line was later transferred to London Transport ownership and incorporated into the new Central Line extension on 31 May 1948.

Design: This station is without question the most complete and attractive example of all those taken over from the LNER by the Central Line in the late 1940s. The main building has a magnificent brick frontage which stretches for over 50m and it is perhaps unfortunate that the main elevation faces merely on to a small car park. Its design is particularly clever, for the central portion is both forward of the main building line and significantly higher than the adjacent blocks. The result is a stepped effect, culminating with a small bell tower and cupola – the only such feature on an Underground station. Large arched windows on either side of the entrance are seen to their best effect from within the virtually unspoiled ticket hall. Although almost half of the rectangular space has been utilised for a UTS ticket office, the height and splendour of the timber-framed pitched roof ceiling can still be appreciated. The majority of the original platform features remain intact, including the standard decorated metalwork and timber elements to the canopies, and a fine open latticed footbridge towards the western end. Early cantilevered wooden seats also survive on bays within the brick retaining walls.

Barons Court

Dist/Picc 6.0m 1.1m Surface Grade II

Layout: Street level ticket hall leading down to two island platforms via staircases.

Above:
The main frontage of Barkingside station, surmounted by the unique cupola.
Hugh Madgin

Below:
The Metropolitan Railway station building at Bayswater.

History: Opened on 9 October 1905 to serve District Railway trains, although the track had been in operational use in 1874. GNP&BR services commenced on 15 December 1906.

Design: The station building is similar in style to the main frontage of Earl's Court. Both were designed by the District Railway's chief architect, Harry Ford, in conjunction with Leslie Green. It is amongst the most attractive on the system, clad with light brown terracotta and featuring arched windows above shop units, embossed name lettering and decorative balustrading at high level. The ticket hall has been modified to incorporate the UTS ticket office but has managed to retain much of the original green glazed tiling, which extends right up to the high ceiling. A relatively new mottled tiled floor surface fits in well with the older finishes. The attractive, canopied platforms are typical of their age and have changed little since their construction, although lengthened and partially rebuilt in the early 1930s. Three timber benches on each platform incorporate the station's name on a blue vitreous panel and are unique to this location.

Features: Many of the station's early features still exist, such as the outrigger lamps and bronze, illuminated poster display panels on the main building's exterior. Egress from the station was originally via exits at the extreme ends of each facade and the arched openings are still visible.

From its opening, the GNP&BR used both sides of the current eastbound platform while the District Railway utilised the westbound. This arrangement was altered prior to the Piccadilly Line being extended westwards on 4 July 1932 with the subsequent creation of cross-platform interchange.

Bayswater

Circ/Dist 5.8m Sub-Surface

Layout: Street level ticket hall leading down to two single platforms via an over-bridge and staircases.

History: Opened as 'Bayswater' on 1 October 1868 on the MR extension from west of Edgware Road to Brompton (Gloucester Road). The station was renamed 'Bayswater (Queen's Road) & Westbourne Grove' in

1923, although the latter part of its title was dropped ten years later. District Line trains first served the station on 1 November 1926 and its name changed again to 'Bayswater (Queensway)' on 1 October 1946, with the suffix being lost over time.

Design: Designed by Sir John Fowler, engineer and architect for the early MR stations, this two-storey, light-coloured brick building is one of the very few of its vintage to remain largely intact, although the loss of high level decorative details by the 1950s and the incorporation of bland shop fronts – especially since electrification of the railway in 1905 – have diminished its appearance. The canopy which once extended across much of the elevation has been modified on several occasions, most recently in 1922 in conjunction with the installation of a cream-coloured terracotta surround to the entrance portal and an extensive modernisation of ticket hall finishes in typical C W Clark fashion. Internally, the hall was enlarged for UTS installation in the mid-1980s through usage of the original Buffet/Tea Room, and none of the earlier decor now survives. An original 1868 iron footbridge remains, from which can be viewed a section of the original overall roof canopy, the majority of which was obscured from the early 1920s by a metal girdered bridge deck. Staircases down to the platform were clad with distinctive green crystal tiling but this has recently been replaced by a bland mauve substitute of little architectural merit. Although the platforms retain their light brown brick walls with deep recesses, these were covered with 1922-vintage metal-framed timber panels until their removal under a modernisation scheme around 1984.

Features: The remainder of the elliptical overall roof survives (albeit in poor condition) above the metal deck. It has been used since December 1925 as a garage storage area. This fascinating relic may be observed from Poplar Place, with the reason for its retention above the deck remaining a mystery.

Becontree

District 1.8m Surface

Layout: Street level ticket hall leading down to two single platforms via staircases.

History: Opened on 18 July 1932 by the LMS to replace the nearby Gale Street Halt, which had been operational since 28 June 1926. The new station was constructed to allow for additional tracks in connection with the introduction of electrification to the terminus at Upminster. District Line trains to Barking first served the station on 12 September 1932.

Design: This small red brick building is almost identical to its sister station at Dagenham East and has remained largely as built despite the addition of unsightly advertising hoardings. The ticket hall has the same UTS tiling, concrete paving and unattractive lighting scheme which have been installed at most stations at this end of the District Line. Neither platform displays any features of particular note.

Features: Derelict remains of the westbound LMS platform (closed around 1960) may still be observed. The equivalent eastbound platform once shared an island platform with the District Line but this area has now been cordoned off.

Belsize Park

Northern 4.0m Tube Grade II (prop.)

Layout: Street level ticket hall leading down to two single platforms via lifts, low level passageways and staircases.

History: Opened on 22 June 1907 on the original section of the CCE&HR.

Design: The surface building is typical of Leslie Green's designs for the early tube stations, with its wide, ox blood faience facade and four arched windows, although the small forecourt area, surrounded by stone column-supported railings, is a particularly unusual feature. Largely untouched until the late 1980s, a joint lift replacement/UTS installation project resulted in completely new finishes being provided in the ticket hall, to a distinctly modern grey and white tiled design. Low level passageways and platforms retain most of their original dark red and cream tile scheme, although their appearance has been altered by the installation of additional tiling on the soffits. Five of the original six tiled station names on the platforms remain exposed

and in good condition. The lift replacement project also resulted in the provision of floor tiling at the base of the lifts in place of the asphalt found elsewhere and vitreous enamel covers over cable ducts beneath the overbridges on the southbound platform.

Features: Belsize Park is one of seven stations on the Northern Line (the others being Camden Town, Clapham Common, Clapham North, Clapham South, Goodge Street and Stockwell), which had air raid shelters constructed adjacently at deep level during the early years of World War 2. It was intended that these should be incorporated within an 'Express Tube' line which would cross London from north to south, but this plan was never implemented.

Bethnal Green

Central 7.6m Tube

Layout: Sub-surface ticket hall leading down to two single platform via escalators and a low level concourse.

History: Opened on 4 December 1946 on the Central Line extension from Liverpool Street to Stratford, although construction work had been largely completed on the outbreak of war in September 1939. While being utilised as an air raid shelter by the local council, this station was the site of one of the worst civilian tragedies of World War 2 when 173 people were killed on 3 March 1943. A plaque commemorating the incident is sited on the headwall above the Roman Road entrance staircase and was unveiled in 1992.

Design: Access to the station is by means of entrances on three of the four corners of the surface road junction, each marked by a silhouette roundel and bronze railings, with some retaining original semi-circular light fittings and inset signage. The walls of the staircases, subway and ticket hall are faced with large, beige faience tiles, with St James's tiling lining the floor. Lower concourse and platform areas of the station are very similar to others designed during the 1930s, such as St John's Wood and Highgate, as one would expect of a station designed by Heaps and Holden. Wall surfaces are clad with small, square, cream tiling with an orange edging, while the ceilings of the escalator shaft and lower concourse are panelled. A distinctive early Central Line extension clock, which makes use of miniature roundels instead of numerals, is to be found on each platform.

Features: As well as being one of only seven stations to have a tiled name frieze on the platforms, Bethnal Green also features distinctive decorative tiles designed by Harold Stabler (showing buildings such as 55 Broadway and St Paul's Cathedral) within the platform wall tiling. In addition, it is noticeable for the existence of the original fluorescent light fittings on the platforms (amongst the first to be installed on the Underground) and the recent blocking-in of the original seat recesses.

Blackfriars

Circ/Dist 10.7m Sub-Surface

Layout: Sub-surface ticket hall leading down to two single platforms via staircases.

History: Opened on 30 May 1870 on the DR extension from Westminster Bridge (later renamed Westminster). The station was originally to be named 'Bridge Street, Blackfriars'. It acted as the terminus until 3 July 1871 when the line was extended further to Mansion House. A covered way to St Paul's station on the LCDR was opened on 13 November 1886. The station was completely rebuilt at street level between 1976 and 1978.

Design: The original surface building was once one of the most stunning and unusual railway structures in London. Four storeys high and featuring two ornate towers, it dominated the street and created an impressive entrance to the station itself. Unfortunately, this magnificent building was largely destroyed by bomb damage in 1940 and only two floors remained until the late 1970s when the site was redeveloped. The ticket hall has been extensively modernised and features orange wall tiling and dark brown quarry tiles on the floor. At platform level, the station has lost its original 50ft elliptical arched roof and finishes now include plain yellowed white wall tiling and a slatted false ceiling.

22

Blackhorse Road

Victoria 3.2m Tube

Layout: Street level ticket hall leading down to two single platforms via escalators and a low level concourse.

History: Opened on 1 September 1968 when services on the initial section of the Victoria Line between Walthamstow Central and Highbury & Islington commenced.

Design: This station features the only significant surface building constructed for the Victoria Line. Designed under the direction of London Transport's Chief Architect, Kenneth Seymour, it is a low, dark brick structure, with a large main entrance canopy and clerestory windows at high level. A cast iron relief of a black horse in a background of blue mosaic is located on the external wall between the two main exits – one of the few examples of significant artwork on the line. The ticket hall is one of the largest on the entire system and is finished with St James's floor tiles, a dark brown mosaic on the walls and a panelled ceiling. There is direct access to the adjacent main line station, although this was not opened until December 1981 when the platforms were relocated from the other side of the bridge to provide improved interchange. The lower levels of the station are typical of all those on the Victoria Line, although the platform ceilings consist of exposed tunnel irons and are only to be found on stations north of Seven Sisters. The platform seating recesses feature a black horse motif on a white and blue background as part of the tiling scheme.

Bond Street

Cent/Jub 21.1m 6.5m Tube

Layout: Sub-surface ticket hall leading down to four single platforms via escalators, low level passageways and staircases.

History: Opened on 24 September 1900 on the original section of the CLR between Shepherd's Bush and Bank, although train services had commenced eight weeks earlier. Although planned as 'Davies Street', the station was never known under this title. It was reconstructed during the mid-1920s, with the creation of a sub-surface ticket hall and the replacement of lifts by escalators, the latter coming into service on 8 June 1926. Further reconstruction work took place throughout most of the 1970s for the introduction of Jubilee Line services, which commenced on 1 May 1979. A metal 'umbrella' was in position over the road junction with Oxford Street between 1972 and 1975 to allow the reconstruction of the ticket hall.

Design: Designed by Harry Measures, the original building was typical of all the early CLR stations, with a small, brown terracotta facade and wide entrance/exit arches. External finishes were modified in the mid-1920s (in 'Morden Extension' style), again around 1930 and most recently in the 1980s, during the construction of the West One shopping development. Additional entrances to the station were also built on the north side of Oxford Street and to the east of Davies Street. The ticket hall is clad throughout with dark brown quarry tiles, while the lower access areas feature beige and yellow wall tiling, a terrazzo floor surface and white ceiling panels. The Jubilee Line platforms are distinguished from adjacent, similar stations by the blue wall tiling which incorporates green, black and turquoise logos above the seat units. The Central Line platforms were amongst the first to be modernised under an extensive 1980s programme and are similar in treatment to those at Oxford Circus and Tottenham Court Road, with use being made of small, cream tiles and prominent line identity elements. The only features which characterise this station are the tile bands over the trackside walls which incorporate the station's name in repeated form as a decorative theme.

Features: The opening of Selfridges in 1909 led to a proposal by the American owner to create a direct link to the station under Oxford Street, with the eventual aim of naming it after the store. Objections by the local authorities and the CLR resulted in the eventual abandonment of this idea.

Borough

Northern 2.6m Tube

Layout: Street level ticket hall leading down to two single platforms via lifts and low level passageways.

History: Opened on 18 December 1890 as part of the original section of the C&SLR between Stockwell and King William Street. The station was known as 'Great Dover Street' prior to opening. It was closed between 17 July 1922 and 22 February 1925 to allow for the enlargement of the tunnels and general modernisation, including lift replacement.

Design: Designed by T. Phillips Figgis, the original surface building was a plain brick structure, featuring the large, glazed dome characteristic of the line south of the river. The structure was extensively modified by Holden in the mid-1920s and was completely rebuilt in the 1970s. The current building is clad with brown and cream tiling to full height and has a distinctive rotunda at high level containing lift control equipment, along with an unusual concrete roundel on a stub, offset tower fairly reminiscent of Chiswick Park. Platforms are finished with white, black and green vitreous wall tiling and concrete paving, installed during the station's temporary closure in the early 1920s.

Boston Manor

Piccadilly 1.3m Surface

Layout: Street level ticket hall leading down to two single platforms via staircases.

History: Opened as 'Boston Road' on 1 May 1883 on the DR branch from Mill Hill Park (now Acton Town) to Hounslow Town. The station was renamed 'Boston Manor' (sometimes with the suffix 'for Brentford & Hanwell') on 11 December 1911. It was rebuilt in conjunction with the introduction of Piccadilly Line services on 13 March 1933, although reconstruction was not completed until 25 March the following year. District Line services ceased on 9 October 1964.

Design: The surface building was designed by Charles Holden but marks a distinct break from the style employed previously on the Piccadilly Line extensions. Although still relying on brick as the main building material, the structure is much smaller in scale compared to the Sudbury box design. It has a tall, thin tower, with internally illuminated glazed panels on one side to act as a beacon to draw people towards the station. Holden is said to have been inspired by the architecture he saw while touring Holland in the early 1930s. The small ticket hall is clad with bricks and St James's floor tiles, while the platforms are of partly wooden construction and date from early DR days. These latter features are perhaps unique as Holden usually rebuilt all areas of stations he was commissioned to redesign. The windows within the western headwalls of the platform buildings are not original and were installed around 1934 to replace the glazed screens which existed previously under the canopies themselves. An original signal cabin survives in good condition at the western end of the eastbound platform, although its previously glazed corners have been panelled.

Bounds Green

Piccadilly 3.9m Tube Local

Layout: Street level ticket hall leading down to two single platforms via escalators.

History: Opened on 19 September 1932 on the Piccadilly Line extension from Finsbury Park to Arnos Grove. However, work was not fully completed until March the following year. A bomb caused serious damage to the westbound platform on 13 October 1940, resulting in the deaths of 19 people and injuries to a further 52.

Design: The form of the surface building is clearly influenced by Holden's Sudbury box style. It was designed in collaboration with another consultant architectural firm, James & Bywaters, and is like no other of this period. The usual concrete-capped brick structure takes an octagonal form, with the glazing occupying the corners rather than being contained within the main facades as found elsewhere. Large silhouette roundels are located on the two street-facing facades as well as on both sides of the tall brick ventilation tower behind the main building. The upper walls are unusual in as much as they are the only examples of where brick finishes in a Holden style ticket hall have been rendered over and painted. Lower concourse and platform areas are similar to others on the Cockfosters extension and feature cream wall tiling with a red trim. One of the original bronze uplighters is still functional in the lower concourse.

Bow Road

Dist/H&C 2.8m Sub-Surface Grade II

Layout: Street level ticket hall leading down to two single platforms via staircases.

History: Opened on 11 June 1902 by the Whitechapel & Bow Railway (nine days after the start of services on the extension from Whitechapel to Upminster), and served by DR trains from that date. The station has been used by Metropolitan (now Hammersmith & City) Line trains since 30 March 1936.

Design: Reputedly designed by C. A. Brereton, engineeer to the W&BR, the surface building consists of a small, one-storey structure constructed from red brick and featuring matching arched doors and windows. Its narrow ticket hall walls are mostly rendered but have brightly painted wooden panels at low level, while the staircases are faced with white, glazed brickwork. The platforms are located in a cutting and partially enclosed. A metal girder roof covers the enclosed area and is supported by massive steel pillars, which along with drab, painted walls result in a rather gloomy atmosphere. The open areas are much more inviting, with glazed canopies and attractive brickwork, further enhanced by an imaginative colour scheme which stresses the more attractive features.

Brent Cross

Northern 1.5m Surface Grade II (prop.)

Layout: Street level ticket hall leading up to one island platform via a subway and staircases.

History: Opened as 'Brent' on 19 November 1923 on the extension of the Hampstead branch of the Northern Line from Golders Green to Hendon Central, and later to Edgware. Passing loops for trains on express services were used at the station between 13 June 1927 and 22 August 1936. Its name changed to 'Brent Cross' on 20 July 1976, following the opening of the nearby shopping centre of the same title.

Design: Designed by Stanley Heaps, with Adams, Holden & Pearson as consultant

Above:
The platform at Blackhorse Road.

Below:
Station entrance at Bow Road.

architects, the station is similar to others built on this extension, which were the first new buildings constructed by LER since its formation in 1910. The surface building is set back a considerable distance from the road and is fronted by a large bus/taxi forecourt and a parade of shops. Its Georgian-style facade, with Portland stone Doric columns and decorative ironwork, is in distinct contrast to those built for earlier sections of the system. Access to the large ticket hall is by means of two sets of wooden entrance doors, one of which cannot be used following the installation of the UTS suite in the 1980s. The black and white chequered tiled floor is a distinctive feature of these Heaps ticket halls, although in this case, the original was replaced in the mid-1980s by a matching design. A valanced canopy covers the southern end of the platform and shelters a small wooden waiting room between the staircases, although this may not be an original feature. Decorative iron railings originally surrounded the staircases but these have now been covered by plain wooden panels, used largely for advertising purposes and as protection from the wind on this exposed platform. The platform structure was rebuilt during 1992, resulting in a reduction in length from nine to seven cars and it being concrete paved.

Features: The original station name was picked out in individual letters on the main facade and the fixing holes for these can still be seen behind the existing frieze plate. The station was originally to be called 'Woodstock' but was changed to 'Brent' not long before the date of opening. On the far side of both sets of tracks may be observed wide gaps which are all that remain of the passing loops last used in 1936.

Brixton

Victoria 16.5m Tube

Layout: Sub-surface ticket hall leading down to two single platforms via escalators and a low level concourse.

History: Opened on 23 July 1971 as the terminus of the extension of the Victoria Line from Victoria.

Design: The station does not have a surface building of its own and is instead incorporated

26

into a shopping and office development. Access to the large ticket hall is by means of a short, orange-tiled staircase contained within a broad, nondescript exterior. UTS gates have recently been installed and the area features a panelled false ceiling, multi-coloured tiled walls and a terrazzo floor. Similar finishes are found in the low level concourse and cross-passageways, with a dark grey wall tile most prominent. The platforms are clad with the usual light grey 'Victoria Line' tiling, although this combines with dark grey tiles on the trackside to indicate advertising sites. Decorative tiling in the seat unit recesses (a key feature of all Victoria Line stations) displays a two-tone orange brick-like pattern on a green background and is designed as a visual pun on the station's name.

Bromley-by-Bow

Dist/H&C/2.4m Surface

Layout: Street level ticket hall leading down to two single platforms via an overbridge and staircases.

History: Opened as 'Bromley' on 31 March 1858 by the LTSR, with the main building being resited on the opposite side of the road on 1 March 1894. DR services commenced on 2 June 1902 and its name changed to 'Bromley-by-Bow' on 18 May 1967. The main entrance was severely damage by a fire on 20 February 1970 and a new permanent building opened in its place on 11 June 1972.

Design: The original street building was an angular, rather ornate structure unlike those designed for the majority of stations on this section of line. Following fire damage, it was replaced by a small, plain one-storey building in complete contrast to its predecessor, with the neat ticket hall being faced with mauve mosaic and terrazzo floor tiling. The overbridge and staircases are contemporary with the ticket hall and are plain in appearance, with corrugated iron ceilings, metal panelled sides and corrugated plastic sheeting in place of glazing. The platform walls have been rebuilt in plain red brickwork and are covered by simple canopies. An asphalt floor surface adds to the general ambience of functionality and indicates a lack of imagination during the station's redesign.

Features: Some of the original ornate canopy support brackets still exist on the eastbound platform. The westbound platform is substantially wider than its counterpart because it occupies almost all of the island platform once shared with LTSR services.

Buckhurst Hill

Central 1.0m Surface

Layout: Street level ticket hall leading down to two single platforms via staircases and a footbridge.

History: Opened as a single-track halt on 22 August 1856 by the ECR (part of the GER from 1862). The station was resited slightly to the east around 1891/92 in connection with double tracking. It was first served by Central Line trains on 21 November 1948 when services were extended from Woodford to Loughton. The secondary ticket office was opened in the same year.

Design: The original ECR station buildings and platform may be observed when approaching from the west. Its successor is a two-storey, red brick structure with two arched windows (with decoratively banded lintels) and a matching doorway. The ticket hall was refinished in a red and white tile scheme for the installation of UTS equipment, although a black asphalt floor remains as do original 1940s globe pendant light fittings. A wooden-roofed staircase leads to the eastbound platform, with access to the other platform being via an impressive latticework-sided footbridge, dating from the 1891 reconstruction. The platforms are particularly attractive and portray their main line origins, with red brick walls, decorative support brackets and valanced canopies, although the station's appearance has been marred by the recent installation of tall, galvanised steel fencing at the western end of the westbound platform.

Burnt Oak

Northern 2.2m Surface

Layout: Street level ticket hall leading down to one island platform via an overbridge and staircases.

History: Opened as 'Burnt Oak (Watling)' on 27 October 1924, 10 weeks after services on the Northern Line extension from Hendon Central to Edgware commenced; the delay being caused by a builders' strike. The main station building was not ready for public use until August 1928, a small wooden hut serving as a ticket office in the interim. The name's suffix has been gradually dropped over the years.

Design: The surface building was designed by Stanley Heaps, although Adams, Holden & Pearson acted as consultant architects. It is similar to the style developed for other stations on the extension, although Heaps decided to forsake Portland stone columns in this case. The ticket hall features a high panelled ceiling, lit by several uplighters and featuring numerous clerestory windows at high level. However, the walls were retiled in 1988 in an uncomplimentary grey design with black, green and white bands. The timber panelled overbridge was orignally open on either side, with windows being installed subsequently. It leads down via staircases to an island platform which retains many of its original features, including six early wooden-framed roundel panels and two wooden seating recesses. The lattice columns and glazed canopy are also contemporary with the station's opening.

Features: The roundel on the bridge parapet outside the station is notable for retaining its original lattice column support.

Caledonian Road

Piccadilly 3.1m Tube

Layout: Street level ticket hall leading down to two single platforms via lifts.

History: Opened on 15 December 1906 on the original section of the GNP&BR.

Design: The two-storey surface building is typical of the style developed by Leslie Green for the early tube stations and features a red, glazed terracotta facade incorporating five identical, evenly spaced glazed arches. The station name is picked out in gold on embossed letters above the entrance. A modernisation scheme, carried out in conjunction with lift replacement and

Above:
Platform ironwork at Burnt Oak.

UTS installation projects, was completed in 1987. New white and green wall tiling, along with a light-coloured terrazzo floor surface, has been installed and this finish has been extended into the cross-passageways at the base of the lifts. The platform walls retain their original three-tone brown tiled finish and still have several of the station name patterns exposed, along with many of the other tiled directional signs, including a rare version on the trackside horizontal tile band of each platform.

Features: To the right of the entrance and retail unit on the facade, one can still make out the raised lettering indicating that the area beneath was the exit to the station prior to lift modernisation. Two of the very early solid roundels, dating from around 1916, may still be seen on the platforms.

Camden Town

Northern 13.1m 2.6m Tube

Layout: Street level ticket hall leading down to four single platforms via a single bank of escalators and low level passageways.

History: Opened on 22 June 1907 as the junction station serving both the Hampstead and Highgate branches of the CCE&HR. Services on the original C&SLR were extended to the station on 20 April 1924 and escalators were brought into service on 7 October 1929. This necessitated the construction of new cross-passages and a low level concourse, with substantial modifications being required at ticket hall level. The station was to have been named 'Camden Road' at an early stage of planning.

Design: The surface building has a layout very similar to that of Chalk Farm, occupying the apex of a junction between two streets, although in this case the end portion of the block comprises a white stone structure (currently used as a bank). It has two red faience facades in typical Leslie Green style. Of these the Kentish Town Road elevation remains largely unaltered. The Camden High Street elevation, by contrast, has been substantially modified twice: first in 1929, when the entire elevation to the right of the roundel was rebuilt, relocating the arched window to its current position directly adjacent to its neighbour; and then in autumn 1940, when the facade containing the left-hand of the original three arched windows was destroyed during an air raid. Nothing of the original ticket hall remains because of the modifications needed for the installation of escalators and later for the UTS ticket office. Its relatively small size and the presence of only two escalators has resulted in considerable congestion, especially during the weekends when the local markets are open. The low level concourse and passageways to the platforms are still clad in black and white vitreous tiling installed during the late 1920s, while the platforms retain their original light blue wall tiling although much is in poor condition with some of the tiled station names damaged beyond repair.

Features: Two of the original outrigger light fittings survive on the Kentish Town Road facade. The unusual red silhouette roundels built into the lattice metalwork above each of the entrances are also of interest, although they are not contemporary with the station's construction.

The entrance portals to the old lifts may be observed in the interchange passageway at the southern end of all platforms. The original portals on the platforms are coordinated with the wall finishes and are denoted by double tile bands on either side. In contrast, the later 1920s portals appear to enter the platform environment at random.

A rare 'To Highgate' sign may be observed within the horizontal trackside tile band at the southern end of platform 3.

Cannon Street

Circle/Dist 5.6m Sub-Surface

Layout: Sub-surface ticket hall leading down to two single platforms via staircases.

History: Opened on 6 October 1884 on the DR/MR extension from Mansion House to New Cross (ELR). The station was reconstructed between 1968 and 1975.

Design: The original surface building was located in the forecourt of the splendid Cannon Street Hotel which fronted the main line station. Given a new Ford-designed frontage around 1910, it was later demolished to make way for the development in which the entrances to both British Rail and Underground stations are now located. The simple ticket hall is accessed by a short flight of stairs from street level and features

little of architectural merit. The dull nature of both wall and floor surfaces creates a rather gloomy atmosphere despite the bright integrated lighting and light orange wall tiles, and these finishes are utilised throughout the rest of the station.

Canons Park

Jubilee 0.9m Surface

Layout: Street level ticket hall leading up to two single platforms via staircases.

History: Opened as 'Canons Park (Edgware)' on 10 December 1932 on the MR branch line from Wembley Park to Stanmore. The suffix was dropped within a year of the station's opening. The branch was transferred to the Bakerloo Line on 20 November 1939 and to the Jubilee Line on 1 May 1979. Each platform was closed for several months during spring and summer 1993 to allow for platform reconstruction and general refurbishment – the station being closed completely in August and September.

Design: The main station building consists of two wings – one either side of the bridge carrying the tracks and each containing a retail unit. Unfortunately, what was once a neat design with decorative brickwork has been defaced over the years and has only recently been restored, although much of the brickwork is still rendered over or clad with concrete. The ticket hall features an impressive vaulted ceiling, attractive skylights, wooden wall panels and a new tiled floor. The recently retiled staircases lead to two small, simple, brick platform buildings with plain glazed canopies, the remainder of the platform areas being exposed.

Chalfont & Latimer

Metropolitan 1.1m 0.3m Surface

Layout: Street level ticket hall leading to two single platforms via a subway accessed by staircases. The southbound platform also has a bay road used as the terminus of the Chesham shuttle service.

Above:
The Kentish Town Road frontage of Camden Town station. *Hugh Madgin*

History: Opened as 'Chalfont Road' on 8 July 1889 on the MR extension from Rickmansworth to Chesham. The station was renamed 'Chalfont & Latimer' on 1 November 1915.

Design: The main building is similar to other stations at this end of the Metropolitan Line. It is almost identical to Chorleywood, although in better condition, having retained its entrance canopy and all of its chimney stacks. The small ticket hall has an unsympathetic tiling scheme which fails to reflect the Victorian feel to the platforms. Many of the buildings are constructed from or clad with painted timber, with little of the original brickwork remaining visible. The canopy on the southbound platform extends some distance further to the north compared to that on the other platform, to provide limited cover for users of the bay road. The only aspects which spoil this generally attractive station are the extensive stretches of welded mesh fencing on the open areas of the platforms and the grey tiled subway link beneath the tracks.

Chalk Farm

Northern 3.1m Tube Grade II (prop.)

Layout: Street level ticket hall leading down to two single platforms via lifts and low level passageways.

History: Opened on 22 June 1907 on the Hampstead branch of the CCE&HR. The station was to have been named 'Adelaide Road' at an early stage of planning.

Design: The surface building occupies the apex of the junction between Haverstock Hill and Adelaide Road. It features typical Leslie Green architecture, with red faience cladding incorporating 13 arched windows on the two facades. Originally, access to the ticket hall was open from both sides but now only one entrance is in use following the installation of a new ticket office in the 1980s. The remainder of the external wall space is used for shop units. Internally, the ticket hall retains much of its original green wall tiling to dado height, although the ticket office and the area around the lifts (which were modernised in the late 1970s) have been reclad in a tile which matches the colour but not the style of the original. A

drab fluorescent lighting scheme and an asphalt floor surface further spoil the appearance of this potentially attractive area. The low level passageways and platforms retain their original cream and red wall tiling, although the former are spoilt by several large pipes and cables which are attached to the walls at head height. The platform walls were until recently covered with commercial advertising and graffitied paintwork, presenting a poor scene to the traveller. A recent refurbishment project has resulted in the replacement of the low level rendered bays by matching tiling and the general rationalisation of the advertising, making these amongst the most attractive surviving Green platforms on the Northern Line. Five of the original six tiled station names remain exposed and in good condition.

Features: The panels above each of the original entrances and the end retail unit feature tiled UNDERGROUND lettering, which was added within a year or so of the station's opening. Occasional tiles may be found at platform level with their manufacturer's name – G. Woolliscroft & Son Ltd – within the design. Chalk Farm is amongst the shallowest deep tube stations on the system to be served by lifts (at 42ft/12.8m below street level).

Chancery Lane

Central 9.0m Tube

Layout: Sub-surface ticket hall leading down via a bank of escalators to a mid-level concourse and a single eastbound platform, linked to the westbound platform by a further flight of escalators.

History: Opened as 'Chancery Lane' on 30 July 1900 on the original section of the CLR from Shepherd's Bush to Bank. A sub-surface ticket hall and escalators to replace the lifts were brought into service on 25 June 1934 after major reconstruction work which had been under way since 16 March 1932. The suffix '(Grays Inn)' was added to the title at the time of the new ticket hall's opening but was dropped gradually thereafter.

Design: The original surface building was very similar to other stations designed by

Harry Measures for the new railway. However, this was made redundant following the station's reconstruction and the ticket hall can be reached only by means of staircases on either side of High Holborn at the junction with Grays Inn Road - each surrounded by standard 1930s style railings. The ticket hall is clad with white faience tiles, while the lower level concourses are finished with standard 1930s yellow tiling. The platforms retain much of their original white wall tiling on the trackside and over the soffits. A modernisation project, completed in 1987, retiled the main walls in a similar style and laid a granite floor surface in place of asphalt. Standard red 'tractor' seats and trunking were also installed under this project.

Features: Construction work on the CLR began in April 1896 on the site of this station, with the shaft being sunk four months later. The original ticket hall building survives largely intact and occupies the ground floor of an imposing pink stone-clad office block at 31-33 High Holborn.

Charing Cross

Bak/Jub/North 24.1m 2.1m Tube

Layout: Two sub-surface ticket halls leading down to six single platforms via escalators and low level concourses, passageways and staircases.

History: Opened as 'Trafalgar Square' on 10 March 1906 as part of the original Baker Street & Waterloo Railway. An unconnected station called 'Charing Cross' was opened on 22 June 1907 on the CCE&HR. This station was renamed 'Charing Cross (Strand)' on 6 April 1914 and 'Strand' on 9 May 1915. The old Trafalgar Square ticket hall was enlarged when the lifts were replaced by escalators (operational from 13 April 1926), and the subway to Cockspur Street was opened by Westminster City Council on 28 September 1928. The Northern Line (as the CCE&HR had become) platforms were closed between 28 September and 7 October 1938, and again between 1 September and 17 December 1939, to allow for the installation of flood alleviation measures. Strand station was again temporarily closed between 16 June 1973 and 1 May 1979 when a new Charing Cross station was opened, encompassing the old

Strand and Trafalgar Square platforms and those of the newly opened Jubilee Line. The Bakerloo Line ticket hall and platforms were modernised four years later.

Design: This station has never had a significant surface building, with the main (ex-CCE&HR) ticket hall being constructed under the forecourt of the main line station. This was completely modernised and enlarged for the opening of the Jubilee Line and features new wall and floor tiling, a metal panelled ticket office and a slatted false ceiling. The smaller ticket hall, located nearer to Trafalgar Square, had been refurbished in similar fashion by 1983. Low level concourses and passageways feature white wall tiling, a terrazzo floor surface and white ceiling panels. Original Northern and Bakerloo Line tiling still exists but has been covered over: on the Northern Line platforms by large screen-printed melamine panels, with stunning murals (depicting the construction of the original Eleanor Cross between 1291 and 1294) by David Gentleman; on the Bakerloo Line side by a selection of National Portrait Gallery pictures. Back wall lighting has been used most effectively on these platforms. The Jubilee Line platforms are similar to those elsewhere on the line but also feature panels depicting Nelson's Column.

Features: The ticket hall under the forecourt was constructed in only six weeks after a fatal accident, involving the collapse of part of the main line station's roof on 5 December 1905, led to its temporary closure.

The tiling beneath the panelling on the walls of the northbound Bakerloo Line platform is plain white in contrast to the more decorative tiling on the southbound and elsewhere on the line. This phenomenon was caused by the suspension of work on the railway's construction in 1901, owing to financial problems, and a subsequent change in design policy on recommencement.

Some original 1906 vintage railings survive around the staircase giving access into Trafalgar Square itself.

Chesham

Metropolitan 0.6m Surface

Layout: Street level ticket hall leading to one single platform (originally with a bay road).

Above:
The northbound Bakerloo Line platform at Charing Cross. *Hugh Madgin*

Below:
The surface buildings at Clapham Common are amongst the first examples of Holden's station redesigns. *Hugh Madgin*

History: Opened on 8 July 1889 as the terminus of the MR extension from Rickmansworth.

Design: The small, dark brick building has changed little since it was first opened and has a curiously lop-sided appearance. It features a narrow wooden canopy supported by square pillars (a third, central pillar existed until at least 1955), with its soffit forming part of the main pitched roof. The original ticket hall retains its timber panelling and fireplace but is now used as an entrance lobby and waiting area, the ticket office having been relocated on the platform itself. The platform has a standard MR canopy for around half of its length, featuring the highly ornate support brackets that characterise the stations at this end of the line, although a crude lighting run spoils the general appearance of this area. An early brick water storage tower survives at the end of the bay road (the latter was in use between 1960 and 1973). In addition, an original signalbox exists in a fine state of repair and faces passengers as they wait on the platform. Refurbished in 1992/93 the station won a first class heritage restoration award in October 1993.

Chigwell

Central 0.2m Surface

Layout: Street level ticket hall leading down to two single platforms via staircases.

History: Opened on 1 May 1903 by the GER on its branch line from Woodford to Ilford. The station was first served by Central Line trains when services were extended from Woodford to Hainault on 21 November 1948.

Design: The street building is in typical GER branch line style: the plain yet pleasing symmetrical brick frontage having distinctive Dutch gables above the upper set of square windows. Rebuilding work around the entrance in the 1940s led to the provision of two sets of collapsible gates, a stub canopy and quarry tile surrounds, with the original large rectangular windows being truncated as a result. The ticket hall originally took a rectangular form but a ticket office has since occupied much of the space. Yellow tiling with a green trim lines

most of the wall space and dates from the 1940s. The overall impression is spoilt by overwhelming glare from the box-shaped ceiling lamps (which replaced the original fittings in the late 1980s) and the lurid orange tiling on the frontage of the ticket office. At platform level, the canopies retain their florid metalwork and serrated valances. Long timber benches, which cantilever from the brick retaining walls between pilasters, date from the early 1900s. The open sections of platform were added in the late 1940s in anticipation of longer Central Line trains; they are notable for being surfaced in asphalt (unlike the originals, which are concrete paved) and feature two concrete lighting/roundel units on each side. Overall, the station has much potential, despite the unpleasant decor and the unsympathetic square 1980s light fittings which 'adorn' the forward girder of each platform canopy.

Chiswick Park

District 1.2m Surface Grade II

Layout: Street level ticket hall leading up to two single platforms via a subway and staircases.

History: Opened as 'Acton Green' on 1 July 1879 on the DR extension from west of Turnham Green to Ealing Broadway. The station was renamed 'Chiswick Park & Acton Green' in March 1887 and adopted its current title on 1 March 1910. It was completely reconstructed around 1932 in advance of the extension of Piccadilly Line services west of Hammersmith. This necessitated the replacement of the two single platforms by new versions set apart to allow space for four tracks.

Design: The main building has much in common with Holden's design for Arnos Grove. Although not a complete drum, it features a wide curved frontage with five windows extending to full height. The high level concrete roof bears the station's name, picked out in individual bronze letters, and a slightly incongruous brick tower offset to one side. The massive ticket hall is accessed by three entrance portals and is faced by dark brown bricks and shop units at low level. The original passimeter has been replaced by a brick UTS ticket office built out from the rear wall. Although attempts have been made to fit in, in terms of materials, the structure is intrusive and spoils the general spaciousness of the hall. The plain, functional staircases and platforms are largely constructed from concrete. They have suffered from general weathering over the years which has diminished the quality of the architecture. The original silhouette roundels are still in position and are located on areas of cream tiles within dedicated poster displays. One of the seating units on each platform is surrounded by a glazed wind-shelter – a feature distinctive of this station and Stamford Brook.

Features: The directional signs at the entrance to the subway under the tracks are contemporary with the station's reconstruction and are amongst the last of this vintage and style to survive. The retail units on the exterior of the building retain their original shop-fronts. In 1964, this station, along with Ravenscourt Park and Stamford Brook, provided a site for the trial installation of AFC (automatic fare collection) equipment prior to its full implementation on the Victoria Line several years later.

Chorleywood

Metropolitan 0.7m Surface

Layout: Street level ticket hall leading to two single platforms linked by a subway accessed by ramps.

History: Opened as 'Chorley Wood' on 8 July 1889 on the MR extension from Rickmansworth to Chesham. The station was renamed 'Chorley Wood & Chenies' on 1 November 1915 but reverted to its original title around 1934. The title names were officially combined as 'Chorleywood' around 1964.

Design: Although the main yellow brick street building is of little architectural merit, the ticket hall and platforms are sufficiently notable to qualify Chorleywood as the outstanding station at the northern end of the Metropolitan Line. The ticket hall contrasts sharply with the dull, unimaginative schemes used elsewhere through the extensive use of timber panelling on the soffit and upper walls. It is completely open

on the platform side – a feature unique to this station. Much of this work dates to the early 1980s when restoration work was carried out following fire damage. The sympathetic painting of the original canopies and supports, the uncluttered nature of the brick wall finishes and the care taken over the flower beds and hanging baskets have combined to produce an extremely attractive travelling environment. Furthermore, a beautiful timber signal cabin survives at the south end of the northbound platform.

Clapham Common

Northern 5.3m Tube Grade II

Layout: Sub-surface ticket hall leading down to one island platform via escalators and low level passageways.

Listing applies to entrance areas only.

History: Opened on 3 June 1900, the station served as the terminus of the first southwards extension to the original C&SLR from Stockwell. The station was closed between 29 November 1923 and 30 November 1924 to allow enlargement of the running tunnels. It was subsequently modernised, including the provision of escalators in connection with the further extension of the line to Morden, along which services commenced on 13 September 1926.

Design: The original surface building was sited at the junction of Clapham Park Road and Clapham High Street, whereas its 1920s replacement was located at the tip of Clapham Common itself. It was amongst the first stations to be redesigned by Charles Holden. The new building consists of a small domed Portland stone structure, containing the entrance to a subway giving access to the sub-surface ticket hall. The ticket hall originally had standard 'Morden extension' finishes but was largely reclad with drab grey and white vertically-aligned tiling during the introduction of UTS. Low level passageways retain their 1920s black and white wall tiling but have been spoilt by a preponderance of cables, advertising and peeling paint. The island platform is very similar to that at Clapham North, with its narrow surface of asphalt and low quality trackside advertising creating a claustrophobic and run-down atmosphere.

TO THE TRAINS   OTHER SIDE DOWN

Above:
Only two tube stations on the system now retain a single island platform. That at Clapham Common is seen as a train of 1959 Stock bound for Edgware arrives.
Hugh Madgin

Below:
Cockfosters circulating area.

WAY OUT

Features: A superb 1920s roundel, complete with dashes above and below the letters, survives on the staircase head wall along with a most unusual pierced arrow 'To the Trains' sign.

Clapham North

Northern 3.5m Tube

Layout: Street level ticket hall leading down to one island platform via escalators and low level passageways.

History: Opened as 'Clapham Road' on 3 June 1900 on the first southwards extension of the original C&SLR, from Stockwell to Clapham Common. It was closed between 29 November 1923 and 30 November 1924 to allow the enlargement of the running tunnels. The station was also substantially modernised during this period, although work was not completed until 29 May 1926 when new escalators were brought into service. This work was co-ordinated with the further extension of the line to Morden on 13 September 1926 and the station's current title was adopted at this time.

Design: The current surface building, replacing that demolished in the mid-1920s, occupies a corner site and consists of a small, one-storey structure constructed from Portland stone. Above the entrance, a flat stone screen with a roundel on a plain background has been incorporated into the design. The substantial ticket hall retains some of the 1920s white and green tiled finishes but the ticket office is clad in an uncomplementary manner. The confused nature of the finishes is compounded by fluorescent light fittings, a glazed focal point, a white metal barrier line and an asphalt floor. At low level, the station is very similar to Clapham Common, although in this case, use is made of concrete paving in place of asphalt.

Clapham South

Northern 5.0m Tube Grade II

Layout: Street level ticket hall leading down to two single platforms via escalators and a low level concourse.

History: Opened on 13 September 1926 as part of the further extension of the original C&SLR from Clapham Common to Morden.

Design: The surface building was the first to be developed by Holden for the Morden extension and presented him with an opportunity to design a completely new station. He created the concept of a three-sided screen, constructed from Portland stone. This incorporated entrances at low level and a glazed roundel within the main window above the canopy. The five-storey building was added in 1934. Original shop units either side of the entrance lobby are surrounded by a most unusual black and white fluted tile while the lobby leads into a large ticket hall, faced with 1920s green and white tiling and standard white tiling on the UTS frontage. The floor tiling has been extensively repaired over the years and now has a distinct patchwork appearance. The low level concourse and platforms are typical of the Morden extension stations, characterised by the use of white wall tiling with black and green trim, and a concrete paved floor feature.

Features: The station was originally to have been called 'Nightingale Lane' and this name still exists hidden beneath the blue bars on the platform roundels.

Cockfosters

Piccadilly 1.3m Surface Grade II

Layout: Sub-surface ticket hall (with street access from both sides of Cockfosters Road) leading to two island platforms with three sets of tracks.

History: Opened on 31 July 1933 as the terminus of the final northwards extension of the Piccadilly Line from Enfield West (later Oakwood).

Design: Unlike most Holden-designed stations, Cockfosters has a very discreet surface building, consisting of a low brick structure with two small towers, with a pole-mounted roundel attached to each. This building, along with a largely timber bus shelter structure and bus stand on the opposite side of the road (opened less than a year after the rest of the station), gives staircase access down to a superb ticket hall. Its size, exaggerated by the high vaulted ceiling, creates a sense of spaciousness unmatched by any other station of the Underground except its 'sister' station at Uxbridge. Lighting is provided by large areas of glazing between the concrete buttresses and globe fittings which extend down from the ceiling. St James's floor tiles are laid throughout the area, while the lower sections of the concrete walls and columns have been painted to match the original colour scheme. The ticket hall leads directly on to the platforms and forms part of the same building, although the floor surface changes to asphalt. Half of the platform area is in the open and trains use three sets of tracks – the central bay being served by both platforms.

Features: The station has remained almost unaltered since it opened. The original bronze-framed passimeter, shop units and signage still exist, along with a distinctive clock on an orange background above the buffers of the central bay. Superb original signs also survive above bus shelter entrances and attached to lamp posts on the adjacent layby island.

Colindale

Northern 2.3m Surface

Layout: Street level ticket hall leading down to one island platform via an overbridge and staircases.

History: Opened on 18 August 1924 on the Northern Line extension from Hendon Central to Edgware.

Design: The original surface building – similar in style to that of Hendon Central – was severely damaged by bombs on two separate occasions during September 1940 and was replaced by a temporary structure on the eastern side of the tracks soon after. This survived until 1962 when the current building, forming part of the ground floor of an office development, was constructed. Shop units occupy most of the wall space either side of the brick entrance. The ticket hall is of modern appearance, with light grey wall tiling, St James's flooring and clerestory windows at high level around the perimeter. The remainder of the station is

almost identical to Hendon Central, except for the lack of original signage and the installation of concrete paving and a brick waiting room in recent years.

Colliers Wood

Northern 2.7m Tube Grade II

Layout: Street level ticket hall leading down to two single platforms via escalators and a low level concourse.

History: Opened on 13 September 1926 on the Northern Line extension from Clapham Common to Morden.

Design: The surface building is almost identical to the entrance at Tooting Bec – an opened-out, triple-faceted screen, constructed from Portland stone and featuring a large roundel within the window design. Ticket hall features include a standard green, black and white tiling design, with the ceiling being supported by several massive, brown-painted columns. The low level concourse and platforms match those of the other stations on this part of the line, with similar wall tiling to that in the ticket hall and concrete paving on the floors.

Covent Garden

Piccadilly 12.7m Tube Grade II (prop.)

Layout: Street level ticket hall leading down to two single platforms via lifts, low level passageways and staircases.

History: Opened on 11 April 1907 on the original section of the GNP&BR, which had commenced services on 15 December 1906. The building above the station was added around 1964.

Design: This Leslie Green-designed building is one of the better surviving examples of his original tube stations. It dominates the junction between Long Acre and St James Street, and features the standard red terracotta tiling, glazed arches (three on each facade) and embossed name lettering on a white tile band. The tiled UNDERGROUND sign above one of the entrances was probably added soon after the station's opening and is therefore not an original feature. The interior was completely redesigned in the late 1980s as part of a major lift replacement project, which also removed the canopies above the entrances, although these have now been reinstated using a modern design. The ticket hall walls have been clad with dark green and cream tiles in the style of the original, while the floor surface features a light-coloured ceramic tile. The low level passageways, staircases and platforms retain their original finishes – orangy brown, white and yellow wall tiling, and integrated tiled signage. The tiling scheme is distinctive in that it does not use the dark reds, greens and browns found at almost every remaining Leslie Green station. Two of the early solid red roundels remain on the platforms.

Croxley

Metropolitan 0.5m Surface Grade II (prop.)

Layout: Street level ticket hall leading down to two single platforms via staircases.

History: Opened as 'Croxley Green' on 2 November 1925 on the joint MR/LNER branch line from Moor Park to Watford. LNER trains stopped using the branch during the General Strike of May 1926 and services were never recommenced. The station's name changed to 'Croxley' on 23 May 1949.

Design: The main building is typical of Clark's style for the MR's new branch lines to Watford and Stanmore. A two-storey brick structure, it features a small, but prominent, glazed canopy supported by two cast iron columns. In all other ways, the building resembles a large suburban house. The ticket hall is similar to Watford's, although little of the original green mosaic tiling survives. The platforms are largely uninteresting, with dark brick walls and plain canopies for part of their length. However, they are redeemed through the presence of 18 1925-vintage decorative lampposts (all with reproduction luminaires), some of which were resited here when the lighting at Watford was replaced in the late 1980s.

Dagenham East

District 1.7m Surface

Layout: Street level ticket hall leading down to two single platforms (plus a bay road at the western end of the eastbound platform) via staircases.

History: Opened as 'Dagenham' on 1 May 1885 by the LTSR. District Railway services were extended from Whitechapel to Upminster on 2 June 1902 but were suspended beyond Barking (except for occasional workings) between 30 September 1905 and 12 September 1932. The station had been taken over by first the Midland Railway (in 1912) and then the LMS. The LMS decided to reconstruct the building in the early 1930s, to allow the introduction of electrified tracks for District Line services, with a bay road on the eastbound platform first used on 24 November 1935. The station was given its current title on 1 May 1949 and ownership transferred to the London Transport Board on 1 January 1969.

Design: The street level building contrasts sharply with those being constructed by Holden and MR architects at around the same time. It consists of a low, dark brick facade with a wide white canopy and a pole-mounted silhouette roundel on the roof. Shop units occupied the windows each side of the entrance at one time. The simple ticket hall has a tiled ticket office frontage and a concrete paved floor. At platform level, the station is similar to many designed around this time, with dark brick walls and plain iron canopies.

Features: Derelict remains of the westbound LTSR/LMS platform and of the footbridge which connected it to the ticket hall (both closed around 1960) may still be observed. The equivalent eastbound platform once shared an island platform with the District Line but this area has now been fenced off.

Dagenham Heathway

District 2.6m Surface

Layout: Street level ticket hall leading down to one island platform via a long ramp.

Above:
The 1925-vintage station building at Croxley. *Hugh Madgin*

History: Opened as 'Heathway' on 12 September 1932 in conjunction with the extension of electrified District Line services from Barking to Upminster. The station's name changed to 'Dagenham Heathway' on 1 May 1949 and ownership transferred to the London Transport Board on 1 January 1969.

Design: The street level building was almost identical to its sister station at Dagenham East when it was first built. However, the left-hand third of the building was demolished in the early 1960s and now forms part of a supermarket. The remaining portion of the building is nondescript and has a rather lop-sided appearance. Internal finishes include a green tiled ticket office frontage and a concrete paved floor, while access to the platform is by means of a long, timber-panelled ramp – a feature found only on some stations on this section of the District Line. The platform has two undistinguished dark brick buildings and a partially glazed canopy for much of its length. A recent refurbishment project has substantially improved its appearance through redecoration and installation of a new signage scheme.

Features: A most distinctive 'Change Here for Fords of Dagenham' sign survives in refurbished form at platform level.

Debden

Central 0.9m Surface

Layout: Street level ticket hall leading to two single platforms via a footbridge.

History: Opened as 'Chigwell Road' on 24 April 1865 by the GER and renamed 'Chigwell Lane' on 1 December the same year. The station was rebuilt around 1893 to allow for the doubling of the line, resulting in the provision of an additional platform. Services were suspended between 23 May 1916 and 2 February 1919. Its name changed to 'Debden' on 25 September 1949 when Central Line services were extended from Loughton to Epping.

Design: The current building replaced the GER ticket hall around 1974 and is a low, plain structure, built from pink brick and featuring a blue name frieze around its entire perimeter. In contrast, the ticket hall is quite attractive, with high level clerestory windows, beige and red wall tiling and a terrazzo floor surface. This leads directly on to the eastbound platform – the westbound accessed by means of a lovely latticework footbridge – with the platform buildings themselves being of little architectural interest.

Dollis Hill

Jubilee 2.2m Surface

Layout: Sub-surface ticket hall (reached by a long subway between Burnley Road and Chapter Road) leading up to one island platform via a staircase.

History: Opened on 1 October 1909 by the MR after pressure from local property developers, although this section of line had been in operation since 2 August 1880. The platform was resited on 18 September 1938 for the inauguration of Bakerloo Line services on 20 November the following year, although Metropolitan Line trains continued to use the station until 7 December 1940. The Jubilee Line took over services from the Bakerloo on 1 May 1979.

Design: The entrances from either side of the tracks are ordinary in appearance, although the passageway from Chapter Road (which did not open until 20 December 1909) has an interesting mixture of finishes, ranging from red brick near the entrance to white glazed brickwork on the ramp and cream tiling at sub-surface level. Ticket hall areas form part of the public subway and were refurnished (with a white panelled false ceiling, cream wall tiling and a two-tone terrazzo floor surface) during UTS installation in the mid-1980s. The remainder of the station dates from the major reconstruction project which took place in the late 1930s for the transfer of the Stanmore branch to the Bakerloo Line. Large, beige faience tiles – typical of this era – line the walls of the staircase, although they are now in poor condition. The platform features an elegant concrete canopy with rounded ends, supported by fair-face red brick buildings. The latter include a waiting room with a large expanse of glazing, occupying the southern end of the structure. Carefully-tended flower beds on the open areas of the platform add to the attractive nature of this station.

Ealing Broadway

Cent/Dist 8.8m Surface

Layout: Street level ticket hall (owned by British Rail) leading down to two District Line platforms (one island and one single) and one island Central Line platform, by separate staircases.

History: Opened on 1 July 1879, as the terminus of the DR extension from just west of Turnham Green. The original street building was reconstructed shortly before World War 1. Central Line services first used the adjacent Great Western Railway station on 3 August 1920, when they were extended from Wood Lane. A new joint ticket hall was opened by British Rail (Western Region) on 5 December 1965 on the site of the original GWR building, with access to the District Line platforms commencing on 13 November the following year.

Design: The second DR building is still in existence but is no longer used for railway purposes. However, the magnificent, white stone facade is in good condition and still proclaims the station name, engraved in the stone at high level. The new street level building is owned by British Rail and is of modern appearance. District Line platforms retain their original train shed and rendered retaining walls, although most of their length is in the open. Six distinctive, timber-framed, solid red roundels survive on the walls under the trainshed roof. The adjacent Central Line platform has also kept its canopy but the original floor surface has been replaced by concrete paving.

Ealing Common

Dist/Picc 2.2m 0.4m Surface Grade II (prop.)

Layout: Street level ticket hall leading down to two single platforms via staircases.

History: Opened as 'Ealing Common' on 1 July 1879, on the DR extension from just west of Turnham Green to Ealing Broadway. The station's name changed to 'Ealing Common & West Acton' in 1886 but reverted to its original title on 1 March 1910. A reconstructed station was opened on 1 March 1931 and the entire South Harrow branch of

the District Line (which had started operations on 23 June 1903) was transferred to the Piccadilly Line on 4 July 1932.

Design: The current surface building is very similar to its sister station at Hounslow West and includes many of the characteristics used by Holden several years earlier for the Morden extension stations. It consists of a two-storey, heptagonal tower, constructed from Portland stone and featuring an uncoloured silhouette roundel within six of the seven clerestory windows. The entrance is flanked by retail units incorporated into the design and is topped by a blue name frieze on a canopy running the width of the building. A pole-mounted silhouette roundel on top of the canopy and a blue tile band just above the window line complete the picture. The ticket hall is one of the most attractive on the system, with its natural lighting, distinctive shape and unusual grey and cream tiling scheme to just above ticket office level. Its spaciousness is spoilt, however, by the presence of a photo booth in the centre of the floor. Cream tiled staircases lead down to the two wide platforms. These feature elegant concrete canopies with unusual clerestory windows and supported by substantial columns. The eastern ends of the platforms have been spoilt by the replacement of the original concrete fencing by galvanised steel railings. Nevertheless, Ealing Common remains an architecturally interesting and attractive station.

Features: The outline of the original passimeter can be seen clearly in the St James's tiling on the ticket hall floor. Some fine 1930s line diagrams survive at the head of the staircases. This station was one of four sites around London which housed a trolleybus headway recording clock. The clock case was salvaged during UTS work.

Earl's Court

Dist/Picc 17.4m 9.2m Misc Grade II

Layout: Two street level ticket halls (Earl's Court Road and Warwick Road) leading down to two island sub-surface District Line platforms via staircases and to two single tube Piccadilly Line platforms via both lifts and escalators.

Listing refers primarily to the District Line train shed.

History: Opened on 30 October 1871 on a section of track served by DR trains since 12 April 1869. The original timber building was destroyed by fire on 30 December 1875 and though repaired as a temporary measure, a replacement station was opened on a new site to the west on 1 February 1878. The main street building, facing Earl's Court Road, was reconstructed in conjunction with the commencement of GNP&BR services on 15 December 1906. The Warwick Road entrance was opened on 9 May 1887 but had been substantially rebuilt by 14 October 1937, along with the construction of an exhibition centre subway, escalator shaft and ticket office.

Design: The Earl's Court Road facade was designed by Harry Ford in liaison with Leslie Green and is similar to their work at Barons Court. It differs from the appearance of the other early tube stations through the usage of golden-brown glazed terracotta instead of ox blood red, and the inclusion of decorative balustrading at high level. The original lettering is still in fine condition, although intrusive shop-fronts and an unattractive 1920s canopy above the entrance spoil the overall appearance. However, one of the original 1906 vintage shopfronts survives to the left of the entrance. The entrance lobby is largely unchanged but the ticket hall has been completely redesigned; additional floor space having been created by rafting over the eastern end of the platforms, and carried out around 1982 in conjunction with the introduction of new lifts. Ticket office, lift surrounds and staff accommodation frontages are faced with light and dark brown vitreous enamel panels. Although reasonably attractive, these finishes are inappropriate and fail to fit in with the prevalent Victorian and Edwardian architecture. The Warwick Road entrance is similar to that of St John's Wood, with its brick construction, glazed rotunda and St James's tiled floor. However, its external appearance has been radically altered through the addition of a glazed drum on top of the rotunda in the early 1960s, designed to contain the control room serving both District and Piccadilly line trains.

The District Line platforms are dominated by a massive train shed covering the full width of the station. Constructed from iron and extensively glazed, this outstanding feature was designed by John Wolfe Barry and gives the platforms a 'main line railway' feel. It is a key reason for the station's listed status. Unfortunately, the remainder of the scene has been spoilt by the installation of the bridge raft mentioned earlier, a high level footpath between the two ticket halls, large advertising panels and cables, which cover the rendered retaining walls. The concourse and staircases beneath the District Line platforms are largely clad with cream-coloured faience tiles which are contemporary with the construction of the Warwick Road entrance and the subway to the Earl's Court exhibition centre. Originally, the concourse was much wider, with a series of tiled columns down each side, but the side aisles were later infilled so as to provide additional staff accommodation. Piccadilly Line platform refurbishment was completed in 1989 but unlike the subjects of many other modernisation schemes, these areas retain the feel of a Yerkes tube station through the use of cream wall tiling with brown and green bands reflecting the style of the original design. Brown terrazzo floor tiling further enhances their appearance.

Features: Earl's Court was the first station in London to have escalators installed. These came into service on 4 October 1911. Thus, the Piccadilly Line platforms became the first, and to date the only, ones to have direct access via both escalators and lifts (other than those intended mainly for use by mobility impaired passengers). The escalators to the exhibition centre feature some of the last remaining original bronze uplighters on the Underground. Consequently, this part of the station has been used frequently by television companies for filming historical scenes. The area was also used for three years from June 1942 as an aircraft components factory, with labour provided on a voluntary basis by London Transport staff. District Line platforms retain four of the wooden seating/roundel units installed in the 1930s and several of the indicator boards provided around the turn of the century. The bands over the Piccadilly Line platforms comprise the original 1906 tiling, although the remainder of the finishes have been replaced.

East Acton

Central 2.1m Surface

Layout: Street level ticket hall leading up to two single platforms via a subway and staircases.

History: Opened on 3 August 1920 on the CLR extension from Wood Lane to Ealing Broadway. Platform rebuilding work was completed in December 1978.

Design: The street level building nestles in the shadow of the adjacent bridge carrying the railway. It is a small, light brick structure with a grey slated roof and an asymmetrical pattern of three windows and two doors. The cramped ticket hall was modernised with the installation of UTS equipment and features low level, white wall tiling and an asphalt floor finish. Severe water seepage has resulted in one of the subway walls being covered by a plastic panelling system. The platforms are amongst the simplest on the Underground and retain their original painted timber waiting rooms. Recent works have led to the reconstruction of the westbound platform, the provision of ugly steel palisade fencing and the installation of a brick electrical switchroom as part of a signalling modernisation project.

Eastcote

Met/Picc 1.8m Surface Grade II (prop)

Layout: Street level ticket hall leading down to two single platforms via staircases.

History: Opened on 26 May 1906 as a halt by the MR, although this section of line had been in operation since 4 July 1904. DR trains first served the station on 1 March 1910. The platforms were lengthened to cater for seven-car trains in 1914 and for eight-car trains in 1927, when new waiting shelters were added. DR services were transferred to the Piccadilly Line from 23 October 1933. The entire station was reconstructed around 1939.

Design: The current station building marks a return by Holden to the square 'Sudbury box' style he had first developed in the early 1930s. It is a dark brick structure with a concrete lid and large glazed areas on the front and back facades only. The entrance area is flanked by two rounded shop units which extend out to the pavement and each features a pole-mounted silhouette roundel above. The ticket hall is similar to that at Northfields, but is smaller in scale. UTS equipment has been tastefully incorporated into the black glazed brickwork below the window level. The platforms are constructed from dark, fair-face brickwork and covered by square concrete canopies for a third of their length. Wooden seating is located within recesses at the base of each staircase and within large, extensively glazed waiting rooms. The open areas of the platforms retain the concrete lighting/advertising units which were once common on stations of this vintage. However, the original lamps have been replaced by plain, modern fittings and the concrete inexplicably painted white. Well-designed flower beds and refurbished 1930s iron-framed seating add to the generally attractive nature of these platforms.

East Finchley

Northern 3.6m Surface Grade II

Layout: Street level ticket hall (also small side entrance) leading up to two island platforms via a subway and staircases.

History: Opened as 'East End, Finchley' on 22 August 1867 by the GNR. A second platform was added on 1 December 1867 and a subway under the tracks constructed in 1873. The station acquired its current name on 1 February 1887. It was reconstructed with two island platforms for the inauguration of Northern Line services north of Highgate (the current Archway station) which commenced on 3 July 1939. The station served as the terminus until the line was extended further to High Barnet on 14 April 1940, with the final steam train services ceasing on 2 March the following year.

Design: The existing building stands to the west of the railway bridge over the High Road, on a site previously occupied by the standard design, yellow brick GNR station which served two single platforms. An inelegant, dark brick structure, it was the last station designed by Holden (in partnership with L H Bucknell in this case) to be opened before the outbreak of World War 2 and is perhaps his least impressive at street level. The symmetrical box and drum forms adopted elsewhere appear to have been rejected here, although the Holden influence in terms of materials and window design is still clearly discernible. The main ticket hall has recently been tastefully modernised through the removal of a 1930s timber passimeter and the installation throughout of attractive beige tiles to match those installed previously on the ticket office frontage. The front of the hall is dominated by a high ceiling and three tall, bay windows. Each entrance porch features fine original light fittings with cleverly detailed timber covers which disguise the electrical conduits. In many ways, the secondary entrance, accessed from a public footpath, is more attractive than the main elevation, although spoilt temporarily by the siting of Portacabins housing staff accommodation on part of the forecourt. This entrance leads into a tall, tiled lobby area with an original integral shop unit. The subway connecting the two entrance halls was clad with its original tiled finishes and feature an extensive bronze barrier along its length, and several attractive original signs. Four tiled staircases lead up to island platforms which are amongst the most attractive examples of 1930s architecture on the system and have remained largely unchanged since they were first built. The concrete canopies are supported by platform buildings and plinths, clad with cream-coloured tiling. The north-western ends of the buildings are rounded and incorporate glazed waiting rooms, while the other ends feature rounded, glazed staircases leading up to staff accommodation above the platforms. The only discordant aspect is the replacement of the original concrete roundel/lighting supports by standard steel lamp-posts.

Features: The most stunning and best-known feature on the station is undoubtedly the lead-coated figure of an archer located on a parapet wall opposite the southern end of the southbound platform and sculpted by Eric Aumonier to represent the vitality and progressive image of the new railway.

East Ham

Dist/H&C 6.8m Surface

Layout: Street level ticket hall leading down to two single platforms via staircases.

History: Opened on 31 March 1858 by the LTSR. The station's buildings were rebuilt to coincide with the quadrupling of tracks and the extension of DR services from Whitechapel to Upminster on 2 June 1902, although it served as a temporary terminus between 30 September 1905 and 1 April 1908. The station has been used by Metropolitan (now Hammersmith & City) line trains since 30 March 1936 and transferred to London Transport ownership on 1 January 1969.

Design: The main building occupies a substantial length of street facade and is constructed of brown brick. The roof features distinctive gables above the three entrances and oddly shaped chimney stacks in between. Its massive ticket hall resembles a large barn, with its ceiling open to the roof and clad with brown and white glazed brickwork. Splendid cast iron railings act as a barrier line and date from 1902. The platforms retain turn of the century decorative valanced canopies and their supporting brackets. Platform buildings are constructed of dark brown brick and have been spoilt by the later construction of an ugly, enclosed footbridge. The westbound platform originally acted as an island platform, serving the main line trains. When these services were stopped in 1970, segregating railings were installed. The eastbound platform and its canopy were extended around 1902 in order to provide an additional stabling bay and the remains of this feature – taken out of service on 26 October 1958 – can still be seen.

Features: The canopy brackets include the letters LTSR within their design at high level. A fine collection of cast iron bench seats dating from the early 20th century survives on both platforms.

Edgware

Northern 2.5m Surface

Layout: Street level ticket hall leading down to two platforms (one island and

Above:
The station frontage at East Ham. *Hugh Madgin*

Below:
The buildings and platform awnings at East Ham date from LTSR days.
Hugh Madgin

one single) via an overbridge and stair-cases.

History: Opened on 18 August 1924 as the terminus of the Northern Line extension from Hendon Central. It had been intended to extend the line further to Bushey Heath as part of a major programme of new works devised in the late 1930s. However, this project was first suspended and then cancelled, owing to 'Green Belt' legislation following World War 2.

Design: The station building retains the neo-Georgian appearance of all the stations designed by Heaps – with Adams, Holden & Pearson as consultant architects – for the Edgware extension. The main brick structure is fronted by a Portland stone colonnade and has had a brick-paviored circular driveway created in the forecourt in recent years. This forecourt originally featured a vegetated island and was flanked by wings matching the design of the main building. However, the eastern wing, along with the bus garage adjacent to the station, was demolished in 1937/38 in order to allow the widening of the cutting as preparatory work for the planned Northern Line extension to Bushey Heath. Meanwhile, the western wing – originally utilised as a bicycle store and as a shelter for bus users – was removed as part of a recent redevelopment of the bus station and access slipway. The eastern wing has since been reconstructed in the style of the original design and once again acts as a shopping parade. The ticket hall originally had a similar layout and finishes to Brent Cross but was altered in the late 1980s to allow for the provision of a new ticket office and resited secondary entrance. An earlier timber overbridge was rebuilt around 1965 and is now of brick construction. The main island platform is covered by a large timber roof supported by cast iron arches, which contrasts sharply with the concrete construction methods used by Holden at Cockfosters less than a decade later. Some original signage may be found on the exterior of the waiting room under the staircase. The single platform is fully exposed and was brought into service from 20 November 1932 in order to increase the reversing capacity of the station.

Features: Further evidence of the proposed extension exists in the form of a derelict platform to the south of platform 1

and the way the tracks extend northwards under the main road (which was specially strengthened in anticipation of further tunnelling work). The main overall roof originally extended as far as the brick headwall at the northern end of the platforms and was cut back to its current extent in the late 1930s in order to carry out enabling works for the extension. The remains of the metal brackets may be observed inset into the wall of the adjacent train depot. Plans existed for the construction of a new street building in typical 1930s style, complete with a prominent tower and integrated bus interchange facilities, but these were not implemented when the extension proposals were dropped in the early postwar years.

The Portland stone pillars which once formed a colonnade in front of the eastern wing were subsequently salvaged and reused during the creation of a side entrance facing the bus slip road.

Edgware Road (Bak)

Bakerloo 2.1m Tube Grade II (prop.)

Layout: Street level ticket hall leading down to two single platforms via lifts, low level passageways and staircases.

History: Opened on 15 June 1907 on the BS&WR extension from Great Central (now Marylebone). The station acted as the terminus of the line until the latter was extended to Paddington on 1 December 1913. It was closed between 25 June 1990 and 26 January 1992 in connection with lift replacement and extensive modernisation.

Design: The main facade is one of the smallest designed by Leslie Green and originally formed part of a substantial parade of shops. The buildings to the south were demolished in the mid-1960s to allow the construction of the adjacent Marylebone flyover, and the station now occupies a corner site. Until 1991, the red terracotta tiling and the surrounds to the two arched windows was covered by garish cream and scarlet paint, but this was removed as part of the recent refurbishment project, when lettering at high level was reinstated. All internal finishes have been completely renewed during the temporary closure but unlike most previous modernisation

Above:
Inside the train shed at Edgware.

Below:
The C. W. Clark station building at Edgware Road (H&C).

schemes, the style of the original station has been retained, with the use of matching green and cream wall tiling and the reintroduction of hexagonal shade light fittings in the ticket hall. The appearance has been enhanced through the installation of a terrazzo floor finish and beige mosaic above dado height in the access passageways and staircases. New facilities include the provision of an integrated trunking system to carry electrical and communications cables, a full passenger security system (comprising alarm points, CCTV coverage and a control point in the ticket hall) and signage to the latest standards throughout.

Features: One of the original name panels within the tiling has been retained as a historical feature at the southern end of the northbound platform. This is recessed, as the new tiling has been laid on top of the old. An early cantilevered lamp bracket remains above the exit door in the Bell Street facade, which retains its white and brown glazed brick finish.

Edgware Road (H&C)

Circ/Dist/H&C 5.6m 0.2m Surface

Grade II (prop)

Layout: Street level ticket hall leading down to two island platforms via an intermediate level concourse and staircases: also access from Marylebone Road by overbridge during peak hours.

History: Opened on 10 January 1863 on the original section of the MR. The platforms were relocated slightly to the east in 1867/68 for the construction of the junction for the new branch to Gloucester Road. Major track layout alterations were carried out from September 1910. The platforms, along with the retaining walls, were then rebuilt as two islands for the commencement of District Line services on 1 November 1926. The opening of the rebuilt station at street level was delayed until 19 January 1928 because of a proposed scheme to link Harrow Road with Marylebone Road.

Design: Fowler's original brick building occupied the site of the existing station and was refaced by Frank Sherrin around 1911. It was replaced in January 1928 with an attractive design devised by C. W. Clark and linked directly to the recently constructed island platforms. As with the other MR stations modernised during the 1920s, it features cream terracotta tiling with embossed lettering at high level and a large cantilevered canopy above the entrance. At the time of opening, the building featured a stepped parapet wall, incorporating a clock within a diamond-shaped motif, high above the entrance. Although this was subsequently removed, almost all other elements, with the exception of crudely filled-in retail units, remain unchanged since construction. The large open ticket hall is accessed by a gloomy, narrow passageway which once acted as an arcade and still features a small area of the green mosaic wall tiling which once lined the whole interior of Clark's ticket hall. It leads directly on to a landing above the tracks where the roof is extensively glazed, giving the area a feel of rare spaciousness. The view to the platforms is diminished by a metal girder bridge carrying Transept Street, installed during the station's 1920s reconstruction and subsequently closed following the construction of the Marylebone Flyover in the 1960s. A stone and brick, Sherrin-designed entrance building, opened on 1 March 1911 at the head of the overbridge access, was closed on 8 April 1958 and replaced by a small structure on the realigned Marylebone Road. The platforms themselves are commonplace, although the glazed canopies and timber overbridge – installed in 1926 to replace the original overall roof and earlier bridge respectively – are not unattractive.

Features: The reorganisation of the platform layout in 1926 was partly in response to a proposed link between the MR main line just north of Kilburn and the Inner Circle at Edgware Road. Although the single platforms were replaced by islands and the train indicator panels (now removed) displayed the northern termini names of Verney Junction and Uxbridge for a short time, the bottleneck between Finchley Road and Baker Street was eventually removed by the opening of the Bakerloo Line's Stanmore branch in 1939 instead.

Elephant & Castle

Bak/North 12.5m 1.4m Tube

Layout: Two street level ticket halls leading down to four single platforms via lifts, low level passageways and staircases.

History: Opened on 18 December 1890 on the original section of the C&SLR between King William Street and Stockwell. A separate station was opened on 5 August 1906 as the terminus of the BS&WR, although services on the main section of the line between Baker Street and Kennington Road (now Lambeth North) had commenced on 10 March of the same year. An interchange passageway to the C&SLR platforms was also constructed, opening five days after the inauguration of the BS&WR station. The C&SLR station was closed between 29 November 1923 and 30 November 1924 to allow for tunnel enlargement, general modernisation and platform lengthening; the surface building entrance also being modified during this period. The building was reconstructed again in 1965 in conjunction with road-widening and a local council-funded subway system, although the lifts were not replaced until around 1983. A substantial modernisation project commenced in May 1990, was suspended in November of the same year and completed in the Bakerloo Line ticket hall area only in autumn 1993.

Design: The Bakerloo Line street building is unlike many of Leslie Green's designs for the original tube stations, for it has two ox-blood red terracotta facades at an obtuse angle to each other. An attractive four-storey brick structure was built on top of the station building at an early stage and this is now used as staff accommodation. Its current isolated position is a result of road improvements in the 1960s which swept away the remainder of the buildings on this site. The external finishes have recently been restored and a glazed extension built to the side of the building, to allow for the creation of a one-way flow through the ticket hall. The ticket hall itself has been completely modernised and features a white false ceiling, cream coloured wall tiling and a mauve terrazzo floor finish. The low level passageways and platforms retain their original red and cream tiled wall finishes but these are in very poor condition and warrant replacement in matching style.

The Northern Line station currently has no surface building other than a horrendous, grey panelled structure (containing the lift machine equipment) on top of a light-grey tiled ticket hall and a temporary booking office within an adjacent Portakabin. The original building was a domed design, typical of the style developed by Figgis for the original C&SLR stations. Low level passageways and platforms feature the black and green-bordered white tiling common to all the Northern Line stations built and refurbished in the 1920s, although original 1890 white tiles survive on the soffit for much of the platforms' length.

Features: Some of the original C&SLR brown and cream decorative tiling remains at the bottom of the spiral staircase from the Northern Line ticket hall and is one of the very few areas remaining intact in an operational Underground station. During the 1924 rebuilding, it was necessary to swap over the pedestrian and track sides on the northbound platform.

The Bakerloo Line tracks extend some considerable distance southwards as it had originally been the intention to extend the line down the Old Kent Road. Plans in the 1930s to extend the line to Camberwell led to the boring of new tunnels being started but the scheme was not completed because of World War 2.

Elm Park

District 2.3m Surface

Layout: Street level ticket hall leading down to one island platform via a long ramp.

History: Opened on 13 May 1935 by the LMS, although District Line services had recommenced over this stretch on 12 September 1932. Ownership transferred to the LTB on 1 January 1969.

Design: The street level building rates as one of the most nondescript anywhere on the system and is certainly the least imaginative of the new stations built on this line in the 1930s. As at Dagenham Heathway, the small ticket hall leads straight into a long timber-clad ramp down to platform level. The rectilinear metal-framed platform canopy is functional in appearance and has none of the contemporary elegance of West Hampstead and Dollis Hill, for example. However, two notable green painted, timber seating units with distinctive rounded ends and dating from 1935 survive in the centre of the platform.

Embankment

Layout: Street level ticket hall leading down to two single sub-surface District Line platforms via staircases and to four single tube platforms via escalators, an intermediate level concourse and low level passageways and staircases.

History: Opened as 'Charing Cross' on 30 May 1870 on the DR extension from Westminster Bridge (now Westminster) to Blackfriars. The Victoria Embankment, under which the railway was constructed, opened a few weeks later on 13 July. The BS&WR platforms opened as 'Embankment' on 10 March 1906 and their name was changed to 'Charing Cross (Embankment)' on 6 April 1914. On the same date, a terminus platform serving 'Hampstead Tube' services was opened under the same title, along with a single track loop under the Thames. Other changes which occurred around this time included the removal of the overall roof covering the District Line platforms and the construction of an intermediate concourse to provide interchange by escalator with the tube platforms, in place of the long sloping subway which had been used previously. The escalators came into operation on 2 March 1914. Both tube stations were renamed 'Charing Cross' on 9 May 1915. Further alterations took place around 1920 with the addition of another ticket office, new subways and a bridge over the District Line platforms.

A new southbound Northern Line platform – along with associated escalators and staircases – was first used on 13 September 1926 when the line was extended southwards to Kennington. Although the loop tunnel had been closed from 26 January the same year, the platform continued in use throughout. Interchange between the sub-surface and deep-tube lines was enhanced when the station was reconstructed in the late 1920s, allowing for an enlarged ticket hall and intermediate concourse; escalators giving access between these two areas being brought into service on 4 December 1928. The Northern Line platforms were closed between 28 September and 7 October 1938, and again between 1 September and 17 December 1939, to allow for the installation of emergency flood prevention gates. The entire station was renamed 'Charing Cross Embankment' on 4 August 1974 and finally 'Embankment' on 12 September 1976. The ticket hall was partially rebuilt in the late 1970s, while low level areas of the station were modernised between 1985 and 1988.

Design: The original brick District Line buildings were replaced in late 1914 by a new structure, designed by H. W. Ford to provide escalator access to the deep-tube platforms. The single-storey, Portland stone building has colonnaded entrances facing the Victoria Embankment and Villiers Street, while the large ticket hall within boasts a black and white chequered floor and prominent columns, although the feeling of space has been reduced through the construction of offices to the rear and the lowering of the ceiling height. Some of the original 1920s green-bordered cream tiling scheme survives on the staircase up from the eastbound District Line platform and also on the walls of the long interchange passageway between the Northern and Bakerloo Line platforms. The District Line platforms built within the Victoria Embankment have been reconstructed several times. The original elliptical glazed roof was removed around the time of World War 1 and later the walls were clad with standard buff-coloured tiles for the 1951 Festival of Britain. This also led to the provision of two escalators from ticket hall level. The latest modernisation utilises extensive areas of white vitreous enamel panels and grey terrazzo, and these finishes have been extended to the concourse below the tracks and the tube platforms. An abstract coloured strip design has been incorporated within the vitreous enamel panels and was created by Robyn Denny.

Features: The earlier tiling survives beneath the vitreous enamel panelling on the tube platforms and may still be seen when areas are exposed.

A set of staircases and an overbridge that once linked the centre of the District Line platforms with the eastern side of the ticket hall were opened in 1951 but later taken out of service, although consideration has been given in recent years to their reinstatement. The small brick access building still survives and may be observed to the right of the Embankment entrance. The 1914 vintage Villiers Street facade originally featured a mosaic roundel at high level but this was replaced by a more standard (and less imaginative) version around 1951.

Above:
The northern entrance to Embankment station, fronting Villiers Street. *Hugh Madgin*

Epping

Layout: Street level ticket hall leading to two single platforms with a footbridge.

History: Opened by the GER on 24 April 1865. Extensive modifications were carried out when the track was doubled in January 1893. The station was first served by Central Line trains on 25 September 1949, when Underground trains were extended from Loughton (although under LT ownership the latter has only ever been served by a shuttle from Epping).

Design: The main station building remains much as it did when it first opened. An asymmetrical red brick structure, it has a two-storey station master's house built to the left and a smaller block housing the ticket office to the right. The section in between is set back from the main building line and contains the ticket hall, entered through a pitched, glazed canopy. The narrow, gloomy ticket hall has little to commend it and leads directly on to the eastbound platform, which retains its original red brick, GER buildings and other early features. It is linked to the westbound platform by means of a typical GER open, latticed footbridge, although its pleasant aspect is marred by the presence of a separate concrete overbridge straddling the tracks and platforms to the east.

Euston

Layout: Sub-surface ticket hall (accessed by escalator from the main BR concourse) leading down to six single platforms via escalators, low level passageways and staircases; notable for not having any direct access from the street.

History: Opened on 12 May 1907 as the terminus of the C&SLR extension from Angel. The line was closed between 9 August 1922 and 29 April 1924 to allow for the enlargement of the tunnels and the construction of a further extension to join up with the 'Hampstead Tube' at Camden Town. The station's CCE&HR platforms were opened on 22 June 1907. The railways were served by lift from separate surface buildings and also by means of a joint sub-surface ticket hall under the main line station, until the former were closed from 1 October 1914. The demolition of the original main line station in the early 1960s resulted in the rebuilding of the sub-surface ticket hall, which opened in its new form in March 1965. Most of the low level areas of the station were reconstructed several years later, in anticipation of the commencement of Victoria Line services on 1 December 1968. This work included the conversion of the original C&SLR island platform into a very wide southbound platform on the Bank branch and the construction of a new northbound platform – both providing cross-platform interchange with the new line. Most of the new facilities, including the escalator link to platform level, were operational from 15 October 1967.

Design: Most of the station is clad with standard 'Victoria Line' finishes, ie light grey wall tiling, white ceiling panels and St James's floor tiling, but in fact pre-date the opening of the new line itself by over a year. The main exceptions are the platforms on the Charing Cross branch of the Northern Line which retained their original blue and cream Leslie Green tiling scheme during the 1960s reconstruction. These were modernised in 1987 and feature large expanses of white vitreous enamel metal panelling, incorporating multi-coloured decorative patterns, and a granite-like terrazzo floor surface. These platforms illustrate the manner in which stations can be improved in an attractive way through the use of modern materials.

Features: The original entrance into the C&SLR island platform can still be seen as one leaves by train from the southbound Northern Line (Bank branch) platform. The interchange between the Bank branch of the Northern Line and the Victoria Line is unusual in that, because of their alignment, the trains on the northbound (and southbound) platforms head in opposite directions.

The original CCE&HR Leslie Green building still survives near the main line station in Melton Street and is used as a substation, but the C&SLR building in Eversholt Street (at its junction with Doric Way) was demolished in 1934 and is now the site of

Euston House, the headquarters of the British Railways Board.

Euston Square

Circ/H&C/Met 7.9m Sub-Surface

Layout: Sub-surface ticket hall (sited in subway under Euston Road) leading down to two single platforms via staircases.

History: Opened as 'Gower Street' on 10 January 1863 on the original section of the MR between Farringdon Street and Paddington (Bishop's Road). A subway connecting the MR station with its main line near-namesake was authorised in 1890 but was never constructed. The station's name was changed to 'Euston Square' on 1 November 1909 and the entrances were reconstructed when the road was widened in 1931 and again in the late 1940s. Cracks in the brick platform vault caused by wartime bomb damage necessitated substantial reinforcement work around 1966.

Design: When the station first opened, it had matching buildings – for eastbound and westbound travellers – on either side of Euston Road, constructed from imitation white stone and having decorative rendered mouldings on their roofs. When Euston Road was widened in 1931, a new ticket hall serving both platforms was constructed under the new road, with C. W. Clark-designed entrance pavilions set back from the original sites. These three-faceted buildings were far less impressive than Clark's efforts at Willesden Green and others during the previous decade but continued to use the same style and building materials. Bomb damage during World War 2 led to the buildings' demolition soon after the cessation of hostilities. Although the station still has two entrances, these are now little more than staircases, on the southern side being built into a large office development constructed in the late 1940s. The ticket hall is on the eastern side of a subway under the road which is open to the public as a road crossing during rail traffic hours. It is finished in light grey wall tiling and dark brown floor paviors dating from UTS installation in the mid-1980s. The overbridge and staircases down to the platforms are clad with white vitreous enamel tiles, with an orange and black border around the advertising sites,

installed at the time of the road widening. The platforms themselves are somewhat gloomy because of the low, metal girder ceiling which replaced much of the original brick arched roof in the mid-1960s. Although small areas of original brickwork still remain visible, the majority has been clad with bland 'Victoria Line' grey tiling, which again dates from the 1960s. One only has to view the platforms at Great Portland Street to visualise how the equivalent areas would have looked when first opened.

Fairlop

Central 0.3m Surface

Layout: Street level ticket hall leading up to two single platforms via a subway and staircases.

History: Opened on 1 May 1903 by the GER on its branch line between Woodford and Ilford. Central Line services commenced on this section of line on 31 May 1948.

Design: The tiny ticket hall building, with its prominent pitched roof, is located next to the railway viaduct and is set back by a considerable distance from Forest Road. A roundel motif within the concrete block paviors in the forecourt was added during a refurbishment project during the 1980s. The ticket hall itself leads almost directly into an arched subway under the tracks. At platform level, the station retains the majority of its GER features, including timber canopy soffits and decorative metalwork. Most notable are some lovely decorative balustrades which surround the access stairwells. The open areas at the Hainault end were added in the 1940s, in order to cater for the longer Central Line trains, and have roundels and lamp-posts on low brick retaining walls, instead of the concrete units provided at the other stations on this section of line.

Farringdon

Circ/H&C/Met 10.5m Sub-Surface

Grade II (prop.) Local

Layout: Street level ticket hall leading down to two single platforms via staircases.

Also, two adjacent single platforms for British Rail Thameslink services.

The station is also locally listed by the London Borough of Islington and contained within the Charterhouse Conservation Area.

History: Opened as 'Farringdon Street' on 10 January 1863 as the eastern terminus of the original section of the MR, with the station being known as 'Victoria Street' during an early stage of planning. The line was extended to Moorgate on 23 December 1865 and the station was relocated a few yards to the east along Cowcross Street. The GNR commenced services on its 'City Widened Lines' using platforms to the west of the Metropolitan's on 1 March 1866 and the old station was closed from that day. The station's name changed to 'Farringdon & High Holborn' on 26 January 1922, before adopting its current title on 21 April 1936.

Design: The original building was a temporary timber structure opened on the site of the old Farringdon Market. Its replacement was typical of the style designed by Fowler for the MR and MDR extensions, and consisted of a wide yellow brick facade similar in form to the building that survives at Bayswater. The existing building dates from November 1923 and was designed by C. W. Clark in common with modernisation works carried out to other early MR stations. Characterised by white terracotta tiling and embossed lettering at high level, this splendid two-storey building dominates the street environment and is matched by a similarly designed shopping parade on the opposite side of the road. The green mosaic tiling which once clad the walls of the ticket hall was removed for the installation of UTS equipment and has been replaced by a garish parody of multicoloured tiles. An iron footbridge that originally linked the platforms was renewed in 1899 and replaced in the 1960s by an extended concourse at ticket hall level.

The platform areas are perhaps the best examples of early MR station architecture still intact and were refurbished in 1988, with the scheme seeking to restore rather than to upgrade, through the removal of timber panelling and the rationalisation of advertising. The original glazed train shed remains, supported by massive iron brackets attached to restored yellow brickwork, although the many changes which have been made to the retaining walls over the years – including the bricking in of the high

level alcoves in the 1920s – are clearly evident. The appearance of the platform areas has been marred by the opening on 8 June 1992 of a plain footbridge at their western end, to provide improved access between Underground and Thameslink services.

Features: A substantial section of the side elevation of Fowler's 1865 building still survives in Turnmill Street and includes a staircase access route to the eastbound platform.

Finchley Central

Northern 3.6m 0.1m Surface

Layout: Street level ticket hall leading down to one island and one single platform via a footbridge and staircases.

History: Opened as 'Finchley & Hendon' on 22 August 1867 by the GNR. The station was renamed 'Finchley' on 1 February 1872 and the track/platform layout altered two months later to allow through trains to High Barnet. Its title changed to 'Finchley (Church End)' on 1 February 1894, and the station was finally given its current name on 1 April 1940. The track layout was altered and the platforms extended at their southern end in advance of the commencement of Northern Line services on 14 April 1940, when the line was extended from East Finchley to High Barnet.

Design: The station has remained largely unchanged since its early GNR days. Accessed by means of a slip road from Regent's Park Road, the ticket hall is housed in a plain, single-storey building constructed from light brown brick. The interior was completely redecorated for the installation of UTS equipment (which resulted in the blocking of one of the two original entrances) and boasts an attractive brown and cream coloured tiling scheme. Platform level is reached by means of staircases off an original GNR footbridge, which is also linked to the secondary entrance in Station Road. This feature is unusual in that its internal surfaces have been clad with timber panels, although the basic latticework is still evident from the outside. The single platform nearest the ticket hall remains largely unaltered since the station's opening, with its yellow brick walls and decorative metalwork to the canopy. By contrast, the island platform has had its canopies and supporting columns replaced over the years, although the ornate scalloped valances match those on the single platform.

Features: The entrance in Station Road was until recently indicated by an unusual sign resembling a compulsory bus stop, probably contemporary with the commencement of Northern Line services in 1940. A similar sign still survives in the forecourt at Mill Hill East. Part of a new platform face was constructed in the late 1930s in preparation for the proposed extension of Northern Line services to Edgware via Mill Hill East, but this work was suspended during World War 2 and not completed.

Finchley Road

Jub/Met 5.9m 6.8m Surface

Layout: Street level ticket hall leading down to two island platforms via staircases.

History: Opened on 30 June 1879 on the M&SJWR extension from its Swiss Cottage station (now closed) to West Hampstead. The station opened with temporary platforms, although the majority of outstanding works were completed by November of the same year. It was renamed 'Finchley Road (South Hampstead)' on 11 September 1885, although the suffix was dropped around 1914. The station was rebuilt to allow for the provision of additional tracks just prior to World War 1, resulting in the provision of an island platform and a new ticket hall building at street level. It was extensively reconstructed again in order to serve Bakerloo Line services, which commenced on 20 November 1939, although the second island platform had been brought into service on 18 September 1938. The Jubilee Line took over the Stanmore branch of the Bakerloo on 1 May 1979.

Design: The original MR station building was a fairly ornate affair, constructed from dull stonework and boasting a splendid clock above the booking office entrance. This was swept away when the station was rebuilt around 1914 and replaced by an attractive, two-storey, stone design by Frank Sherrin, which originally had

entrances in the far left and right bays facing Canfield Gardens and Finchley Road respectively. This was modified in the late 1930s when a plain Portland stone facade containing a new entrance was inserted into the earlier building at the apex of its two elevations. The lobby area and ticket hall have standard 1930s finishes (ie cream faience wall tiles, St James's floor tiles). Two brick-lined staircases lead down to unexciting platforms, covered for much of their length by a glass and panelled canopy supported by plain metal columns.

Finsbury Park

Picc/Vict 17.1m 13.1m Tube

Layout: Street level ticket hall leading down to four single platforms via sub-surface passageways and staircases.

History: Opened on 14 February 1904 as the terminus of the Great Northern & City Railway. The GN&CR was run by the MR from 1 September 1913 and the Northern Line from 1939, before finally transferring to British Rail on 8 November 1976. The station also served as the terminus of the original section of the GNP&BR, which opened on 15 December 1906, with the line being extended to Arnos Grove on 19 September 1932. The GN&CR platforms were closed from 4 October 1964 to allow for the construction of the Victoria Line and the rerouting of the Piccadilly Line (see 'Features'). Victoria Line services commenced on 1 September 1968, although construction of the new ticket hall building and bus interchange facilities was not completed for another six years.

Design: The main ticket hall on Wells Terrace was built on the site of an earlier entrance for the introduction of Victoria Line services. It is linked to an auxiliary entrance from Seven Sisters Road by a white tiled subway which dates from the early 1900s. The fabric of this entrance remains almost exactly as built and originally had swan-neck light fittings dropping down from the roof and the station's name picked out in individual letters on the panel below the stub canopy feature. The subway to the main British Rail ticket hall is clad for much of its length with light grey phenolic glass reinforced plastic panels and brown paving

Above:
The Montgolfier brothers-inspired balloon reliefs can be seen in this view of the eastbound Piccadilly Line platform at Finsbury Park.
Hugh Madgin

57

Above:
The impressive frontage of Fulham Broadway.

installed as part of a modernisation scheme around 1985. Finishes to the Victoria Line platforms are typical of their type, although much of the grey wall tiling has come off in recent years. The Piccadilly Line platforms were refurbished under the modernisation project and now feature mauve wall tiling and a beige tiled floor surface. These finishes, along with the decorative mosaic around the portals and the large mosaic balloon reliefs on the trackside walls, make these platforms amongst the most attractive of their type on the Underground.

Features: Finsbury Park is one of only two tube stations (the other being Arsenal) whose platforms can be reached by staircase only. The original lifts served interchange traffic only and were taken out of service on 25 April 1921 after serving evening rush hour uses only for many years because of low patronage at other times. However, the shafts and the ticket hall serving them still exist to the rear of the BR subway.

It is rumoured that the balloon reliefs, designed by Annabel Grey, were chosen

because Finsbury Park was the location of the first flight by the Montgolfier brothers in England, but this event in fact took place at Finsbury *Fields* near Broadgate!

The GN&CR platforms were converted in the 1960s to serve westbound Piccadilly and southbound Victoria Line services. Some of the original tiling may still be observed on the soffits of these platforms. The original westbound Piccadilly Line platform was modified for use by northbound Victoria Line services, in order to allow cross-platform interchange between the lines.

Fulham Broadway

District 5.5m Surface Grade II

Layout: Street level ticket hall leading down to two single platforms via an overbridge and staircases.

History: Opened as 'Walham Green' on 1 March 1880 on the DR extension from

58

West Brompton to Putney Bridge & Fulham (now Putney Bridge). The street level building was rebuilt c1905 at the time of the electrification of the railway and the station given its current name on 2 March 1952.

Design: The original street level building was a fairly undistinguished brick structure occupying a corner site. In contrast, the current building, designed by Harry Ford, boasts a much more impressive facade, utilising brown terracotta blocks with a stepped parapet wall above cornice level. In many ways, it is totally unlike any other station on the system. One passes beneath a standard 1920s canopy before entering the extensive ticket hall which features a lovely glazed pitched roof and retains much of its original timber-framed ticket office facade, into which the ticket machines and windows have been carefully integrated. 'DR' (District Railway) monograms may be observed on the stonework just below the cornice. A parade of shops occupies the opposite elevation and its crude display material and signage diminishes the overall ticket hall environment. The magnificent, wide platforms are distinguished by an original 1880 vintage timber and glass overall pitched roof and high, arched retaining walls. Unfortunately, the brickwork has been rendered over and painted, but the walls retain their shape and style nevertheless. The platforms are connected by a broad overbridge and associated staircases, all of which retain their open balustrades. At the time of writing, several advertising posters dating back to the 1920s survive in an exposed state on the headwall of the overbridge. The symmetry of the station is muted by the existence of a low level canopy added around 1905 over the open end of the eastbound platform, but this is more than compensated for by the survival of two rare free-standing roundel panels dating from the 1920s. Indeed, much of the signage on the station dates from this era and greatly enhances the general ambience.

Features: The north bank of the Chelsea Football Club's Stamford Bridge ground – visible as one approaches the station from the east – is constructed from the spoil created by tunnelling during the construction of the GNP&BR during the early years of this century.

Gants Hill

Central 2.6m Tube

Layout: Sub-surface ticket hall (located beneath Gants Hill Cross roundabout and accessed by means of numerous staircases and ramps) leading down to two single platforms via escalators and a low level concourse.

History: Opened on 14 December 1947 on the Central Line extension from Leytonstone to Newbury Park.

Design: The staircase entrances are marked by distinctive pole-mounted silhouette roundels, while the staircases themselves, subways and ticket hall are faced with orange-bordered cream tiling and St James's floor tiling. The lower concourse has matching finishes but its distinctive feature is a high barrel-vaulted panelled ceiling, which was inspired by similar designs on the Moscow Metro. The platforms are similar in style to those for St John's Wood and Bethnal Green, although they differ strongly through the large number of entrances from the 'Moscow Hall' and the installation of panelled false ceilings over the tracks. A major modernisation project, completed in early 1994, resulted in the exact replication of all wall tiling and the reinstatement of the false ceilings which had been missing for many years. The 'twinning' of Gants Hill with a station on the Moscow metro is proposed.

Gloucester Road

Circ/Dist/Picc 9.9m 0.8m Misc Grade II

Layout: Street level ticket hall leading down to two sub-surface platforms (one island and one single, plus one single disused) via staircases and to two single tube platforms (serving the Piccadilly Line) via lifts and low level passageways.

History: Opened as 'Brompton (Gloucester Road)' (although also referred to on station signs as 'Gloucester Road Station Brompton' and 'Gloucester Road for Brompton') on 1 October 1868 as the temporary terminus of the MR extension from just west of Edgware Road. The line was extended further to South Kensington on 24 December of the same year. The station also acted as the terminus of the DR when it extended its services from Earl's Court on 12 April 1869. An additional footbridge linking the western end of the MR and DR platforms was installed in 1906, in order to relieve interchange congestion. The GNP&BR opened its platforms on 15 December 1906 and the entire station was renamed 'Gloucester Road' the following year. Replacement of the overall roof above the sub-surface tracks by standard umbrella canopies also occurred at around this time. Piccadilly Line platforms were closed between 30 August 1987 and 21 May 1989 during the implementation of lift replacement works.

Design: The original DR building still exists and is one of the few early stations to survive largely intact. An attractive two-storey, yellow brick structure, it was partially rebuilt during the mid-Edwardian era, resulting in the removal of the high level parapet, the installation of white lettering on a green mosaic background above the upper tier of arched windows and the reshaping of some ground floor features. The parapet features and a modern interpretation of the original pitched, glazed canopy have been reinstated, along with the restoration of the remainder of the facade, in conjunction with ticket hall modernisation. This work also resulted in the conversion of the building back to its original use after many years of housing shop units, although the new entrances are located where windows were sited in the original design. Ticket hall areas have been completely retiled and feature a stunning glazed barrel-vault feature.

District Line platforms retain their original brick retaining walls but have recently been rafted over for a shopping development overhead, the original overall roof having been removed in the 1900s. The old asphalt floor finish has been replaced by an attractive green terrazzo finish and large globe pendant light fittings resembling the original design have been suspended from the ceiling, along with the retention of a turn of the century train describer. Concealed illumination from behind the advert panels completes the effect and shows how sensibly handled air-space development can enhance the travelling environment.

The original GNP&BR ticket hall occupies a site adjacent to the earlier building and its exterior is faced in standard Leslie Green, red terracotta. Original cantilevered light brackets still exist on the external facades. The building has recently been refurbished as part of the development scheme. In contrast, the Piccadilly Line platforms have not been touched by modernisation and are perhaps the most attractive of all Green's designs, featuring particularly fine dark green and cream-coloured tiling.

Features: The single eastbound District Line platform was in use until February 1970, when the track layout was altered and the island platform widened. Hoardings and grime that had covered its brick retaining wall were finally removed around 1985. The entrance to the MR ticket office was located directly to the right of the DR's building, until it was made redundant following the MR's incorporation into the LPTB in 1933.

Golders Green

Northern 5.8m Surface

Layout: Street level ticket hall leading up to two island platforms (also one single platform not in passenger use) via subways and staircases.

History: Opened on 22 June 1907 as the terminus of the Hampstead branch of the CCE&HR. The line was extended further to Hendon Central on 19 November 1923 and this necessitated substantial track layout revisions, through the provision of an additional platform face to the north of the original 'arrivals' bay (now platforms 4 & 5). The northbound single platform was extended and an extra exit provided down the embankment in 1928.

Design: Almost all of the fabric of the original station remains intact, although the entrance has twice been radically altered, most recently through the addition of a new ticket hall forward of the old building line. Constructed of red brick, the main facade fronts on to a large bus forecourt, for this station has long been one of the most important train/bus interchanges in north-west London especially since 1912 when the LGOC was incorporated into the LER. Part of the original valanced canopy survives to the left of the entrance. The original main ticket hall is now largely occupied by the UTS ticket office, with the new ticket

Above:
The now historic train describer survives at the modernised Gloucester Road, surrounded by reproduction light fittings. *Hugh Madgin*

Below:
The red faience Leslie Green buildings at Goodge Street surmounted, as intended, by further development.

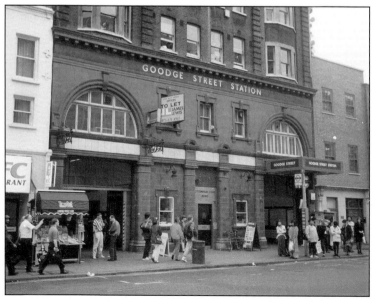

hall featuring an ill-matching, light blue wall tiling scheme. The secondary entrance from Finchley Road was opened on 18 December 1911 to serve as an electric tram interchange route and is approached by means of a timber-roofed footpath. Its associated ticket hall features orange, embossed lettering within the cream faience above the entrance doors and one of the few wooden passimeters to survive on the system. Passageways under the tracks and the staircases up to the platforms are faced with original cream wall tiling, which features green patterns and brown borders. This is the only surface station where 'Yerkes tube' finishes have been deployed, although interestingly not on the external elevations. The platforms retain their valanced canopies and timber seating units. Staff accommodation blocks have been added at the northern end of platform 1 and this platform is now used only for access to these facilities.

Features: The area within the Finchley Road entrance was substantially altered c1924, with the introduction of *two* passimeters in place of the earlier ticket office. Some extremely rare timber barriers and standard 1920s tiling are still to be found in good condition.

Goldhawk Road

Hammersmith & City 1.7m Surface

Layout: Street level ticket hall leading up to two single platforms via a subway and staircases.

History: Opened on 1 April 1914, although services on this section of the Hammersmith & City Line had been in operation since 13 June 1864.

Design: The ticket hall is built within two arches of the brick viaduct carrying the railway and is accessed by means of discrete entrances on either side of the adjacent bridge. It was extensively modified for the installation of the UTS suite and features a light grey and blue-bordered tiling scheme. This has been extended to the subway under the tracks. The staircases leading to the platforms have timber panels and extensive areas of glazing. The platform buildings are also con-

structed from timber and are fairly plain in design, although recent redecoration works and passenger security measures have compensated for this to some extent.

Goodge Street

Northern 7.4m Tube

Layout: Street level ticket hall leading down to two single platforms via lifts and low level passageways.

History: Opened as 'Tottenham Court Road' on 22 June 1907 on the original section of the CCE&HR. The station was renamed 'Goodge Street' on 9 March 1908 to avoid confusion when an interchange connection was made between the CLR station at Tottenham Court Road and CCE&HR's Oxford Street.

Design: The simple red terracotta facade is typical of those designed by Leslie Green and is now incorporated into a larger building. Arched windows are located above the halls giving access to and from the lifts, with the facade having a perfect symmetrical design. It also features an unusual vitreous enamel blue name frieze at high level and two of the original decorative light brackets. The ticket hall was modernised in the late 1980s at the same time as the three high speed 1930s lifts were replaced. A green and cream wall tiling scheme predominates, with dark brown quarry tiles on the floor. The low level passageways and platforms were similarly retiled at around the same time. Unfortunately, the dull nature of the asphalt floor surface tends to diminish the potentially attractive nature of the pattern at platform level. Original wall tiling survives in the spiral staircase and presents an interesting comparison with the 1980s scheme.

Grange Hill

Central 0.2m Surface

Layout: Street level ticket hall leading down to two single platforms via an overbridge and staircases.

History: Opened on 1 May 1903 by the GER on its branch line between Woodford and Ilford. The buildings were reconstructed for the commencement of Central Line services on this section of line on 21 November 1948.

Design: The original station buildings were designed by the GER's own architects and were typical of the style still to be found elsewhere on this part of the Central Line. The existing street building is very similar in style to that of White City, although on a much smaller scale. Inside, it is simply furnished and has little to commend it, especially since the installation of the crude box light fittings which have also defaced Chigwell. The original 1903 platforms are quite attractive, with their red brick retaining walls and decorative iron columns supporting the canopies, although several of the brick bays were lost during the 1948 reconstruction of the ticket hall building. However, the appearance of these areas has been diminished quite substantially since the installation in recent years of corrugated metal canopies which lack the charm and elegance of the original timber versions they replaced. With the exception of Roding Valley, this station has suffered more alterations than any other on the Hainault loop.

Features: As at Chigwell and other stations on this section of line, the platforms were extended for the inauguration of Central Line services and these sections are identified by a large number of combined concrete roundel/lighting units which date from that time.

Great Portland Street

`Circ/H&C/Met 5.3m Sub-Surface Grade II`

Layout: Street level ticket hall leading down to two single platforms via an overbridge and staircases.

History: Opened as 'Portland Road' on 10 January 1863 on the original section of the MR. The station was renamed 'Great Portland Street' on 1 March 1917 but was changed again to 'Great Portland Street & Regent's Park' in 1923. Street level buildings and access to the platforms were rebuilt in the late 1920s, opening in their new form on 28 June 1930. The station regained its existing title in 1933.

Design: The original building was similar to the others designed by Fowler for stations on this section of line, although in this case, particular efforts were made to fit in with the other buildings on the Crown Estates' land, such as nearby Park Crescent. Faced with imitation stonework and topped by a decorative parapet, it was notable for the small domed towers located either side of the entrance porch, although these lasted for less than a decade after the date of opening. The current building is an oval, cream terracotta-clad structure, designed by C. W. Clark, the resident architect for the MR. It is one of the very few stations on the Underground system that occupies an island site and was accessible originally from all directions, although the western entrance has been blocked to facilitate the construction of the UTS ticket office. Retail units occupy much of the exterior wall space. The ticket hall is very distinctive, with eight square columns forming a circular colonnade around the UTS gates. Finishes consist of cream vitreous enamel wall tiling and a beautifully patterned brown tiled floor, although the central portion was crudely replaced at the time of gate installation. Similar tiling lines the walls of the staircases and overbridge. The platforms were similar to Euston Square's when first built, but by the 1930s much had been covered by metal-framed timber panels. Most of these were removed under a modernisation scheme in the early 1980s and the brickwork behind restored. The result bears a close resemblance to the restoration scheme at Baker Street, although the lack of alcoves of sufficient depth prevented the introduction of the imaginative lighting that had been so successful on the earlier scheme. Nevertheless, the overall impression of the platforms is most pleasing, with their vaulted yellow brick ceiling and surviving timber panels, the latter painted in an attractive purple and cream colour scheme.

Features: The proximity of the Royal National Institute for the Blind has resulted in this station being chosen to trial various measures designed to assist the partially sighted. These include tactile signs on the walls and bright yellow seating units.

In addition to the removal of glazing from the alcoves, a further substantial opening was created at the western end of

Above:
The late-1920s station building at Great Portland Street.

the platforms in the late 1860s in order to address the severe ventilation problems faced by this section of line during the days of steam locomotion, and this feature may still be observed.

Greenford

Layout: Street level ticket hall leading up to one island platform (although see 'Design' below) via an escalators and staircase.

History: The original station on this site was opened on 1 October 1904 by the GWR. It was rebuilt to act as the temporary terminus of the Central Line when services were extended from west of North Acton on 30 June 1947, although the platforms were served by a temporary entrance building until late the following year. The Central Line platform was transferred from GWR to LTE control on 1 January 1948 and the line was extended further to West Ruislip on 21 November the same year. The station served both services until 17 June 1963 when the adjacent GWR platforms were closed. Reconstruction of the platform and associated buildings was completed in late 1993.

Design: Designed initially by Lewis and implemented postwar by Curtis, the single-storey street level building is constructed largely of red brick but dominated by chequered clerestory windows (of small pane glass set in concrete frames) and a canopy across the entire width of the structure. A silhouette roundel is to be found high up on the brickwork of the railway viaduct. The external shop units and the main walls of the majestic curved ticket hall are clad with small cream-coloured tiling, although the ticket office frontage is faced with a dull, grey tiled finish. St James's floor tiling has been laid throughout, while the high ceiling and clerestory windows dominate the appearance of the area. The platform is unusual in that it is very wide for part of its length and divides into two narrow islands at the eastern end; the space in between acting as the terminus bay for local NSE services to Paddington. Owing to subsidence problems, the platform buildings were reconstructed using green and white vitreous enamel panelling during 1993.

Features: The subway leading to the old GWR platforms is now partially used for staff accommodation and was accessed from the wall facing the base of the escalator shaft. The escalator itself was the first, and now the only surviving example, on the Underground serving surface platforms at high level; the fixture at Alperton having been taken out of service in 1988.

Green Park

Jub/Picc/Vict 16.8m 16.4m Tube

Layout: Sub-surface ticket hall leading down to six single platforms via escalators, and low level concourses and passageways.

History: Opened as 'Dover Street (St James's)' on 15 December 1906 on the original section of the GNP&BR. The station was renamed 'Green Park' on 18 September 1933 to mark the bringing into service of a new ticket hall and escalators in place of the earlier lifts. Further extensive modifications took place for the inauguration of Victoria and Jubilee Line services on 7 March 1969 and 1 May 1979 respectively.

Design: The original GNP&BR building was located in Dover Street and was very similar in style to the Leslie Green structure that still survives in Down Street, although it had wider arched windows. It was demolished in the mid-1960s and its site at 5-7 Dover Street is now occupied by an apartment block. The new ticket hall was located beneath the main road and is accessed by means of staircases from within Devonshire House on the north side and a covered pavilion adjacent to the Park itself. 1930s faience tiled finishes were replaced when the hall's layout was modified to allow for the installation of escalators to the new Victoria Line. The Victoria Line access passageways and platforms have standard line finishes, ie grey wall tiling and white soffit panels. Piccadilly Line areas were modernised around 1985 through the installation of a multi-coloured tiling scheme inspired by the Park. This replaced the light blue and cream wall tiling that had been in place since 1906, although some of the original

finishes remain as bands over the tracks and in cross-passageways. Jubilee Line areas are similar to those at Baker Street, the only difference being the inclusion of a leaf pattern within the red wall tiling.

Hainault

Central 1.4m Surface

Layout: Street level ticket hall leading up to one island and one single platform via a subway and staircases.

History: Opened on 1 May 1903 by the GER on its branch line between Woodford and Ilford, although it was closed between 1 October 1908 and 2 March 1930. The station was substantially rebuilt, including the reconstruction of the western platform, prior to the commencement of Central Line services on 31 May 1948.

Design: Nothing remains of the original GER station at street level, having been replaced in the late 1940s by an undistinguished brick structure on the south side of New North Road. The elliptical ticket hall presents an attractive space and, along with the 1903 vintage subway and staircases, is clad with cream faience tiles incorporating a turquoise trim. Unfortunately, the original globe pendant light fittings have been replaced by uninspiring ceiling-mounted versions. Platform 1 remains almost unchanged since its opening and is typical of the style adopted on this GER branch line. The other platform, by contrast, was substantially rebuilt for the inauguration of Central Line services, so as to allow for the provision of tracks on either side, thereby permitting a high degree of operational flexibility. This work led to the replacement of the original decorative canopy by a rather plain 1940s design, although partially compensated for by the installation of stylish concrete roundel-cum-lighting standards, five of which survive – in various states of repair – on the open section of the platform. Two particularly attractive flower beds are also located in this area.

Features: The ticket office passimeter, supplanted in the mid-1980s by UTS, may now be found at the entrance to the London Transport Museum in Covent Garden.

Hammersmith (Dist)

Dist/Picc 14.0m 6.1m Surface

Layout: Two street level ticket halls leading down to two island platforms via over-bridges and staircases.

History: Opened on 9 September 1874 as the terminus of the DR extension from Earl's Court. The building was severely damaged by fire on 20 January 1882 and rebuilding work was not completed until 23 August of the same year. The platforms and street entrances were rearranged for the commencement of services on the GNP&BR on 15 December 1906. Hammersmith served as the terminus for the Piccadilly Line (as the GNP&BR later became) until 4 July 1932 when the railway was extended to South Harrow. The platforms were rebuilt in connection with this extension between 1930 and 1933. Work has recently been completed on the reconstruction of the entire station as part of a major redevelopment covering the whole island site adjacent to Hammersmith Broadway.

Design: Prior to their demolition as part of the redevelopment, the station featured two street level frontages – one designed by Heaps in Holden's 'Morden Extension' style, and the other by Ford, which was very similar to the one that still exists at Earl's Court. Until superseded by a combined station built in 'Holdenesque' style in the early 1930s, the Piccadilly Line had its own separate station adjacent to, and to the north of, that used by the District, consisting of two island platforms in a configuration similar to that found at Golders Green. Use was made of the simple steel-framed, concrete-clad style typical of stations of this era but was not perhaps one of the better examples of its type. The new station has a bright and airy feel, owing mainly to the extensively glazed canopies that cover the entire platform areas. Several of the 1930s integrated signage/seating units have been retained as part of the overall design. The spacious main ticket hall can be accessed by means of a shopping arcade in a similar fashion to High Street Kensington, built over 80 years earlier.

Features: The remains of the tiled name frieze and pilasters which once adorned the exterior of Ford's building have been incorporated into one wall of the new ticket hall, above a large stylised representation of Hammersmith Bridge using turquoise tiling. Solid brick ruins of a viaduct, which once carried LSWR and MR trains from the Hammersmith & City Line to Richmond, may be observed as one approaches the station from the west. The station on this line at Grove Road was closed in June 1916 and finally demolished 38 years later.

Hammersmith (H&C)

Hammersmith & City 6.4m Surface

Layout: Street level ticket hall leading directly to one island and one single platform.

History: Opened on 13 June 1864 as the terminus of the semi-independent H&CR, with services provided by the GWR from Farringdon Street. MR trains first served the station on 1 April 1865 and the line became the joint responsibility of the MR and GWR from 1 July 1867. The station was relocated to its current site on 1 December 1868 because of disturbance caused by the installation of the LSWR tracks from Kensington to Richmond (now used by the District Line). Modifications to the track layout were carried out around 1908 through the construction of two island platforms, and again in 1939, although the outbreak of World War 2 caused completion of the work to be delayed until 1948.

Design: The original timber building was replaced in 1907-09 by the elegant brick structure that exists today. Designed by the GWR architect, P. E. Culverhouse, it features a fine clock embedded in stonework at the apex of the central gable. Most of the frontage is occupied by shop units and originally had a canopy across its full width. Access to the arcaded ticket hall is by means of an entrance to the extreme right. The interior concourse created by Culverhouse presents a very pleasing impression, with the extensively glazed pitched roof complemented by recently installed chequer-board floor tiles. It also features a rounded ticket office which sits in the middle of the floor space and was originally clad with green 'mosaic' tiling. Inappropriate yellow tiling was added under UTS but vestiges of lettering from the earlier finishes are still discernable at high level. An access passageway from the entrance facing Hammersmith Broadway was added around 1912 and is considerably less attractive in nature compared to its neighbour. The platforms are accessed directly from the ticket hall and have attractive iron-framed, glazed canopies with crenellated valances. the one on the single platform being supported by cantilevered brackets from a plain brickwork retaining wall. Fine reproduction cast iron benches have recently been installed and add to the general ambience of these areas.

scheme common to the low level areas of the station. This latter is similar to the other tube stations on this branch, ie cream coloured tiling with a strong banding of deep red, although much of this had been removed at the time of writing.

Features: The station was originally to be called 'Heath Street' and this is the name which appears within the tiling on the platforms. However, a decision was made to alter its title prior to its official opening. Hampstead is well known for being the deepest station on the Underground (at 192ft/58.5m below ground level).

Hampstead

Northern 3.4m Tube Grade II (prop.)

Layout: Street level ticket hall leading down to two single platforms via lifts and low level passageways and staircases

History: Opened as 'Hampstead' (although see 'Features' below) on 22 June 1907 on the Golders Green branch of the CCE&HR.

Design: The surface building is one of the most unusual of Green's designs, for it has red glazed terracotta facades on three planes, with the main elevations either side of the original entrance each having two arched windows and the short connecting wall facing the adjacent road junction having only one. Occupying a corner site, the station originally had two entrances, but the main one was blocked off in the late 1980s to allow the installation of a retail unit within the ticket hall – the original shop having been demolished to accommodate a new ticket office. The station name is picked out in individual letters above the old entrances although these are not contemporary with the building's construction. Ticket hall areas have been extensively modified in recent years as part of lift replacement and UTS installation projects. Although most of the original finishes have been replaced, the original decorative green tiled ticket office windows have been replicated, along with the installation of overly ornate green wall tiles and use of a complementary quarry tile floor. The overall effect is most impressive, although spoilt by a crude lighting scheme. The upper and lower lift lobbies have been reclad with brown and cream tiling which fails to match the pattern and colour of the

Hanger Lane

Central 1.4m Surface Grade II (prop.)

Layout: Sub-surface ticket hall (accessed by means of an extensive subway network) leading down to one island platform via an overbridge and staircase.

History: Opened on 30 June 1947 on the Central Line extension from west of North Acton to Greenford. Ownership was transferred from the GWR to the LTE on 1 January 1948, with the construction of the new station buildings being completed on 2 January the following year.

Design: Initially designed by Lewis and then developed to completion by Curtis after World War 2, the circular surface building located in the middle of the infamous gyratory system is one of the most distinctive Underground structures. Although similar in form to Southgate, it has no surface level entrances and access is by means of staircase only. The staircase entrances leading to the local council-owned subway system are identified by pole-mounted silhouette roundels in a similar way to Gants Hill. Originally two staircases led down to ticket hall level, but one was later closed off, although it still remains intact behind a false wall. The ticket hall itself resembles a smaller version of Arnos Grove – completed 16 years earlier. Its tall brick walls, circular design and St James's tile flooring are all similar to the earlier station, although high level clerestory windows and brown wall tiling below are noticeable differences. It also boasts original torpedo fluorescent light fittings around the perimeter and a prototype design of uplighter/seating unit in the centre of the floor, installed in the late 1980s. The platform was never provided with a concrete canopy as found elsewhere on the West Ruislip extension and instead features an ugly, metal structure supported by an angular steel frame and covered with corrugated iron sheeting. Original 1940s line diagrams surround the lower half of the two columns nearest the base of the staircase.

Harrow-on-the-Hill

Metropolitan 5.8m 0.5m Surface

Grade II (prop.)

Layout: High level ticket hall leading down to three island platforms (one for NSE services) via staircases.

History: Opened as 'Harrow' on 2 August 1880 as the terminus of the M&SJWR extension from Willesden Green. Services were extended further to Pinner and beyond on 25 May 1885, and to Uxbridge on 4 July 1904. GCR trains began to use the station from 1890 and its name changed to 'Harrow-on-the-Hill' on 1 June 1894. A revised platform layout (accommodating four platforms instead of the original two) was inaugurated on 21 June 1908 and the entire station was completely rebuilt in 1938-39 as part of the major New Works Programme, although some of the work, especially at platform level, was not completed until as late as 1954. In the early 1980s, the College Road building was demolished and the station entrance incorporated into a new office development.

Design: The original station building was located off Lowlands Road, on the site of the existing secondary entrance and resembled the structure which survives at Ruislip. When the station was rebuilt to accommodate six platform faces, the ticket hall was positioned on a new overbridge, with access gained by means of staircases from brick entrance buildings on either side, of which the one facing College Road was considerably more prominent. Illumination is provided by large barrel-vaulted sky-

Below:
Inside the station building at Hanger Lane.

lights, as well as 'seagull' fluorescent fittings. The three platforms are similar in style to those at Dollis Hill and West Hampstead, which were opened around the same time. Their canopies feature false ceiling panels and are supported by quarry tile-clad columns. Retail units, waiting rooms and staircases are constructed from red fairface brickwork – the latter having a similar profile to those of Park Royal. A subway beneath the tracks dates from the platforms' 1908 reconstruction and is faced with brown and white glazed brickwork in very poor condition.

Features: Harrow-on-the-Hill is amongst the largest and busiest surface stations on the Underground. It is also the only one to have lifts installed, although they are no longer used, which were originally intended for the movement of mail boxes between the local post office and the platforms, and also for parcels to the adjacent MR sorting office.

Hatton Cross

Piccadilly 1.6m Sub-Surface

Layout: Street level ticket hall leading to one island platform via staircases.

History: Opened on 19 July 1975 as the temporary terminus of the Piccadilly Line extension from Hounslow West. Services to Heathrow Central (now Heathrow Terminals 1,2,3) commenced on 16 December 1977.

Design: Access to the station is by means of a huge entrance lobby containing seating and shop units. Doors within the floor-to-ceiling glazed side walls lead to the adjacent bus station and on to the Great South West Road. The ticket hall is separated from the lobby by a series of glass doors, with the door handles shaped as half-roundels – a feature that would not be tolerated today! The hall itself is fairly simple in design, with brown wall and floor tiles the predominant finish used. Access to the platforms takes a rather unusual form for an Underground station, for it is by means of open staircases down to a concourse landing, from which two wide staircases extend to low level. The platform is typical of the sub-surface design developed for the Heathrow extension, although the colour scheme of dull green on

the train-ward facing walls, beige on the trackside walls and bright orange on the inner faces of the columns is by no means the most attractive.

Heathrow Terminals 1, 2, 3

Piccadilly 10.5m Sub-surface

Layout: Sub-surface ticket hall leading down to one island platform via two separate banks of escalators for entry and exit traffic.

History: Opened as 'Heathrow Central' on 16 December 1977 as the terminus of the Piccadilly Line extension from Hounslow West. The construction of a further extension led to the station's name being changed to 'Heathrow Central (Terminals 1,2,3)' on 3 September 1984, and to its current title on 12 April 1986, in conjunction with the inauguration of the new station serving the airport's fourth terminal.

Design: As with the other stations on the Heathrow extension, extensive use has been made throughout this station of marble-effect terrazzo on the floors, along with blue mosaic and orange tiling on the walls and columns. The overall effect is quite pleasing but looks a little dated, especially when compared with its counterpart at Terminal 4, opened less than 10 years later. The appearance at platform level has been enlivened by the use of a stunning Concorde logo on the wall panels beneath the escalators, designed by Tom Eckersley.

Heathrow Terminal 4

Piccadilly 2.1m Sub-surface

Layout: Sub-surface ticket hall leading directly on to one single platform.

History: Opened on 12 April 1986 on a single line loop extension from Heathrow Terminals 1,2,3. The station was built in order to serve the new terminal building in the airport.

Design: The ticket hall, which is linked directly with an access route to the terminal, is one of the most spacious and beautiful on the system. It forms a large oval, with the high, rough stone finish supported by massive beige marble-effect columns. The same finish is used for the floor and a pilaster 'colonnade', which stretches around the perimeter, with ticket office facilities and shop units occupying the bays in-between. Illumination is by means of concealed uplighters at the head of each pilaster and spotlighting flush with the ceiling finish. The platform has identical wall and floor finishes, with the former incorporating a striped '4' motif in relief above each seating bay. The roundels are of the three-dimensional silhouette type also used at Mansion House. The overall appearance is somewhat angular and contrasts markedly with tube platforms constructed elsewhere on the system. Nevertheless, the general impression is one of high quality and is let down only by the poor level of illumination.

Features: When it opened, several banks of television monitors were located on the trackside wall and relayed advertising to the waiting passengers, although this experimental system was subsequently removed.

Hendon Central

Northern 3.6m Surface

Layout: Street level ticket hall leading down to one island platform via an overbridge and staircases.

History: Opened on 19 November 1923 as the temporary terminus of the Northern Line extension from Golders Green. The line was extended further to Edgware on 18 August 1924.

Design: The main building originally consisted of an attractive one-storey Georgian-style structure, constructed from Portland stone and featuring four pairs of Doric stone pillars and a decorative ironwork balustrade on the porch roof. Although the station itself has remained largely unchanged, it has been incorporated within a larger building, constructed within three years of the station's opening. The facade still dominates the junction of two major roads but the flower-adorned roundabout that once existed was replaced in the 1960s. A large entrance lobby features the black and white chequered floor which is distinctive of

Heaps' stations on this section of line. The ticket hall is accessed through three sets of splendid wooden doors and is very similar to that at Brent Cross, with its high level clerestory windows and black bordered white wall tiling. Overbridge and platform areas are almost identical to those at Colindale, although at this site some of the original signage still remains between the staircases, along with fine timber benches.

Features: Original 1920s light fittings survive at the base of the disused staircase to Queen's Road.

High Barnet

Northern 1.6m Surface

Layout: Ticket hall at footpath level, with direct access to a footbridge and staircases leading to one island and one single platform.

History: Opened on 1 April 1872 by the GNR. The station commenced service as the terminus of the Northern Line extension from East Finchley on 14 April 1940.

Design: The station is approached by means of a long sloping footpath from Barnet Hill, with the original GNR building located at the bottom facing on to the car park. The current entrance building was opened in 1896 and is located further up the path, giving direct access on to an original latticed footbridge which is marred only by a crudely positioned train indicator, probably installed for the inauguration of Northern Line services. At platform level, the station has changed little since its opening and displays a high degree of Victorian charm, with the canopies retaining their highly decorated valances and ornate support metalwork, most notably on the island platform. There is also an attractive pair of matching, glazed waiting rooms at the southern end of the island platform, with a beautifully restored signal cabin on platform 1.

Highbury & Islington

Victoria 9.4m Tube

Layout: Street level ticket hall leading down to two single platforms via escalators and low level passageways and staircases, also cross-platform interchange with main line services.

History: Opened as 'Highbury' on 28 June 1904 by the GN&CR, although the service between Moorgate and Finsbury Park had commenced on 14 February of the same year. The GN&CR was taken over by the MR on 1 September 1913 and operated by the Northern Line from 1939. The station's name changed to 'Highbury & Islington' on 20 July 1922. Substantial reconstruction, including the provision of two new platforms, preceded the introduction of Victoria Line services on 1 September 1968. A new entrance and escalators were brought into service on 7 April the same year. Northern Line GN&C services were transferred to BR operation on 16 August 1976, having been suspended on 4 October the previous year.

Design: The existing entrance was built for the Victoria Line and is located behind a post office, set back a considerable distance from the main road. A nondescript timber entrance leads into a typical Victoria Line station, with large expanses of grey wall tiling and St James's flooring. It differs from the other stations through the extensive usage of grey, mosaic tiling on the walls of the access areas. The pattern within the seat recesses on the platforms is arguably the most attractive on the line, featuring a medieval castle on a hill within an octagonal frame on a dark blue and red background.

Features: The current ticket hall occupies the site of an earlier GNR station, known as 'Islington', which had been opened on 26 September 1850. A small portion of this earlier building survives directly to the left of the new entrance. The original GN&CR station building – disused since April 1968 – still exists on the north side of Holloway Road, although largely obscured by large poster panels. A small single-storey structure, it is faced with white terracotta tiles and has five glazed arches – the middle and far right ones originally serving as the entrance and exit doors respectively. Some of the original lettering can still be made out at high level.

The southbound Victoria Line platform makes use of the original GN&CR northbound tunnel and the glazed white tiling can still be seen on its soffit. Two new platforms were constructed in order to allow cross-platform interchange between the two lines.

Highgate

Layout: Sub-surface ticket hall leading down to two single platforms via escalators and a low level concourse.

History: The original GNR station was opened on 22 August 1867 and services on this line continued to serve the station (which was at surface level) until 5 July 1954, when British Railways closed the former LNER branch line to Alexandra Palace.

The Underground station was opened in an incomplete state on 19 January 1941, although trains first used the extension of the Northern Line between Archway (qv) and East Finchley on 3 July 1939 and it had been used as an air raid shelter during the Blitz. It was originally intended for the Northern Line to take over LNER's Alexandra Palace branch and extensive rebuilding work was carried out at platform level. In the event, the onset of war lead to the project's suspension and eventual cancellation.

Design: The station has no significant surface buildings, with the ticket hall being accessed by means of a staircase towards the bottom of the car park approach road and a small brick entrance from Priory Gardens. Staircase, ticket hall and low level concourse areas are clad in finishes typical of those installed during the late 1930s, ie cream wall tiling, with a green border, and St James's floor tiling. The platforms are very similar to those at St John's Wood, with their tiled lettering at name frieze level and concrete paved floor surfaces. They are notable for being capable of serving nine-car trains, unlike any other 'tube' platforms. The station's location at the base of a steep hill led to provision being made for an escalator link between the ticket hall and a small brick structure close to the junction of Archway Road and Muswell Hill Road. Although planned from an early stage of the station's redevelopment, this connection – modified to allow for one escalator only, instead of the two originally planned – was not brought into service until 26 August 1957.

Features: The largely timber-constructed GNR building was located on the eastern side of the tracks at the end of what is now the car park approach road. A covered footbridge gave access to two widely spaced single platforms, with an additional set of tracks in-between (an island platform was provided in their place around 1883) and surrounded by copious vegetation. The station was radically altered for the proposed start of Northern Line services, including the removal of the footbridge and the remodelling of the main platform buildings. It served main line trains for several years, alongside one small remaining GNR platform building (which was subsequently demolished), with access by means of a staircase from the main sub-surface ticket hall directly below the GNR platforms. The angular concrete canopy and the remains of the platforms can still be seen through the foliage as one walks down the steep footpath from Wood Lane. Parts of the original brick GNR buildings may also be observed.

High St Kensington

Circ/Dist 12.5m Sub-Surface

Layout: Street level ticket hall leading down to one island and two single platforms via staircases.

History: Opened as 'Kensington (High Street)' on 1 October 1868 on the MR extension from west of Edgware Road to Brompton (Gloucester Road). The station's name was originally to have been 'Kensington' and changed to 'High Street Kensington' over time. DR services commenced on 3 July 1871 and involved the reorganisation of the platform layout. It was largely rebuilt around 1907, with further modifications to the ticket hall in 1937/38. A minor congestion relief scheme, completed in 1992, resulted in a direct link between platforms 4 and platforms 2 & 3 at their northern end.

Design: The original street level building was a prominent, brick design in typical Fowler style, which was demolished around 1907 to make way for a splendid arcade, designed by George Sherrin in art nouveau style. This originally gained direct access to neighbouring department stores on either side. The existing ticket hall finishes date
72

from the late 1930s and consist of cream coloured faience wall tiles, St James's flooring and globe pendant lamps, although most of the area's illumination comes from the high level clerestory windows and fluorescent lighting. The overall glazed roof over the platforms was removed around 1905 and replaced by independent glazed, valanced canopies, designed by Sherrin. However, the original brick retaining walls remain in restored condition, although until recently these were largely obscured by green panels installed during the 1930s at the same time as the rafting over of the northern end of the platforms to allow for the enlargement of the ticket hall.

Features: The island platform has three rare examples of the combined seating/roundel units dating from the 1930s, which once graced many stations of this kind. An ornate semi-circular metal grille which at one time adorned the arch above the arcade entrance now forms part of the London Transport Museum collection.

Hillingdon

Met/Picc 0.8m Surface

Layout: Footbridge access to high level ticket hall leading down to two single platforms via staircases.

History: Opened on 10 December 1923 as a halt on a section of line first used by the MR on 4 July 1904 and by the DR on 1 March 1910. Its name changed to 'Hillingdon (Swakeleys)' in April 1934 but the suffix was gradually lost over time (although still retained on platform signage). District Line services were taken over by the Piccadilly Line on 23 October 1933. The station underwent complete reconstruction between January 1991 and autumn 1993 in conjunction with a major scheme to reroute the nearby A40 trunk road. It is interesting to note that the station's reconstruction had been planned as early as 1938 with the construction of a 'Sudbury box' design and associated free-standing tower. However, this ambitious scheme was cancelled following the onset of war.

Design: The original station survived largely unchanged until the reconstruction project led to its demolition in September 1992. Most surfaces of the mock-Tudor ticket hall building, as well as the platforms, were constructed from timber and were typical of the style developed by Clark for all the halts built for the MR around that time. It was linked to the platforms by means of an attractive latticed footbridge. By contrast, the new station is extremely modern in design, with large expanses of glass and white metal framework. Notable features include the long footbridge giving access from Long Lane, the heavily glazed waiting rooms on each platform and the lifts for mobility impaired passengers.

Holborn

Cent/Picc 18.2m 12.4m Tube

Layout: Street level ticket hall leading down to five single platforms via escalators, intermediate level concourses and low level passageways and staircases.

History: Opened on 15 December 1906 on the original section of the GNP&BR. Services on the Aldwych branch line commenced on 30 November 1907. The station's name was changed to 'Holborn (Kingsway)' on 22 May 1933 in connection with a major reconstruction project, which started in October 1930 and resulted in the opening of interchange passageways and two flights of escalators from an enlarged ticket hall. Central Line platforms and escalators were not brought into service until 25 September 1933. The name's suffix has been dropped gradually over the years.

Design: The surface building occupies a corner site at the junction of High Holborn and Kingsway, and is rather different in appearance to other stations of its vintage. Although having many of the features of a typical Leslie Green design, such as arched windows and decorative pilasters, it was only partially faced with the standard, red terracotta which characterised his buildings. The corner facade and the two end bays on the Kingsway elevation were – and still are – clad with a brown stone finish and are of an appearance consistent with the other buildings constructed along the new Kingsway thoroughfare, which was opened in October 1905. The major reconstruction scheme which commenced in October 1930 resulted

in the replacement of each terracotta facade by a plain, Portland stone frontage. This is the only example of where a Holden design has been superimposed upon an existing Green building. The ticket hall was partially rebuilt in the mid-1970s and is faced with St James's flooring and beige faience wall tiles. These finishes once continued throughout much of the station. However, the lower areas were extensively modernised between 1985 and 1989, with much use being made of vitreous enamel panels and terrazzo floor tiling. The design of the platforms is most distinctive, with the black panels portraying artefacts from the nearby British Museum and the floor featuring an attractive, black and white chequered pattern.

Features: The eastern tunnel platform on the Aldwych branch is still used for passenger services and retains its original multi-coloured 'Yerkes tube' tiled finishes, with a very rare signal cabin surviving at its southern end. It was closed as a wartime measure between 21 September 1940 and 1 July 1946. Trains transfer into the western tunnel just south of the station. The western tunnel platform has not been used since 16 August 1917 and now serves as a private storage facility.

The white tiled platforms of the original CLR station of British Museum can still be seen as trains approach/leave the western end of the Central Line platforms. It had been planned in 1908 (ie soon after the opening of the Piccadilly Line station) to construct a subway link between Holborn and British Museum but this idea was never implemented and by 1914 the resiting of the latter had been authorised, although not realised immediately because of the onset of World War 1.

Disused areas of the station were employed during World War 2 as an emergency headquarters of the London Passenger Transport Board.

Holland Park

Central 2.3m Tube

Layout: Street level ticket hall leading down to two single platforms via lifts and low level passageways and staircases.

History: Opened on 30 July 1900 on the original section of the CLR from Shepherd's

Bush to Bank. The provisional title given to the station in 1891 during the planning stages was Lansdowne Road.

Design: The surface structure is one of only six original CLR buildings to have survived largely intact and is perhaps the best preserved at street level. Designed by Harry B. Measures, its small size and beige, decorated, unglazed terracotta facade give it a discreet yet attractive street presence. The overall appearance is only slightly marred by the presence of a glazed rotunda towards the rear of the flat roof, installed as part of a lift replacement project in the late 1980s. Inside, the ticket hall has been beautifully modernised through the use of a deep green wall tile and cream-coloured terrazzo. The ticket office occupies a significant part of the floor space but has been integrated fairly well, although it encloses one of the original four fluted metal columns – each with a decorative capital – which support the rear area of the hall. An original and highly ornate timber balustrade survives around the head of the spiral staircase, while a most distinctive stepped, semi-circular ceiling detail may be observed above the entrance to the lifts. The walls of the low level passageways and platforms were originally faced in white tiling but this has been painted over for many years, with beige tiling having been applied to the lower walls of the platforms in the 1980s.

Holloway Road

Piccadilly 4.0m Tube Grade II (prop.)

Layout: Street level ticket hall leading down to two single platforms via lifts and a low level passageway and staircase.

History: Opened on 15 December 1906 on the original section of the GNP&BR.

Design: The surface building has perhaps the simplest design of the larger Green stations and overall, its finishes survive in better condition than any other. Its wide, red faience facade contains six identical arched windows and features original gilded lettering, with the appearance spoilt by an ugly canopy above the entrance and the crude blocking-in of old entrances and shop units. The ticket hall retains much of its original deep green wall tiling and all three decora-

tive ticket office windows. Recently installed beige floor tiling and pendant light fittings have further enhanced this area. The low level passageway and platforms have kept their original cream and two-tone brown patterned tiling – the distinctive repeated chevron design on the platform walls being the only example of its type still visible at surviving early tube stations.

Features: When the station was first built, a double spiral moving walkway was installed on an experimental basis in a secondary shaft alongside that for the lifts. Although apparently successful, it was not brought into passenger service and much of the equipment was removed soon after. In March 1993, maintenance work at the base of the shaft revealed the remains of the staircase and parts of these have now been removed for permanent display at the London Transport Museum. The shaft still exists and the access portals can be observed adjacent to the lifts at lower landing level.

Hornchurch

District 1.6m Surface

Layout: Street level ticket hall leading down to two single platforms via an overbridge and staircases.

History: Opened on 1 May 1885 by the LTSR. DR services were extended from Whitechapel to Upminster on 11 June 1902 but were suspended beyond East Ham and later Barking (except for occasional workings) between 1 October 1905 and 11 September 1932. The station had been taken over by first the Midland Railway (in 1912) and then the LMS, and it was the latter which decided to reconstruct the building to allow the introduction of electrified tracks for District Line services. Ownership was transferred to the LTE on 1 January 1969.

Design: The street level building is very similar to those constructed at around the same time at Dagenham East and Dagenham Heathway, with its low, dark brick facade, white canopy and pole-mounted silhouette roundel on the roof. The simple ticket hall has no features of note, while at platform level the station resembles

74

others designed around this time, with dark brick walls and plain iron canopies.

Features: Derelict remains of the westbound LTSR/LMS platform and of the footbridge which connected it to the ticket hall (both closed around 1960) may still be observed. The equivalent eastbound platform once shared an island platform with the District Line but this area has now been fenced off.

Hounslow Central

Layout: Street level ticket hall leading up to one island platform via a passageway and staircase.

History: Opened as 'Heston Hounslow' on 1 April 1886 by the DR, although services on the extension to Hounslow Barracks (now Hounslow West) had commenced on 21 July 1884. The station was rebuilt in conjunction with the doubling of the single track, which had prevailed since the extension's opening: this work was completed by 19 October 1912. It was renamed 'Hounslow Central' on 1 December 1925. Piccadilly Line trains first served the platforms on 13 March 1933 and District Line services ended on 9 October 1964.

Design: The original street level building was only a temporary structure and has been described as a very small 'tin shed'. Its modest cottage-like replacement of 1912 was designed by Harry Ford and has been superbly restored. The bronze notice case to the left of the entrance and the window to the right are in fact replicas of the originals that remain. Ticket hall features include a high pitched roof ceiling and an early timber ticket office frontage. This area has been enhanced by the provision of a black and white chequered tiled floor surface and new timber entrance doors. The passageway and staircase to platform level have been tastefully refinished using white tiling with a blue decoratively moulded dado course and floor tiling to match the ticket hall. A simple timber-valanced canopy cov-

Below:
The entrance to Hounslow Central.

ers the platform for around half of its length and two attractive timber waiting rooms. A recently completed refurbishment project resulted in the resurfacing of the platform with concrete paving slabs and the installation of new seating and signage.

Hounslow East

Piccadilly 2.9m Surface

Layout: Mid-level ticket hall (located on staircase between street and eastbound platform) leading up to two single platforms via staircase (although see design below).

History: Opened as 'Hounslow Town' on 2 May 1909 by the DR, although services on the extension to Hounslow Barracks (now Hounslow West) had commenced on 21 July 1884. The station's opening coincided with the closure of the nearby branch terminus of the same name. It was renamed 'Hounslow East' on 1 December 1925 and Piccadilly Line trains first served the platforms on 13 March 1933. District Line services ceased on 9 October 1964. A new waiting room and canopy were installed on the eastbound platform c1965.

Design: Little of the original buildings designed by Ford has survived and the station presents a nondescript appearance, especially at street level. There is no main building as such and access to the platforms is by means of individual staircases. The ticket hall is located half-way up the staircase to the eastbound platform and has few features of interest. The only platform buildings of note are located on the eastbound side: an undistinguished metal canopy, supported by a dark brick wall with clerestory windows, – installed around 1964 – and the original staff accommodation office at the western end. The remaining areas are bounded by ugly steel palisade fencing.

Features: The westbound platform is unique in having no buildings whatsoever other than a small waiting shelter. The route of the branch line to the original Hounslow Town can still be observed as one approaches the station from the east.

76

Hounslow West

Piccadilly 2.3m Sub-Surface

Grade II (prop.)

Layout: Street level ticket hall leading down to one island platform via a long covered passageway and staircases.

History: Opened as 'Hounslow Barracks' on 21 July 1884 as the terminus of the DR extension from Osterley & Spring Grove. The station was served by a shuttle service from that station until 1 April 1886 when through trains were introduced. It was renamed 'Hounslow West' on 1 December 1925 and the ticket hall building opened in reconstructed form on 5 July 1931. Piccadilly Line trains commenced using the station on 13 March 1933, with District Line services ending on 9 October 1964. New platforms and a link from the ticket hall were built for the extension of the line to Hatton Cross, which opened on 19 July 1975.

Design: The original building was an asymmetrical brick structure which was typical of DR architecture of its time. Its replacement is very similar in appearance to that of Ealing Common and marks a further stage in the development of the architectural style created by Holden for the Morden extension of the Northern Line, with the ample use of Portland stone and multi-faceted glazed screens. It differs from Ealing Common largely through the inclusion of one-storey shop units within the design either side of the main structure. The ticket hall retains its wooden passimeter (currently utilised by a newspaper vendor). A vertical chevron pattern within the beige tiling above head height is picked out in dark pink and presents a striking appearance, although its effect is diminished by the protruding ticket office. The floor has recently been attractively retiled, with the pattern reflecting the unusual polygonal shape of the area. The timber telephone recesses look contemporary with the other fittings but in fact were installed later (probably in the late 1930s) in place of a W. H. Smith kiosk. Access to the platform is by means of a long, dog-legged corridor, constructed from timber and corrugated metal sheeting. The platform itself is in excellent condition and reflects the simplicity of design used at stations on the Heathrow extension. Although strictly an island, the two sides of the platform are divided by a series of square, tiled columns which support a slatted metal false ceiling under the main structural girders. The combination of light-coloured terrazzo floor tiling, the false ceiling and new lighting results in a bright and attractive environment. The only significant changes to this area of the station have been the replacement of the original oval plastic benches by standard blue 'tractor' seats in the mid-1980s and the installation of a new signage scheme in early 1993.

Features: Remains of one of the platforms provided for the introduction of Piccadilly Line services in 1933 may be seen from the car park to the rear of the ticket hall building. The car park has been built over most of the track alignment but part of the canopy and the staircase down from the ticket hall are still clearly distinguishable.

On 1 October 1993, a trial stair-lift was brought into operational service, to provide wheelchair users with a means of access between ticket hall and platform levels.

Hyde Park Corner

Piccadilly 4.2m Tube

Layout: Sub-surface ticket hall leading down to two single platforms via escalators and a low level concourse.

History: Opened on 15 December 1906 on the original section of the GNP&BR. Work to install escalators and a new ticket hall beneath the central traffic island was completed on 23 May 1932. Access to the station was modified further in the early 1960s, with the construction of a road underpass and associated subway network.

Design: The station has no surface features and is accessed by means of a public subway network. The ticket hall was modernised in the 1960s and features unusual blue mosaic tiling on the columns in place of the earlier multi-facetted display cases, which still survive at Manor House and Marble Arch. Escalators lead down to a small concourse, which opens directly on to the

two platforms. The latter remain largely as built, with typical Leslie Green wall finishes (brown bordered cream tiling with a repeated yellow cross pattern) and an asphalt floor surface. Although in reasonably good condition, they are marred by the poor state of the tiled signage and the presence of badly matched wall tiling where entrance portals have been blocked up.

Features: The original Green surface building still survives and occupies a site on the south side of Knightsbridge. It is currently used as a pizza parlour and its red faience facade is in fine condition, although the protruding white stone portal appears incongruous with the rest of the architecture. The lift shafts and corridors to the platforms also survive and access to the latter may be observed in one of the cross-passageways, opposite original tiled directional signage which survives in very good condition.

Ickenham

Met/Picc 0.9m Surface

Layout: Street level ticket hall leading down to two single platforms via staircases.

History: Opened as 'Ickenham Halt' on 25 September 1905, following pressure from the local parish council, on a section of line first used by the MR on 4 July 1904. DR services commenced on 1 March 1910 and these were subsequently taken over by the Piccadilly Line on 23 October 1933. The station's buildings were largely reconstructed around 1971.

Design: The current street level building is located above the tracks and is constructed from dark red brick, with identification by means of a pole-mounted roundel. The ticket hall has a very simple design, making use of clerestory windows and St James's floor tiles. An unusual feature is an access staircase leading directly between the ticket hall and the adjacent car park. The platforms have a functional but not unattractive feel to them, with the short covered areas featuring metal canopies and brick walls and the open areas bounded by copious vegetation. An almost completely glazed waiting room was provided on the westbound platform in early 1993.

Kennington

Northern 3.0m 3.5m Tube Grade II

Layout: Street level ticket hall leading down to four single platforms via lifts and low level passageways and staircases.

History: Opened on 18 December 1890 on the original section of the C&SLR. The station was closed between 1 June 1923 and 5 July 1925 to allow for the enlarging of the running tunnels. Further reconstruction and modernisation work was carried out in advance of the extension of the 'Hampstead Railway' to the station on 13 September 1926, including the provision of a 'reversing' loop to the south of the station and new platforms flanking those of the C&SLR.

Design: Unlike the other original C&SLR stations designed by Figgis, Kennington remains largely as built – at least externally. The basic red brick structure survives, along with a distinctive grey dome towards the rear and the original station exit facing Braganza Street. The only major changes are the provision of a standard canopy and a Holden-designed tiled fascia above the entrance. The ticket hall, however, was completely remodelled in the mid-1920s during reconstruction work and features the finishes (ie green and white vitreous wall tiles, St James's floor tiles) common to the other stations on this section of line. Likewise, the low level passageways and platforms make ample use of black and white wall tiles and dark brown concrete paving. However, the overall impression is diminished by the horrendous lime green paintwork which dominates the lower areas.

Features: For many years, the station was also referred to as 'Kennington New Street'. The platform floor surfaces were removed during the tunnel enlarging works – the resultant space used for temporary sidings – and reinstated on completion, although it was deemed necessary to swap over the pedestrian and track sides on the northbound City platform.

Kentish Town

Northern 3.6m Tube

Layout: Street level ticket hall leading down to two single platforms via escalators and low level staircases.
History: Opened on 22 June 1906 on the

Below:
The oldest tube station surface building in the world is at Kennington.
Hugh Madgin

original section of the CCE&HR. Escalators between ticket hall and platform levels were brought into operation on 21 November 1932. The ticket hall was redesigned in 1980/81 to allow replacement of the separate British Rail/London Underground ticket offices by a single facility.

Design: The original Leslie Green-designed surface building still survives and retains many of its early features, such as station name lettering at high level. Its single face frontage has five arched windows, with the centre one separated from the remainder by two much smaller rectangular windows. To its left, a most distinctive angular canopy previously connected to the Midland Railway station still stands. The ticket hall was modernised for the introduction of UTS and the improved interchange with the NSE platforms, and two-tone brown wall tiling and St James's floor tiling now predominate. The staircases and platforms have retained their attractive cream and brown wall tiling, and this has been enhanced in recent years by the installation of an additional metre of cream tiling above the name frieze. Otherwise, the platforms remain largely untouched, with the usual preponderance of unco-ordinated advertising covering over decorative wall patterns and tiled signage.

Features: New entrances on to the platforms were provided for the introduction of escalators in the early 1930s and the intrusive nature of these is evidenced by the way they cut across the original tiling pattern. The access passageways to the redundant lifts may be observed at the northern end of each platform.

Kilburn

Jubilee 4.9m Surface

Layout: Street level ticket hall leading up to one island platform via a staircase.

History: Opened as 'Kilburn & Brondesbury' on 24 November 1879 on the M&SJWR extension from West Hampstead to Willesden Green. The entrance and ticket hall were reconstructed in connection with

track widening between Wembley Park and Finchley Road on 31 May 1915, although the station work itself was not completed until 22 June the following year. It was rebuilt in connection with the transfer of services to the Bakerloo Line on 20 November 1939, although Metropolitan Line trains continued to use the station until 7 December 1940. The station was renamed 'Kilburn' on 25 September 1950 and Jubilee Line services commenced on 1 May 1979.

Design: The entrance to the station is located beneath and adjacent to the bridge carrying the tracks over the Edgware Road. Other than an attractive curved latticed window above the entrance itself, the exterior is rather bland and warrants considerable upgrading. Massive stone piers, which hold up the bridge carrying the southbound tracks, have been cleaned in recent years but nevertheless add to the gloomy nature of this area. The main station identification is found on an angular canopy on the northern side of the bridge, supported by columns clad (unusually) with faience tiling. The location of the ticket hall and the station's history have resulted in it assuming a rather awkward shape and this has been made worse by the intrusion of the UTS suite, resulting in an uncomfortable mixture of 1930s and 1980s finishes. The long staircase to the platform is partially faced in cream glazed brickwork, while the platform itself is typical of others rebuilt in the late 1930s, such as West Hampstead and Dollis Hill. It features a white-panelled canopy, a distinctive rounded waiting room at the northern end and several original silhouette roundels.

Features: The additional bridge over the Edgware Road, installed in early 1915 as part of the track widening project, has lettering proclaiming 'METROPOLITAN RAILWAY' within the metalwork. This feature was picked out in paint during a recent redecoration project and may be observed to best effect from any passing northbound train.

Until the late 1930s, the station was served by two single platforms, either side of what are now the northbound Metropolitan and Jubilee Line tracks. Once the 'up' platform had been converted into the existing island from 18 September 1938, the old 'down' platform was removed and all surface buildings demolished. However, grey brickwork matching that of the surviving staircase may be observed behind advertising hoardings at their eastern end and also from street level.

Kilburn Park

Bakerloo 2.8m Tube Grade II

Layout: Street level ticket hall leading down to two single platforms via escalators and a low level concourse.

History: Opened on 31 January 1915 on the Bakerloo Line extension from Paddington. The station served as the line's terminus for 11 days before services were extended further to Queen's Park. It was known as 'Kilburn & Cambridge Avenue' prior to opening.

Design: The surface building is amongst the most attractive on the Underground and follows the style developed by Leslie Green for the original Tube railways. Its design differs from those of earlier stations through the reduced prominence of the arches, the use of a more finely meshed lattice pattern within the windows and the inclusion of the distinctive UNDERGROUND lettering within the signage at high level. Access to the station was once by means of a splendid barrel-vaulted canopy which stretched out almost to the road, and this survived for over 20 years before being replaced by a more standard design. In the ticket hall, the original timber retail unit remains and the new ticket office frontage has been finished in cream and green tiling to match the original design. The presence of the UTS suite and St James's floor tiling (in place of the original mosaic) have changed its appearance significantly since it was first built, although a recently completed restoration scheme has installed a wholly appropriate pendant lighting scheme and new wall tiling in the original style throughout. The low level concourse and platforms retain much of their original tiling and have been enhanced in recent years through the installation of light-coloured flooring.

Features: A passimeter, which was installed in the ticket hall on 16 December 1921, was the first to be provided on the system and its timber 1930s successor survived until as recently as 1989.

Kingsbury

Jubilee 2.1m Surface

Layout: Street level ticket hall leading down to two single platforms via an overbridge and staircases.

History: Opened on the MR branch line between Wembley Park and Stanmore, with services commencing on 10 December 1932. The branch was transferred to the Bakerloo Line on 20 November 1939 and then in turn to the Jubilee Line on 1 May 1979.

Design: The station building is typical of the style developed by C. W. Clark for the MR prior to it joining the remainder of London's Underground services, under the control of the London Passenger Transport Board, in 1933. Its entrance is contained within a two-storey parade of shops – marked by a steeply pitched roof and dormer windows – and is identified by means of a pole-mounted silhouette roundel at high level. The ticket hall features a high, vaulted ceiling, beige wall tiling and attractive wooden detailing around the telephone recess and shop unit. Whilst the appearance of the covered areas of the platforms, with their dark brick wall finishes and small metal canopies, is fairly functional, they are not unattractive. The only substantial changes to these areas since construction have been recent resurfacing of the floor with concrete paving and the conversion of part of the northbound waiting room into staff accommodation. The station's location within a deep cutting means that the open sections of the platforms are surrounded by a multitude of shrubs, trees and flowers, making them amongst the most attractive on the line. This is tribute to the foresight of the Stanmore Village Preservation Society, who had insisted on the extensive landscaping of the cutting when the line was first built.

King's Cross St Pancras

Circ/H&C/Met/North/Picc/Vict

70.8m 6.0m Misc

Layout: Two sub-surface ticket halls – one leading directly to two single sub-surface platforms (serving Circle, Metropolitan and Hammersmith & City Lines); the other leading down to six single tube platforms via escalators, and low level passageways and staircases.

History: Opened as 'King's Cross' on 10 January 1863 on the original section of the MR. The GNR started services on the Metropolitan's 'City Widened Lines' using MR platforms on 17 February 1868. A subway link – funded jointly by the MR and GNR – was opened on 20 June 1892 to link the station with the main line terminus. Construction of a new road bridge necessitated the demolition of the original building in 1910 and the opening of new entrances on Pentonville Road and King's Cross Bridge, giving access to a wide sub-surface ticket hall. A separate entrance giving access to the 'City Widened Lines' was opened a year later in Pentonville Road on the site currently occupied by the Thameslink ticket hall. This part of the station was renamed 'King's Cross & St Pancras' in 1925 and given its current title eight years later. New Metropolitan Line platforms were brought into service on 14 March 1941 in place of the original areas located approximately 250m to the east, and out of use since 16 October 1940 because of bomb damage.

The platforms belonging to the GNP&BR were opened on 15 December 1906 as 'King's Cross', while the C&SLR platforms – opened on 12 May the following year – had the suffix 'for St Pancras'. The GNP&BR station assumed the same title in 1927 and the entire station was renamed 'King's Cross St Pancras' in 1933. A new circular ticket hall was opened on 18 June 1939 under the forecourt of the main line station, to supersede the original Leslie Green surface building previously on this site and which was eventually demolished in 1963. Installation of escalators in place of lifts and provision of a subway link to St Pancras main line station was also carried out, with work not being completed until 1941. Two of the lift shafts were subsequently brought back into use between 1948 and 1953 as a congestion relief measure.

The C&SLR platforms (now used by Northern Line services) have been closed for long periods on two separate occasions: between 9 August 1922 and 19 April 1924 in order to allow for tunnel enlargement and general modernisation; and between

19 November 1987 and 5 March 1989 in the wake of a major escalator fire, which resulted in the deaths of 31 people.

Services to the Victoria Line platforms commenced on 1 December 1968, necessitating the enlargement of the main ticket hall and the provision of two additional escalators.

Design: The original MR station was located at the junction of King's Cross Road and Pentonville Road and was, when opened, the most prestigious building on the new line. It featured a massive arched, glazed roof spanning between high, brick retaining walls — similar in style to the surviving platforms at Notting Hill Gate — while the exterior featured the two-tone imitation stone finish favoured by John Fowler for all the surface buildings on the original section of the railway. Platform lighting was provided by globe pendant fittings suspended from the roof. The entire structure was removed in 1910 and a standard canopy over the new island platform was provided, along with a lean-to structure on the 'down' Circle Line side. The current platforms are located each side of a wide central concourse (constructed within the bay platform created in 1941 within old running tunnel and converted in 1963) and feature tiling similar in style to their contemporaries at St John's Wood and Highgate.

The main tube ticket hall was completely refitted after the 1989 fire and features green and white wall tiling along with beige-coloured terrazzo. Low level areas constructed for the Victoria Line are clad with finishes typical of the line, with the tiling in the seat recesses portraying five crowns in the shape of a cross. The main concourses retain yellow tiling installed during the late 1930s, while the modernisation of the platforms for both Northern and Piccadilly Lines was completed in 1987, making ample use of an abstract, multicoloured tiled pattern designed by Paul Huxley.

Features: The remains of the original westbound Metropolitan Line platform can be observed as one approaches the station from Farringdon, while most of the old eastbound platform now serves northbound British Rail Thameslink trains. The small 1912 entrance buildings designed by Frank Sherrin still exist on King's Cross Bridge and Pentonville Road, and are currently used as London Underground offices and as a grocery store respectively. Lift shafts which once extended directly up to ticket hall level may be observed in a cross-passageway between the two Northern Line platforms.

Knightsbridge

Piccadilly 16.1m Tube

Layout: Two sub-surface ticket halls leading down to two single platforms via escalators and low level passageways (Sloane Street entrance only).

History: Opened on 15 December 1906 on the original section of the GNP&BR. The original building and lifts were replaced on 18 February 1934 by a sub-surface ticket hall and escalators leading down to platform level. A second entrance and ticket hall adjacent to Harrods were brought into service on 30 July of the same year.

Design: The original surface building faced on to Knightsbridge to the left of its junction with Hooper's Court and although designed by Leslie Green, featured embellishments in the terracotta between the three arched windows which made it unique. A separate secondary entrance was located in Basil Street and this, along with some red faience finishes in the adjacent side road, survive largely. An attractive commercial building, constructed from Portland stone and located at the junction with Sloane Street, incorporates the current station entrance. The blue bar signs protruding from the walls above each entrance are unique to this station and Queensway – both opened in 1934. Walls to the entrance, the attractive circular ticket hall and two other staircases are faced with the cream faience tiles common to stations reconstructed during the 1930s although much has since been renewed. The entrance adjacent to Harrods is similar in style to that in Sloane Street and access to the escalators is by means of a long, narrow passageway, incorporating retail units and a ticket office. Low level concourses and platforms were refinished with a plain

yellow tiling scheme in the 1930s, with new floor tiling being installed during the mid-1980s.

Ladbroke Grove

Hammersmith & City 4.7m Surface

Layout: Street level ticket hall leading up to two single platforms connected by a subway and staircases.

History: Opened as 'Notting Hill' on 13 June 1864 by the semi-independent H&CR, with services provided by the GWR from Farringdon Street. MR trains first served the station on 1 April 1865, and the line became the joint responsibility of the MR and GWR from 1 July 1867. The station's name was changed to 'Notting Hill & Ladbroke Grove' in 1880 and 'Ladbroke Grove (North Kensington)' on 1 June 1919, the suffix eventually being deleted around 1938. The original timber platforms and structural supports were rebuilt around 1900-02 because of a severe deterioration in their condition over the years since construction. The street level building to the south of the railway bridge was reconstructed in the late 1980s and now forms the sole means of access to the station.

Design: Located to the south of the railway bridge, the street building features a plain brick frontage and a cantilevered glazed canopy with a pitched roof. The ticket hall is notable for its high, corrugated metal ceiling and a distinctive, suspended uplighter fitting. At platform level, the station is amongst the most attractive on the H&CR, with its dominant semi-glazed canopies and red brick retaining walls strongly reminiscent of its near contemporary at Hammersmith.

Features: The high crime rate on the Hammersmith & City Line led to the installation of the Underground's first specialist security control room on the eastbound platform. This forms the focus of control for passenger security works at all the stations on the line, these including designated safe waiting areas, alarm points and closed circuit television systems.

An old station entrance, opened before World War 1, still exists to the north of the railway bridge.

Above
Platform view at Ladbroke Grove.

Below
The newly-retiled platform at Lambeth North.

Lambeth North

Bakerloo 2.1m Tube

Layout: Street level ticket hall leading down to two single platforms via lifts and low level passageways and staircases.

History: Opened as 'Kennington Road' on 10 March 1906 as the temporary terminus of the BS&WR. The further extension of the line to Elephant & Castle on 5 August of the same year coincided with the station being renamed 'Westminster Bridge Road'. Its name was changed again on 15 April 1917 to 'Lambeth (North)' and finally to its current form around 1928.

Design: A standard Leslie Green design with three equal arched windows, the surface building originally formed part of a parade of shops, but those to the north were demolished in the 1960s to allow the construction of Baylis Road. The area currently serving as the ticket hall once was the exit from the station, with the entrance located beneath the right-hand arch. However, this had been partially blocked in by the mid-1920s and is currently used as access to staff accommodation. The ox blood red faience tiling was for many years hidden under garish white and beige paint, but this has now been removed. Modernisation of the ticket hall has been carried out in recent years, resulting in the installation of cream wall tiling with a dark green decorative band at dado height and the reinstatement of pendant light fittings. Extensive improvement work has also taken place at platform level, including the replacement of the wall tiling in the lower passageways and on the platforms in the style of the original, and the provision of floor tiling throughout.

Features: Until retiling was completed in 1992, the remains of the original 'Kennington Road' lettering could be observed at intervals along the platform walls beneath the commercial advertising. These platforms were unique in that they were the only ones on the Bakerloo Line to incorporate glass 'Way Out' and 'No Entry' signs within the wall tiling.

Lancaster Gate

Central 3.9m Tube

Layout: Street level ticket hall leading down to two single platforms via lifts and low level passageways and staircases.

History: Opened on 30 July 1900 on the original section of the CLR. It was intended to call the station 'Westbourne' at an early stage of planning.

Design: The original brown terracotta CLR building and five-storey, Delissa Joseph-designed Park Gate Hotel constructed above were demolished in the mid-1960s and the station frontage is now incorporated within the ground floor of the Royal Lancaster Hotel which was built in their place. The ticket hall was extensively modernised in the mid-1980s to allow for the installation of new lifts and UTS equipment, resulting in the replacement of the earlier tiled facade by an attractive glazed screen. In contrast, the low level staircases and platforms have changed little in over 90 years and display some of the last remaining areas of original CLR white tiling in operational use, albeit in poor condition. It is interesting to note the bright nature of these areas caused by the reflective nature of this tiling.

Latimer Road

Hammersmith & City 2.0m Surface

Layout: Street level ticket hall leading up to two single platforms via staircases.

History: Opened on 16 December 1868 by the MR, although services had commenced on this section of line on 13 June 1864. The buildings were reconstructed in 1914.

Design: Awkwardly positioned beneath the raft carrying the eastbound platform over the main road, the station entrance is built discreetly within the brick railway viaduct. The arched roof in the ticket hall is an attractive feature and the whole area was modernised in the mid-1980s with new wall and floor tiles during the reconstruction of the ticket office. Both platforms are of timber construction, although the floor surface has been overlaid with asphalt boarding and plain brick structures have been provided at the western ends to provide staff accommodation. The only features of note are the ornate Corinthian capitals to canopy supports.

Features: Access to the ticket hall was

Above:
Platform scene at Leyton.

Below:
Authentic Central London Railway tiling at Lancaster Gate.

once possible from the northern side of the viaduct and the blocked-in entrance and windows are still evident.

Leicester Square

Picc/North 26.1m 7.5m Tube Grade II (prop.)

Layout: Sub-surface ticket hall leading down to four single platforms via escalators, and low level passageways and staircases.

History: Opened on 15 December 1906 on the original section of the GNP&BR. CCE&HR services commenced on 22 June 1907. Much of the station was reconstructed between October 1930 and 4 May 1935, resulting in the provision of three additional entrances, the creation of a new ticket hall beneath the road junction and the replacement of the lifts by six escalators in two shafts, the latter coming into service on 27 April 1935. An additional interchange passageway between the Piccadilly and Northern lines was opened on 5 July 1948.

Design: The original Leslie Green facades still exist and contain staircase entrances from Charing Cross Road and Cranbourn Street (both opened on 8 June 1936), although the remainder of the frontage is occupied by retail units. An attractive four-storey building, now known as Transad House, was constructed above the station by the mid-1920s. Of the entrances provided during the 1930s reconstruction, the building adjacent to St Martin's Court is of most interest – a simple facade of Portland stone in the style of Holden's earlier designs for stations at the southern end of the Northern Line. The staircases and large circular ticket hall have been faced with materials typical of their age – cream faience wall tiles and St James's floor tiles. A dado frieze, containing a unique LT repeated pattern, features within the tiling. The impressive nature of the area is spoilt, however, by the presence of an unsympathetic lighting scheme, garish retail units and ugly telephone kiosks. A station control room is currently being constructed in the centre of the hall. The 1930s finishes which once also extended down to platform level still remain on the original access areas. Both sets of platforms were modernised in 1985 through the installation of new wall

tiling (black/white for the Northern Line: blue/white for the Piccadilly Line), designed to reflect the station's position as the cinema heart of London. Vitreous enamel portals around the entrances were also installed, although these had to be modified around 1990 when they had been found to reduce the platform width to an unacceptable extent. The dull asphalt floor finish, which diminished the effectiveness of the modernisation work, was replaced in 1993 by light grey tiling, which has improved illumination levels considerably.

Features: A sign in raised lettering proclaiming 'J. Wisden & Company' may be observed within the facade in Cranbourn Street; the floor above the station once serving as the offices of the company producing the famous cricketing almanac. The escalators to the Piccadilly Line platforms were, at 161ft, the longest in the world when first built. One of the original entrances provided during the 1930s reconstruction was taken out of use during the 1980s but the stone-clad building may still be seen at the junction of Little Newport Street and Charing Cross Road.

Leyton

Central 5.0m Surface

Layout: Street level ticket hall leading down to two single platforms via an overbridge and staircases.

History: Opened as 'Low Leyton' on 22 August 1856 by the ECR. The station was renamed 'Leyton' on 27 November 1868, with the current ticket hall building constructed on a new road bridge (replacing the earlier level crossing) in 1879. An additional entrance was opened at the eastern end of the platforms in 1901. Central Line services commenced on 5 May 1947.

Design: The original ECR ticket hall building survives at the western end of the eastbound platform and is best viewed from the car park. The street level building is a simple affair, located on the apex of the bridge over the tracks. Radically altered for the start of Central Line services, recent UTS and refurbishment projects have resulted in the installation of new cream tiling on both the internal and exterior walls of the ticket hall. At platform level, the station remains largely as built, dominated by large valanced canopies supported by decorative iron pillars and brackets. However, the retaining walls have been covered by a cream paint system in recent years in order to disguise the irregular and poorly patched nature of the original red brickwork. A small brick building was installed by a major resignalling project in 1992 at the eastern end of the eastbound platform and this structure effectively blocks off access to the secondary exit in Langthorne Road.

Leytonstone

Central 4.8m 0.1m Surface

Layout: Sub-surface ticket hall (accessed by long subways) leading up to one island and one single platform via staircases.

History: Opened on 22 August 1856 by the ECR. The station was reconstructed first around 1892 and later to coincide with the commencement of Central Line services on 5 May 1947, the latter including the provision of an extra platform face.

Design: The existing main street entrance in Church Lane was built for the inauguration of Central Line services and acts mainly as an access point to a long subway leading to the sub-surface ticket hall beneath the tracks. The subways, the ticket hall itself and staircases to the platforms are all faced with the cream faience wall tiling typical of the period. No pre-1947 features survive at platform level and the only features of note are the curved, glazed skylights located within the canopy soffits.

Liverpool Street

Cent/Circ/H&C/Met 34.3m 3.7m Misc

Layout: Three ticket halls (one at street level, the other two leading directly off the main line station concourse) leading to two single sub-surface platforms via over-bridges and staircases and to two single tube platforms (serving the Central Line) via escalators and low level concourses.

History: Opened as 'Bishopsgate' on 12 July 1875, although MR services had been running into platforms 1 and 2 of the GER's Liverpool Street main line station since 1 February the same year, prior to the completion of the MR's own station. The MR station was renamed 'Liverpool Street' on 1 November 1909 and a new terminus station for the CLR provided on 28 July 1912 following its extension from Bank. Access was provided to the nearby Broad Street station on the North London Railway through the installation of escalators to street level on 10 October 1912 and lifts to platform level on 23 February the following year. Two escalators also provided access to the GER's main line station at around the same time. Extensive modifications to the Central Line ticket hall, including the provision of an additional escalator, were completed on 19 May 1925. Work commenced before the outbreak of World War 2 to reconstruct the stations, in order to provide improved interchange prior to the extension of the Central Line eastwards, which opened on 4 December 1946. Further works, completed by early 1951, included the provision of two new escalators to Central Line lower concourse level and a new sub-surface ticket hall below part of the main line station. A major development of the main line station has resulted in the recent opening of a new ticket hall leading off the BR concourse and will eventually lead to the modernisation of all Underground areas.

Design: The main entrance to the station is via the refurbished BR concourse. Its magnificent new ticket hall is one of the largest on the system and features an 'egg-crate' false ceiling, unusually-coursed off-white wall tiles and a terrazzo floor finish. The latter incorporates patterns reflecting details from No 50, Liverpool Street, which was demolished in the redevelopment of the main line station. The secondary ticket hall beneath the main line platforms is finished in a similar manner.

A particularly distinctive ceiling, featuring square moulded raised panels, lines the soffit of the escalator shaft leading down to the Central Line areas. The platforms until recently retained their original CLR tiling, albeit in very poor condition. These areas have now been modernised in a most pleasing manner, making use of new white tiling in a similar bond and proportion to the original. Terrazzo flooring and white vitreous enamel ceiling panels, continuing the design theme of the concourses and ticket halls, have also been installed, along with silhouette roundels and back-wall lighting.

The original 80ft span overall roof over the Circle Line platforms was removed in 1911-12 and its place taken by a steel and concrete raft, upon which a long shopping arcade, designed by Frank Sherrin, was constructed. A ticket hall was incorporated at its western end at the junction with Old Broad Street, this opening on 11 March 1912. This frontage has since been refaced and now has a rather drab appearance. The platforms now present a muddled appearance with finishes of a variety of vintages, not helped by the dull nature of the metal girder soffit above. A recent modernisation scheme has installed large sheets of white vitreous enamel metal panelling in order to achieve design consistency. The disused platform to the south was previously a terminating bay for trains and was first used in this role on 1 February 1910.

Features: An unusual feature – passenger luggage lifts – was installed at this station around 1897/98. The escalators brought into service in 1912 for the opening of the new CLR platforms were the first on the 'underground' network to act as the primary means of access to and from platform level. A timber and brick signalbox dating from 1875 survives at the western end of the outer rail platform.

London Bridge

Northern 14.3m Tube

Layout: Sub-surface ticket hall leading down to two single platforms via escalators and low level passageways.

History: Opened on 25 February 1900 when the C&SLR extended services to Moorgate. A subway link to the SER main line station, with associated lifts and ticket office, was opened on 2 December 1901. Services were suspended between 29 November 1923 and 30 November 1924 to allow the enlarging of the running tunnels and general modernisation, including the replacement of the original lifts, although work was not fully completed for almost three years. The platforms were closed

again between 7 September 1939 and 18 May 1940 for the installation of flood alleviation measures because of the danger of bomb damage to the nearby tunnels under the Thames. A new sub-surface ticket hall beneath the bus station and escalators leading to platform level were brought into service on 19 November 1967, with a further subway linking it to the BR forecourt opening eight years later.

Design: The sub-surface ticket hall is accessed from three staircases from the bus station and is faced in standard 1960s grey 'Victoria Line' tiling. It differs from other stations refurbished during this period through the use of black and white chequer-board tiling as the floor finish. As with so many other stations, the POM enclosure intrudes on to the floor space, thereby hindering the movement of passengers. The low level passageways have recently been retiled to full height in a pseudo-1920s design with black borders around poster sites and this has substantially improved these areas. The platforms retain the standard green-trimmed tiling common to all Northern Line stations modernised in the 1920s. Some of the earlier white C&SLR tiling may be observed at the bottom of the trackside walls and under paint on the soffits. A trial integrated trunking system, installed in the late 1980s, runs throughout the low level areas of the station.

Features: The original C&SLR building still remains largely intact at the junction of London Bridge Street and Station Approach, and served as one of the station's entrances until the mid-1960s.

Loughton

Central 1.7m Surface Grade II (prop.)

Layout: Street level ticket hall leading up to two island platforms via a subway and staircases.

History: Opened on 22 August 1856 by the ECR, which became part of the GER in 1862. The station served as a terminus until the branch was extended to Ongar on 24 April 1865, from which time it was resited from its original position near the High Road on to the new line. The proposed transfer to the LPTB resulted in the station's complete reconstruction by the LNER (which had incorporated the GER in 1923); the new buildings first being used on 28 April 1940, although Central Line services did not start until 21 November 1948.

Design: The large entrance building is the most significant surface structure built for the eastern extensions of the Central Line. Designed by John Murray Easton (of architects, Easton & Robertson), it consists of a brown brick, two-storey box with a single large arched window dominating the front and rear elevations. The ticket hall is most impressive; the massive arched ceiling contrasting with the square form of the exterior. A tiled floor finish has been carried through into the wide subway under the tracks and staircases to the platforms. The platforms themselves are perhaps the most elegant examples of their type, with their rounded concrete canopies supported by discreet columns. Roundels built into the railings at the top of the staircases and within the seating units are a particularly distinctive feature of this station. The only discordant note is the blocking in of the glazed skylights within the canopies during structural works in the late 1980s.

'Tiffany' lamps remain in position on the frontage. The walls above the staircase to the ticket hall feature an attractive beige and green tile pattern, incorporating mosaic versions of the UNDERGROUND roundel at high level. The ticket hall itself and the area around the top of the escalators are clad with white tiling, bordered by a green chequered pattern. A decorative capital at the head of the column in front of the ticket office is of particular interest. The original multi-coloured mosaic floor surface can still be seen in places but most is covered by a layer of asphalt. Lower level areas of the station are very similar to the other tube stations built on this extension. Although the basic tiled fabric is fairly attractive, its appearance has been marred through the installation of particularly ugly escalators and the preponderance of poorly co-ordinated advertising. The crenellated appearance of the roundels was modified in the 1930s in conjunction with the introduction of the name frieze.

Features: A superb 1920s pole-mounted sign stands remote from the station at the junction of the Edgware Road with Abercorn Place and features its original roundel graphics on one side. A similar feature also survives at Warwick Avenue.

Maida Vale

Bakerloo 2.2m Tube Grade II

Layout: Sub-surface ticket hall leading down to two single platforms via escalators and low level concourse.

History: Opened on 6 June 1915, although services on the Bakerloo Line extension from Paddington to Kilburn Park had commenced on 31 January of the same year.

Design: Maida Vale, along with its sister station at Kilburn Park, is generally regarded as one of the most attractive and important examples of railway architecture in London. Although constructed by Heaps in the same style as the buildings designed by Leslie Green for the original section of the line, it is somewhat smaller in scale, with shallower window arches, a distinctive lattice pattern within the glazing and embossed lettering within the white faience at high level. Three examples of the original

Manor House

Piccadilly 6.3m Tube

Layout: Sub-surface ticket hall leading down to two single platforms via escalators and a low level concourse.

History: Opened on 19 September 1932 on the initial stage of the Piccadilly Line's eastern extension from Finsbury Park to Arnos Grove. Early plans for what became the Victoria Line showed the route taking over Manor House station from the Piccadilly Line.

Design: Perhaps Manor House has the least prominent street presence of any of the stations designed by Holden for this extension. The only surface building of note is a plain brick structure, which acts as an entrance porch to the staircase leading to ticket hall level. Access is also by means of three open staircases at the corners of the

Above
Loughton station entrance from the north.

Below
Maida Vale station frontage.

nearby road junction, linked by long passageways. The ticket hall itself presents an unattractive appearance because of the intrusion of the UTS suite and an ugly lighting scheme. Nevertheless, some interesting features survive, most notably a circular patterning applied to the false ceiling soffit, a timber retail unit with a curved frontage (currently disused) and a cylindrical glazed notice case positioned around a pillar in the centre of the floor. The lower concourse and platforms are similar in appearance to those elsewhere on the line north of Finsbury Park, with decorative metal grilles within the platform walls designed by the artist, Harold Stabler.

Mansion House

Circ/Dist 3.6m Sub-Surface

Layout: Sub-surface ticket hall leading down to one island and one single platform via an overbridge and staircases.

History: Opened on 3 July 1871 when the DR extended its services from Blackfriars. The station was known as 'Cannon Street' prior to its opening. It served as the terminus until the line was extended eastwards on 6 October 1884. Substantial modifications to the platforms' layout were carried out in 1910/11 for electrification and again c1956. The ticket hall was rebuilt around 1912/13 in conjunction with subway construction by the Corporation of London. The street entrance was rebuilt around 1928 and the entire station was remodelled before and during redevelopment of the property above in recent years. This necessitated its closure between 29 October 1989 and 10 February 1991.

Design: The original station was built in a cutting in the style of other MR and DR stations of the time and originally had two island platforms, with three sets of tracks. An additional set of tracks was provided from around 1884 and standard umbrella canopies had replaced the overall glazed roof by the mid-1890s. The platforms were later built over. Modernisation work resulted in the provision of a Portland stone facade (very similar in appearance to that provided at Clapham South on the Morden extension) and faience wall finishes throughout.

Further improvements, especially those carried out during the station's recent closure, have resulted in the creation of a very attractive environment; white wall tiles, a proprietary ceiling system and mottled brown terrazzo flooring being the main features. A modern signing scheme, new lighting and extensive passenger security measures complete the impression of quality that pervades these areas.

Features: The metal railings at the entrances to the subways date from the latter's construction, which is commemorated by a plaque marking their opening by the Lord Mayor. The unusually wide single platform results from it serving as an island between 1910 and 1968, when the northern bay tracks were removed and subsequently blocked off. The route of these tracks is still visible as one approaches the station from the west.

Marble Arch

Central 10.4m Tube

Layout: Sub-surface ticket hall leading down to two single platforms via escalators, low level passageways and staircases.

History: Opened on 30 July 1900 on the original section of the CLR. Work commenced in September 1930 on the construction of a new ticket hall beneath Oxford Street, the rebuilding of the surface building and the replacement of lifts by escalators – the latter coming into service on 15 August 1932. Further modernisation work, especially at platform level, was completed in 1985.

Design: The original surface building matched those still existing at Queensway and Oxford Circus, and located on the northwestern corner of the junction with Old Quebec Street. During the 1930s reconstruction, a plain stone facade was provided and this has been altered in recent years by the addition of a curved, glazed canopy over the entrance. The ticket hall features faience-clad walls, a St James's tiled floor and glazed hexagonal display cases around two structural columns. These finishes, along with the black and white wall tiling on the low level passageways and staircases, all date from the 1930s. The platform walls have been clad with white vitreous enamel panels featuring highly decorative areas around the seating units, designed by Annabel Grey, while the floors have been relaid in a distinctive dark grey terrazzo.

Features: Standard 1930s metal railings surround the staircase access to the council-owned subway network on the south side of Oxford Street.

Marylebone

Bakerloo 4.7m Tube

Layout: Street level ticket hall (within British Rail station concourse) leading down to two single platforms via escalators and low level passageways and staircases.

History: Opened as 'Great Central' on 27 March 1907 as the temporary terminus of the BS&WR extension from Baker Street. Services were extended further to Edgware Road on 15 June of the same year. The station's name was changed to 'Marylebone' on 15 April 1917. Its surface building was bombed during World War 2 and a new ticket office was opened in early 1943 within the main line station, along with escalators to take passengers to lower concourse level.

Design: White vitreous enamel panels were applied to the walls of the ticket office in the late 1980s. The escalator shaft and low level passageway leading to the platform areas feature panelled false ceilings, installed in early 1992. Almost all of the wall tiling at platform level was replaced in 1990 in a style and colour matching the original. Beige ceramic floor tiles have been installed throughout, along with new seating and signing to the latest standards.

Features: Although Marylebone was the name chosen originally, the title 'Lisson Grove' was used in early literature prior to opening. It is suggested that the station was opened as 'Great Central' at the insistence of Sam Fay, the general manager of the recently opened main line railway, then known under that title. A tiled panel incorporating this legend has been retained at

the northern end of the northbound platform.

The original surface building was sited on the northern side of the junction of Harewood Avenue and Harewood Row. Although clad with the red terracotta typical of the early deep tube railway stations, its appearance was more akin to that of Maida Vale than its contemporary at Edgware Road, lacking the wide arches at first floor level that characterised most of Green's stations and explained by the location of the ticket office at basement level. This building was demolished in February 1971. The timber passimeter removed from the ticket hall has been donated to the proposed Museum of Ticketing and is currently housed in the Manchester Bus Museum.

Mile End

Cent/Dist/H&C 7.5m 22.3m Sub-Surface

Layout: Sub-surface ticket hall leading down to two island platforms via overbridges and staircases.

History: Opened on 2 June 1902 by the Whitechapel & Bow Railway and served by District Railway trains. The station was completely reconstructed to allow for Central Line services, which commenced on 4 December 1946, although the rebuilding was largely completed before the outbreak of World War 2 in 1939.

Design: The original station resembled those built around the same time at Bow Road and Stepney Green but was considerably larger, boasting seven arched bay windows. The reconstructed surface building was designed under Heaps' control and marks a return to the flat, Portland stone screen design used by Holden in the early 1930s. Faience and St James's tiled finishes in the ticket hall were renewed in the late 1980s to a complementary design. The platforms are of a style unique to this station and remind one of a scene from the New York subway with its numerous pillars. These areas were modernised in the late 1980s, resulting in the use of white vitreous enamel panels on the trackside walls, panelled false ceilings and a green and white tile pattern.

Mill Hill East

Layout: Street level ticket hall leading up to one single platform via a staircase.

History: Opened as 'Mill Hill' on 22 August 1867 by the GNR and renamed 'Mill Hill East' on 1 March 1928. Northern Line trains first served the station on 18 May 1941 as the initial stage of an extension of the line from Finchley Central to Edgware via LNER tracks, which was never completed because of World War 2. The extension to Mill Hill East was completed during wartime only because of the station's proximity to Inglis Barracks.

Design: One of the simplest stations still in existence on the system, Mill Hill East remains largely in its original form. The main low brick building is typical of the style developed by the GNR and is spoilt only by the crude infilling of windows to the right of the entrance for the installation of the UTS ticket office. The building is fronted by a substantial bus forecourt and contains a small discreet ticket hall of no particular architectural merit. The elevated platform is reached by means of an attractive, brick-lined staircase and served by a single track. It is notable for being largely of wooden construction – the only example that survives on the Underground following the demise of Hillingdon – although recently covered by asphalt panels. The 'traditional' look of the station is further enforced by the small brick waiting room building in the centre of the platform and the open horizontal railings along its rear.

Features: The metal girder bridges carrying the railway over roads south of the station were installed in anticipation of the Northern Line extension to Edgware: note the space available for a second set of tracks on the southern side. The viaduct carrying the railway over the Dollis Brook marks the Underground's highest point above street level (60ft/18.46m).

Monument

Layout Sub-surface ticket hall leading down to two single platforms via an over-bridge and staircases.

History: Opened as 'Eastcheap' on 6 October 1884 on the DR extension from Mansion House. The station's name changed to 'The Monument' on 1 November of the same year and the definite article has been gradually lost over time. The street level building was rebuilt around 1909 to a George Sherrin design and this allowed for the construction a new sub-surface ticket hall. An escalator link connecting the station to Bank came into service on 18 September 1933. The ticket hall was enlarged in 1935, with the original entrance being supplemented by open staircases linked to a local authority-owned subway network. Further reconstruction and modernisation work has been under way since the late 1980s.

Design: Access to the station is by means of an inconspicuous entrance in the ground floor of an office development facing Fish Street Hill. The ticket hall has been extensively modified and modernised in recent years and is now amongst the best designed anywhere. Mottled grey wall tiling and two-tone grey terrazzo, identical to that used at Bank, are also utilised here, with the eventual intention of integrating the design of the two stations. The spacious nature of the ticket hall is enhanced by the presence of concealed lighting within the ceiling cornice and distinctive triangular uplighters on the pillars. These finishes have been extended to the over-bridge and platform level concourses, and at the time of writing are being installed on the platforms themselves. On completion, this station will serve as a fine example of modern station architecture through the use of high quality finishes.

Features: This station was originally to be called 'King William Street' prior to its opening. The Corporation of London-owned subway network is notable for some fine bronze signage and a plaque commemorating its opening on 2 December 1935. Bronze railings around the four staircases are almost identical to those found at Knightsbridge, with some of the original station name panels still surviving within the metalwork.

Moorgate

Circ/H&C/Met/North 13.7m 3.6 Misc Grade II

Layout: One surface and one sub-surface ticket hall leading to two island and two single platforms (partly used by NSE Thameslink services) via a subway and staircases and to two single tube platforms (serving the Northern Line) via escalators and low level passageways and staircases.

Listing applies to C&SLR building only.

History: Opened as 'Moorgate Street' on 23 December 1865 as the terminus of the MR extension from Farringdon Street. The station was modified for the extension of the line to Liverpool Street in 1875 and completely rebuilt from 1894, resulting in the replacement of the dangerously unstable overall roof by individual platform canopies and the provision of a new ticket hall building, which came into service on 17 June 1896.

The C&SLR extended its services to this station on 25 February 1900 and the platforms served as the terminus of the line until it was extended once more on 17 November the following year. The station also served as a terminus for the GN&CR from 14 February 1902 under the title of 'Moorgate'. Interchange was provided between the deep level lines and the MR platforms from 2 September 1912. A new street level ticket hall and entrance was created when the Delissa Joseph-designed 'Britannic House' – built for the Anglo-Persian Oil Company (later to become British Petroleum) – was opened on the eastern side of the Moorgate thoroughfare in 1924.

The C&SLR platforms were closed between 29 November 1923 and 19 April 1924 for the enlargement of the running tunnels and finishes were modernised during this period. These areas of the station were renamed 'Moorgate' from the time of reopening. The MR station was renamed similarly on 24 October of the same year. Escalators, giving access from a new subsurface ticket hall to the Northern Line and GN&CR platforms, replaced the station's four lifts on 3 July 1924 and 2 October 1936

respectively. Northern Line platforms were closed again between 7 September 1939 and 18 May 1940 for the installation of flood alleviation measures, because of the danger of bomb damage to the nearby tunnels under the Thames.

The GN&CR platforms, which had been taken over by first the MR and then by the Northern Line, were closed between 6 September 1975 and 8 November 1976 to allow for modifications as part of the line's transfer to British Rail control. Metropolitan Line platforms and access areas were also extensively rebuilt in the late 1960s in connection with the Barbican development.

Moorgate was the site of the worst accident ever experienced at an Underground station, on 28 February 1975. A Northern Line train on the Northern City section crashed into the end of one of the terminus platforms, resulting in 42 fatalities and a further 74 persons being seriously injured.

Design: The original MR station entrance originally consisted of small pavilions either side of Moorfields,but no evidence of these has survived. In contrast, the C&SLR entrance building remains almost untouched. Designed by T Phillips Figgis to serve as the headquarters for the railway, this splendid building occupies an 'end of block' location and features Portland stone finishes at ground level, incorporating highly decorated panels and an attractive curved section around the apex. The station's name is picked out in individual lettering on each of the three facades, although the original entrance on the Moor Place elevation has since been blocked in. A grand porticoed entrance to the 1896 ticket hall, designed by George Sherrin, was rebuilt in the late 1960s and the new entrance to the station – opened in 1969 – is somewhat less attractive, being lost in the base of a large office development. The Britannic House elevation remains largely unchanged, although the original exit is the only one of the three access points that survives and now contains a staircase to Northern Line ticket hall level. Both ticket halls have been substantially rebuilt over the years and now consist of unco-ordinated 1960s and 1980s finishes.

The Metropolitan Line platforms were covered over by an office development in the late 1960s and now have a somewhat claustrophobic atmosphere, caused by a low false ceiling and the areas over the tracks being painted black. Northern Line platform areas feature off-white, 1960s wall tiling and a slatted ceiling system, although some of the original 1920s finishes are still evident, most notably below the advertisements on the trackside walls.

Moor Park

Metropolitan 0.5m 0.1m Surface

Layout: Street level ticket hall leading up to two island platforms via a subway network and staircases.

History: Opened as 'Sandy Lodge' on 9 May 1910 in order to provide access to a nearby golf course of the same name. Services on this section of line had commenced on 1 September 1887. The station's name was changed to 'Moor Park & Sandy Lodge' on 18 October 1923 and to 'Moor Park' on 25 September 1950. The original timber structures, consisting of two single platforms connected by a footbridge, were completely rebuilt to accommodate the quadrupling of the tracks, the new island platforms being brought into use on 23 April 1961.

Design: This station is quite distinctive, especially at street level. The main building is faced with mosaic tiles and timber panelling, while the attractive ticket hall has an unusual pitched roof and again makes ample use of timber finishes. Dull tiling, which until recently lined the subway and staircase walls, has been replaced by a most attractive design. The platforms have a pleasantly open design, with simple canopies covering around half of their length and extensive glazing within the walls of the staircases and waiting rooms. The station's location on the edge of woodland means that it has a very rural setting.

Morden

Northern 4.1m Surface Grade II (prop.)

Layout: Street level ticket hall leading down to one single and two island platforms via overbridges and staircases.

History: Opened on 13 September 1926 as the terminus of the Northern Line's southwards extension from Clapham Common.

Design: The main station building is the largest on the southern extension of the line and is arguably the most impressive. In common with the other sites, the exterior uses a plain, three faced, Portland stone design with a roundel incorporated within the glazing, although it differs by having the side elevations at right angles to the main structure and by the extension of the blue name frieze across the top of the shops to either side of the entrance. The inappropriately designed building which encloses the station was constructed around 1963. The ticket hall takes an octagonal form and is centred around a similarly shaped skylight. Poorly designed lighting and the poor state of the floor surface tend to diminish the appearance of this potentially attractive area. Access to the platforms is by means of a system of overbridges and staircases, the walls of which have been clad on both sides using standard 1920s vitreous enamel tiles. The platforms themselves are partially covered over by a steel trussed, timber and glass roof, not dissimilar in style to the example constructed at Edgware two years earlier. The track layout consists of single bays between each pair of platforms. In common with the tube stations on the extension, the floor surface has been concrete paved and large timber advertising panels dominate the trackside walls. In addition, some original hardwood benches and timber-framed signs survive.

Mornington Crescent

Northern 1.7m Tube Grade II

Layout: Street level ticket hall leading down to two single platforms via lifts and low level passageways and staircases.

History: Opened on 22 June 1907 on the original section of the CCE&HR. The station was originally to have been known as 'Seymour Street'. It was closed on 23 October 1992 to allow for the replacement of the original lifts and general refurbishment, although the project was suspended later the same year because of budgetary restrictions.

Design: The surface building retains many of the original features used on Leslie Green designs, such as name lettering at high level and decorative lamp brackets (although the latter were originally positioned above the glazed arches and are currently in storage). It occupies a corner site and, for several years, access was by means of an entrance to the left of the arch on the elevation facing Camden High Street. The ticket hall was substantially rebuilt in the mid-1980s for the installation of the UTS ticket office and equipment, resulting in the entrance being relocated to under the right-hand arch on the longer, Hampstead Road elevation. Installation of decorative wall tiling to match the original and pendant light fittings was also carried out. Low level passageways and staircases retain their original dark blue bordered tiling, although cream tiling was applied to the soffits in the late 1980s. The finishes on the platforms remain as installed originally and are now in a very poor state of repair. Substantial modernisation work will be carried out once the lift replacement project resumes and will result in the retiling of all surfaces in a style consistent with the original design.

Neasden

Jubilee 2.1m Surface

Layout: Street level ticket hall leading down to one island and two single platforms via an overbridge and staircases.

History: Opened as 'Kingsbury & Neasden' on 2 August 1880 on the M&SJWR extension from Willesden Green to Harrow (later Harrow-on-the-Hill). The station was renamed 'Neasden & Kingsbury' on 1 January 1910 and finally 'Neasden' on 1 January 1932 to avoid confusion with the Stanmore branch line station at Kingsbury, which was to open under a year later. Responsibility for the station transferred to the Bakerloo Line on 20 November 1939, although Metropolitan Line trains continued to use the facilities until 7 December 1940. Jubilee Line services commenced on 1 May 1979.

Design: The original MR street building still exists but has been heavily modified over the years and now presents a somewhat confused appearance. The central part of the structure was rebuilt *circa* 1969 and again in the mid-1980s for the installation of UTS facilities, resulting in the provision of a vertical glazed screen at high level set back from the main frontage. Either side of this remain the original parts of the building, constructed from red brick and featuring pitched roofs and narrow arched windows. The ticket hall is not unattractive but is spoilt by the intrusive nature of the new ticket office, which previously had been located on the site of the current retail unit. Platform areas have also been extensively rebuilt, through the conversion of the original single 'up' platform into an island and the provision of an additional single platform in January 1914 so as to allow fast and slow trains through the station. New canopies were provided throughout and much of the accommodation replaced, although the original red brick finishes of the (now largely disused) 'down' Metropolitan platform remain.

Features: The subway at the northern end of the station was provided in 1922 to allow train staff access to the nearby Neasden Depot without needing to use the hazardous level crossings that existed previously.

Newbury Park

Central 2.2m Surface Grade II

Layout: Street level ticket hall leading down to two single platforms via an footbridge and staircases.

Listing applies to forecourt canopy only.

History: Opened on 1 May 1903 by the GER on its branch line between Woodford and Ilford. Services on the newly extended Central Line commenced on 14 December 1947.

Design: The dull ticket hall area is accessed directly from the bus forecourt (see 'Features'). It leads on to a simple, painted concrete overbridge installed in the late 1940s, with similarly decorated staircases to platform level. The platforms themselves are typical of the GER stations of this vintage, with their ornate bracketry (incorporating the Railway's initials at high level), slatted timber roof panels and dark red brick retaining walls. Distinctive timber benches dating from the 1900s are located in the bays between the brickwork pilasters and are contemporary with the wooden poster frames above. Overall, the station is notable for the extreme contrast between the 1940s finishes at street level and the turn of the century architecture on the platforms, although it should be said that the staircases and overbridge have been surprisingly well integrated, without destroying the cohesion of the original station.

Features: The bus forecourt in front of the station is covered by a vast concrete roof. Designed by Oliver Hill and opened on 6 July 1949, it was given a Festival of Britain award by the Council for Architectural Town Planning & Building Design two years later and is now a Grade II listed structure. The original GER building was demolished in 1957 when the bridge carrying the Eastern Avenue over the railway was rebuilt.

North Acton

Central 2.3m 0.1m Surface

Layout: Ground level ticket hall (accessed by two long sloping footpaths) leading down to one island and one single platform via a footbridge and staircases.

History: Opened on 5 November 1923, although services on this section of the Central Line – in conjunction with the GWR – had commenced on 3 August 1920. The station was initially to have been called 'Victoria Road'. There were originally two further platforms on the adjacent GWR tracks. These had replaced an earlier station, located around 23 chains (500m) to the west on Park Royal Road, which had been served between 1 May 1904 and 31 January 1913. The existing footbridge once extended over the GWR platforms, which were closed on 30 June 1947 when the Central Line extension to Greenford was opened.

Design: The two footpaths from street level are bounded by ugly galvanised steel palisade fencing. Although the small, red brick building is quite attractive, this is diffi-

cult to appreciate given its location half-way down a hillside. The ticket hall has a pleasant, intimate feel but is spoilt by insensitive lighting. The eastbound platform has recently undergone extensive modification involving its conversion into an island, as part of a project to resignal the whole Central Line. This has necessitated the partial demolition of the original timber buildings on this platform and their replacement by heavily glazed modular structures. An attractive wooden building remains on the other platform, built into the brick retaining wall which extends the entire length.

North Ealing

Piccadilly 0.8m Surface

Layout: Street level ticket hall leading down to two single platforms via footbridge and staircases.

History: Opened on 23 June 1903 on the DR extension from Ealing Common to South Harrow. Services were transferred to the Piccadilly Line on 4 July 1932.

Design: North Ealing is unusual in that it is one of the very few stations on the sections of line taken over by the Piccadilly Line in the early 1930s which was not extensively rebuilt. Indeed, it has remained almost unaltered since it was first constructed. The main entrance building resembles a large detached house with its pebble-dashed walls, prominent chimney stacks and gabled roof. A heavy metal canopy above the wooden entrance doors is cantilevered off the wall and supported by ties from above, while the windows and doors at low level are marked by a red brick border. The small ticket hall has largely painted finishes and retains few original features. The westbound platform is reached by means of a short staircase, above which is to be found a fine early enamel sign indicating 'To Trains For Harrow And Uxbridge', and features a very attractive valanced canopy over part of its length. In contrast, the eastbound platform is accessed via a crude metal footbridge, with a small timber waiting room being the only feature of note.

Features: North Ealing was the last surface station to retain a full set of the distinc-

Above:
Lengthy platform shelters and seats abound at Newbury Park. *Hugh Madgin*

Below:
The suburban style of North Ealing.

tive large platform roundels installed during the 1920s (although isolated examples still remain at Burnt Oak and Morden). Their poor condition led to replacement by near replicas around 1989.

Features: The remains of a high level walkway which linked the station with Weymouth Avenue until 1942 may be observed to the north of the tracks while travelling towards South Ealing.

Northfields

Piccadilly 2.9m Surface Grade II (prop.)

Layout: Street level ticket hall leading down to two island platforms via an overbridge and staircases.

History: Opened as 'Northfield (Ealing)' on 16 April 1908, although services had been running on this section of the DR since 1 May 1883 and a halt had existed since electrification in June 1905. The station's name changed to 'Northfields & Little Ealing' on 11 December 1911. The constuction of a new depot nearby required the provision of an underpass, which led to the resiting of the station to its current location, the new buildings first being used under the name of 'Northfields' on 19 May 1932. Piccadilly Line services commenced on 9 January 1933 and District Line trains stopped using the station on 9 October 1964.

Design: The main station building is very similar in style and scale to that of Sudbury Hill. In many ways an archetypal 1930s Holden station, it features a broad blue name frieze extending across the edge of the canopy which extends forward from the main brick box elevation. The entrance lobby and ticket hall are faced with the distinctive black bricks at low level which Holden and his colleagues specified for four stations only. New staff accommodation and the UTS suite have been built into the previously open concourse to the south; the decline in symmetry being 'sweetened' through the use of matching brickwork. The floor space features two combined uplighter/seating units which were installed in early 1993 and complement the surrounding finishes well. The platform canopies are simple and attractive in design, although the poor state of the concrete supports has necessitated their painting in recent years. Concrete lamp standards dating from 1932 were replaced around 1983 by simpler, less attractive fittings.

North Harrow

Metropolitan 1.2m Surface

Layout: Street level ticket hall leading up to two single platforms via staircases.

History: Opened jointly by the MR and GCR on 22 March 1915 as a halt on a section of line first used on 25 May 1885. The station was rebuilt at street level in conjunction with a road widening scheme, with all work being completed in early 1931.

Design: The ticket hall is accessed by an entrance to the north of the bridge carrying the railway over Imperial Drive. This entrance remains almost exactly as built, making use of the cream terracotta tiling favoured by C. W. Clark. This material extends over the adjacent parade of shops, creating a unified appearance for the area. In contrast, the original entrance to the south of the bridge, which once matched its northern neighbour, was poorly rebuilt in the early 1960s when a second railway bridge was installed (in conjunction with Metropolitan Line four-tracking north of Harrow-on-the-Hill) and has been blocked off in recent years. The ticket hall retains many of its original faience finishes, especially on the columns supporting the high ceiling. Four large skylights provide ample illumination during day-time hours and this area has recently been enhanced through the laying of a cream-coloured tiled floor finish. The staircases to the platforms were for many years covered with timber panelling but have now been upgraded through the use of beige wall tiling (with burgundy borders around the poster sites) and stainless steel handrails. Original black-painted, timber buildings and extensively glazed canopies survive at platform level, and contrast quite sharply with the finishes found elsewhere on the station.

Northolt

Layout: Street level ticket hall leading down to one island platform via a staircase.

History: Opened on 21 November 1948 on the Central Line extension from Greenford to West Ruislip. An earlier station on the GWR was opened on 1 May 1907, but was closed when the new station opened in its current location on the other side of Mandeville Road.

Design: A temporary ticket hall building survived for over a decade after the station's opening, before being reconstructed in its current form c1960. The yellow brick surface building is located over the tracks and is dominated by the raised, square structure of the ticket hall behind. Curtis's original design allowed for a much wider entrance and substantially higher roof, with vertical clerestory windows. Beige tiling, which originally lined the walls, has been largely replaced by light blue on the ticket office frontage and grey elsewhere. The installation of the UTS suite has ruined the symmetry of the ticket hall by intruding out into the floor space. Platform areas are dominated by an elegantly curved canopy, constructed from concrete and featuring early fluorescent light fittings.

North Weald

Layout: Street level ticket hall leading directly on to one single platform.

History: Opened on 24 April 1865 by the GER and transferred to LTE ownership on 25 September 1949, although services were provided by steam trains hired from BR until the electrification of tracks in November 1957.

Design: The original red brick GER building still survives in almost unaltered form, although spoilt by the addition of a large roundel at first floor level. It consists of three blocks of progressively smaller dimensions containing the old station mas-

ter's house, ticket hall and toilets respectively. The only notable feature to have been altered is the roof, which has lost its distinctive GER chimney stacks. Many original features, such as the fireplace and timber window seat, survive in the ticket hall. The platform still in use is on the northern side of the tracks and, in common with the other stations on the Ongar extension, has no canopy worthy of the name or any substantial built structure, other than a low brick wall to the rear. The concrete bridge at the eastern end of the platform was not completed until after World War 2 but is now disused. A passing loop and additional platform were opened on 14 August 1949, in order to allow more than one train to operate on the line at a time. However, these were taken out of use from 17 October 1976 owing to the low patronage of the line.

Features: A splendid timber signal cabin, located almost opposite the main station building, is believed to date from c1888 and was restored in 1992 by the Ongar Railway Preservation Trust.

Northwick Park

Layout: Street level ticket hall leading up to one island platform via a staircase.

History: Opened as 'Northwick Park & Kenton' on 28 June 1923 as a halt on a section of line first operated by the MR on 2 August 1880. The platform was rebuilt in a slightly different position around 1930/31 in order to allow quadrupling of the tracks between Wembley Park and Harrow-on-the-Hill. The station was renamed 'Northwick Park' on 15 March 1937.

Design: The main entrance is reached by means of a short access road from Northwick Avenue. A small, red brick structure, the building dates from the station's opening but has been substantially modified since; this being most evident from the truncated window arches either side of the entrance. The small entrance and corridor also act as a public right of way under the railway tracks. The ticket hall is located off this subway and was reconstructed by the UTS project in the mid-1980s when brown

Above:
A light dusting of snow at the lonely Central Line outpost of North Weald. *Hugh Madgin*

Below:
Northwood Hills station exterior.

and white tiling, to match the finishes throughout the remainder of the lower areas of the station, was installed. Original 1931 brick and timber accommodation buildings still exist at platform level.

Northwood

Metropolitan 1.4m Surface

Layout: Street level ticket hall leading down to two single platforms via staircases.

History: Opened on 1 September 1887 on the MR extension from Pinner to Rickmansworth. Substantial reconstruction took place in the early 1930s to coincide with the opening of a new sister station at Northwood Hills and again in the early 1960s in connection with four tracking to Moor Park. The new street level facilities were opened on 15 January 1961, although work to the station was not completed until the following year.

Design: The existing station has a somewhat muted street presence, consisting of a low, undistinguished brick building which compares poorly with the Chalfont & Latimer-like building that preceded it. A small ticket hall features a panelled false ceiling above clerestory windows and leads via staircases to the simple, brick-walled platforms, each covered by a plain, corrugated metal canopy. These areas are typical of 1960s functional style.

Northwood Hills

Metropolitan 0.9m Surface

Layout: Street level ticket hall leading down to two single platforms via staircases.

History: Opened on 13 November 1933 by the Metropolitan & Great Central Joint Committee, although services had commenced on this section of the MR on 1 September 1887.

Design: The street building is located over the top of the tracks and is dominated by a most distinctive trapezium-shaped canopy that stretches out to the road side. A plain

yet attractive brick facade is spoilt by the needless blanking out of the right-hand retail unit for the installation of UTS accommodation; the retention of the windows – even if blocked-in from behind – would have maintained the elevation's previous symmetry. UTS was also responsible for the intrusion of a ticket office into the wide ticket hall area, although partial amends were made through the installation of a simple yet appropriate tiling, using a beige and burgundy colour scheme, throughout this part of the station. The platforms bear a striking resemblance to those at Kingsbury, opened only 11 months earlier, especially regarding the brick buildings at the northern end. The main difference is the presence of a brick flanking wall on the northbound side, which separates the station from the adjacent fast lines.

Notting Hill Gate

Cent/Circ/Dist 11.3m 6.7m Misc Grade II

Layout: Sub-surface ticket hall leading to two single sub-surface platforms via staircases and to two single tube platforms (serving the Central Line) via three banks of escalators.

Listing applies to District Line platforms' overall roof only.

History: Opened on 1 October 1868 on the MR extension from just west of Edgware Road to Brompton (Gloucester Road). A separate station was opened on the original section of the CLR on 30 July 1900. Services on the District Line were extended over the Metropolitan's tracks from 1 November 1926 and reconstruction of the street level building was completed 18 months later. A road widening scheme resulted in the demolition of the two street-level buildings in the late 1950s, along with the construction of a new joint ticket hall and an interchange link between the platforms. Most of the facilities of the rebuilt station were opened on 1 March 1959, although the main bank of escalators was brought into service a month earlier. Work was not completed fully until 31 July the following year.

Design: The original MR and CLR station buildings were largely typical of those built by these companies, although the latter featured an unusual peaked section above the normally flat roof. Examples of these designs may still be seen at Bayswater and Holland Park respectively. The MR building was replaced in the late 1920s with a standard C. W. Clark cream terracotta frontage, featuring a wide staircase from street level giving access to a new sub-surface ticket hall. The current sub-surface ticket hall is accessed by means of a pair of staircases on each side of the main road and is clad in light blue wall tiling with a dull yellow/green floor surface. These finishes extend down to both intermediate and low level concourses. The Central line platforms were modernised in the late 1950s through the application of beige wall tiling. This has not aged well and presents a rather depressing environment, which is exacerbated by the dark nature of the concrete paving on the floors. The Circle/District Line platforms were until recently in very poor condition, with the original finishes covered by paint and wooden panels at low level. A refurbishment completed around 1989 resulted in the restoration of the yellow brick retaining walls and the redecoration of the magnificent timber and glass overall roof. Perhaps more than any other, these areas give an idea of how the early stations looked in their prime.

Oakwood

Piccadilly 1.8m Surface Grade II

Layout: Street level ticket hall leading down to one island platform via a staircase.

History: Opened as 'Enfield West' on 13 March 1933 as the temporary terminus of the Piccadilly Line extension from Arnos Grove, although work was not fully completed until March the following year. It was renamed 'Enfield West (Oakwood)' on 3 May 1934 and finally 'Oakwood' on 1 September 1946.

Design: Oakwood is possibly the most advanced example of the 'Sudbury box' design developed by Holden for the Piccadilly Line extensions, although another external architect, C. H. James, was responsible for this particular station. The area in front of the station is used as a car park

and bus lay-by, but is distinguished by the tall lighting column-cum-seating unit which was a feature of several stations on this end of the line. The building itself is dominated by the huge, rectangular ticket hall structure. Although similar in style to several others in the series, it is notable for its sheer scale, the high proportion of glass to brick, and the presence of full height windows on the side elevations as well as those at front and back. The central bay on the main frontage contains one of the few remaining original 1930s roundels, most of which were inexplicably replaced in the 1950s. Under the concrete canopy between two retail units, one finds a wide lobby area, designed as a waiting area for bus passengers. The ticket hall is entered via attractive timber doors and is amongst the largest in terms of volume on the entire Underground system. In common with Northfields and Rayners Lane (amongst others), it uses black, glazed bricks up to the height of the ticket office, above which the hall is dominated by a large expanse of red brick and glass. The passimeter (currently used by a newspaper vendor), green-painted, free-standing kiosk and blue clock facing the ticket office are all contemporary with the station's opening and are of considerable interest. The island platform is a contrast in scale with that of the ticket hall. However, the concrete canopy has a certain degree of design merit, and the light fittings on the open section at the western end are amongst the more aesthetically pleasing examples installed in recent years.

Old Street

Northern 8.7m Tube

Layout: Sub-surface ticket hall leading down to four single plaforms (two served by Great Northern & City line) via escalators, low level passageways and staircases.

History: Opened on 17 November 1901 on the C&SLR extension from Moorgate Street to Angel. Services on the separate GN&CR platforms commenced on 14 February 1904, with responsibility being transferred to the MR on 1 July 1913 and the Northern Line from 1939. The C&SLR platforms were closed between 9 August 1922 and 19 April 1924 to allow for tunnel widening works and general modernisation of the station, with escalators being brought into service on 19 August 1925. A new joint street level building, serving a sub-surface ticket hall, was also opened to replace the previous entrances to the station. This building was subsequently demolished in the mid-1960s for road junction reconstruction and the ticket hall was resited beneath the central island of the new roundabout, connected to the platforms by means of escalators. The GN&CR services were suspended between 7 September 1975 and 7 November 1976 to allow for modifications in connection with the transfer of the line to British Rail ownership.

Design: The ticket hall is reached by means of a local council-owned subway and shopping arcade network. Low level passageways to the Northern Line platforms make ample use of cream wall tiling and a mottled terrazzo floor surface, with a mosaic finish being applied to the curved wall areas. In contrast, the corridors leading to the Great Northern platforms are largely painted. The Northern Line platforms were modernised in the mid-1970s and have been clad with two-tone grey wall tiling and a distinctive profiled metal ceiling so designed for its sound absorbing properties. The dull nature of this ceiling and the black asphalt floor tend to diminish the appearance of these potentially attractive areas.

Ongar

Central 0.03m Surface Grade II

Layout: Street level ticket hall leading directly on to one single platform.

History: Opened on 24 April 1865 by the GER. Services on the Central Line were extended to this station on 25 September 1949, although steam trains continued to be used until the advent of electrification on 18 November 1957.

Design: The appearance of this station has remained almost unchanged since its opening. The small, red brick ticket hall building resembles a country cottage and is flanked by asymmetrical accommodation structures in typical GER style. Direct access is

afforded from the attractively furnished ticket hall, with its superb timber parallel ticket office frontage, to the platform, which features a red brick waiting room integrated with the main building.

Features: A main line goods yard was located to the south of the station until it was closed on 18 April 1966.

Osterley

Piccadilly 1.6m Surface Grade II

Layout: Street level ticket hall leading down to two single platforms via an overbridge and staircases.

History: Opened as 'Osterley & Spring Grove' on 1 May 1883 on the DR extension to Hounslow (later Hounslow Town). Piccadilly Line trains used the facilities between 13 March 1933 and 24 March 1934 prior to the inauguration of a completely new station, opened as 'Osterley' and located approximately 300m to the southwest, serving both lines. District Line services ceased on 9 October 1964.

Design: The new street building marked a new stage in station design as developed by Holden. In contrast to the box and drum forms used almost uniformly on the Piccadilly Line extensions, Osterley has a fairly low ticket hall building lit by clerestory glazing, dominated by a tall brick tower with a thin, illuminated beacon on top – modelled on a 'cactus' lantern of the Dutch impressionist style. Holden attempted to be radical and, to some extent, he succeeded but the design has not aged well, although this must be put down partially to its poor maintenance over the years and the recent profusion of cabling and ducting. The ticket hall and platforms are functional yet not unattractive, but pale in comparison with the more dramatic designs utilised elsewhere, such as Chiswick Park and Oakwood.

Features: The Osterley & Spring Grove station building and platforms still survive, the former facing Thornbury Road and currently used as a bookshop.

Oval

Layout: Street level ticket hall leading down to two single platforms via escalators, low level passageways and staircases.

History: Opened as 'The Oval' on 18 December 1890 on the original section of the C&SLR, although sometimes referred to as 'Kennington Oval'. The station was renamed simply 'Oval' around 1894. It was closed between 29 November 1923 and 30 November 1924 to allow for the widening of the running tunnels and the opportunity was taken to modernise the finishes and replace the lifts with escalators, the latter coming into service on 29 May 1925.

Design: The original C&SLR building was greatly altered during the 1920s modernisation but had once resembled the station that still exists at Kennington. The main dome was removed and the facade rebuilt in a style very similar to that at Clapham North, with a flat Portland stone screen above the entrance although mosaic tiling surrounds were added in the 1970s. Internal areas of the station are clad with standard black and green bordered white tiling and whilst this is in reasonable condition, the general impression is one of neglect, caused by the absence of ceiling panels in the ticket hall, the extensive use of asphalt and failing paint finishes.

Features: Access to the lower lift lobby and some 1890s tiling survive at the base of the spiral staircase.

Oxford Circus

Layout: Sub-surface entrance ticket hall leading down to six single platforms via escalators, intermediate level concourses and low level passageways and staircases.

History: Opened on 30 July 1900 on the original section of the CLR. A separate station on the BS&WR opened on 10 March 1906, with interchange facilities available between the lines from that date. Work to rebuild the BS&WR station commenced in November 1912, with the construction of a new concourse hall in the basement of the street level building. This concluded in the bringing into service of escalators on 9 May 1914, and the subsequent withdrawal of lifts to the Bakerloo line. The new ticket hall under Argyll Street was enlarged in the early 1920s in order to serve both lines, with escalators to the CLR platforms being introduced on 30 June 1925; the redevelopment was fully operational on 16 August of the same year. Reconstruction took place again during the 1960s in anticipation of the opening of the Victoria Line platforms on 7 March 1969. This work included the building of a new circular ticket hall directly below the junction of Regent Street and Oxford Street, which necessitated the provision of a steel 'umbrella' over the road surface for almost five years so as to allow traffic to continue to flow. A major fire occurred on 23 November 1984 on one of the platforms, causing a considerable amount of damage (see 'Design' below) although no one was killed as a direct result.

Design: The original CLR and BS&WR buildings still exist either side of Argyll Street and are typical of their type, clad with beige and ox-blood coloured terracotta tiling respectively. Both now serve as exits from the secondary ticket hall, the station being entered by means of staircases located at each corner of the road junction. Although similar to the general layout of Piccadilly Circus, the main circular ticket hall fails to match the grandeur of the earlier design, largely because of the relatively poor quality of materials used. The long, lower concourses and Victoria Line platforms make use of the grey wall tiling, curved ceiling panels and terrazzo flooring that characterise stations rebuilt during the late 1960s and early 1970s. However, the 1984 fire led to the replacement of ceiling and wall surfaces with vitreous enamel panels on the northbound Victoria Line platform. Finishes on the other two lines were replaced in the early 1980s and feature colour co-ordinated wall fixtures, a patterned mosaic wall finish (designed by Nicholas Munro) and small, cream ceramic floor tiles.

Features: The escalators leading down to the Bakerloo Line platforms were the longest in the world when they were first installed. This station has more escalators (14) than any other on the system. The BS&WR building features a fine example of Edwardian vandalism, with the original gilded letters reading 'CIRCUS' having been obliterated by a blue tiled 'UNDERGROUND' logo around 1908 in an attempt at corporate identity for the early tube railways.

Paddington

Bak/Circ/Dist/H&C 23.5m 1.8 Misc

Layout: Sub-surface ticket hall (Praed Street) leading to two single sub-surface platforms via staircases, and two sub-surface ticket halls (Bakerloo and Lawn) leading to both the sub-surface and the two tube platforms (serving the Bakerloo Line), the latter via escalators.

History: Opened on 10 January 1863 as 'Paddington (Bishop's Road)' as the western terminus of the original section of the MR. A separate station named 'Paddington (Praed Street)' was opened on 1 October 1868 on the branch line to Brompton (Gloucester Road), with District Line trains first serving these platforms on 1 November 1926. The Bakerloo Line was extended to this station on 1 December 1913 and a new ticket hall (referred to as the 'Lawn' ticket hall) opened beneath the newly built GWR arrival platform concourse on 26 June 1916. A subway linking the Bakerloo Line ticket hall with the MR platforms was also opened on the latter date. The Metropolitan and Circle/District Line stations changed their names to 'Paddington' on 10 September 1933 and 11 July 1948 respectively.

Design: The original MR building stood on Bishop's Road, grafted on to the side of the main line GWR terminus and designed in 'French Renaissance' style. This was demolished in the late 1920s and since 1933 access to the Hammersmith & City Line platforms has been via the main line station only. None of the early station can now be seen and the atmosphere at platform level is more akin to that of a main line station than to that of the Underground. A canopy matching those on the main line platforms covers the island, with much of the area above the eastbound tracks being enclosed by an access road.

The original Praed Street building, designed by Fowler and resembling that at

Below:
Inside the Circle and District Line trainshed at Paddington.

Bayswater, was rebuilt around 1914/15 in a style typical of the Metropolitan's chief architect, C. W. Clark. Its imposing, two-storey facade is faced with cream terracotta and features embossed lettering at high level, giving it a dominant street presence, although diminished by the poor quality of shopfront design. The ticket hall and staircases were redesigned in the mid-1930s with considerable use being made of beige faience blocks and St James's floor tiles. Much of this survived until very recently but has now been replaced by modern finishes to match those installed on the ticket office frontage for the installation of UTS. The platforms retain their original glazed roof and yellow brick retaining walls, these being fully restored during a modernisation scheme completed in 1986, following the removal of timber panelling installed in 1915. An attractive iron latticed overbridge half-way along the platforms also dates from the surface building's reconstruction. The generally impressive appearance of these areas is marred by the installation of surface-mounted, steel trunking and the retention of ugly light brackets at high level, first provided in the 1930s but subsequently re-lamped.

The Bakerloo and Lawn ticket halls, the interchange passageways and Bakerloo Line platforms were upgraded under the 1980s modernisation project by the installation of beige wall and floor tiling throughout. The artwork within the wall tiling, designed by David Hamilton, is derived from a drawing of I. K. Brunel's tunnelling shield and depicted fully in the Bakerloo Line lower concourse. Fragments are depicted in an abstract form elsewhere, and the whole scheme reflects Brunel's influence on the GWR station above.

Features: The headwall above the staircase leading to the Praed Street ticket hall has one of the few internally-mounted 1930s UNDERGROUND silhouette roundels to remain on the system. The exterior wall of the staircase to the Bakerloo Line ticket hall retains the red terracotta tiled finishes which are characteristic of Yerkes' deep-tube stations.

Park Royal

Piccadilly 0.9m Surface Grade II

Layout: Street level ticket hall leading down to two single platforms via an overbridge and staircases.

History: A station known as 'Park Royal & Twyford Abbey' opened on 23 June 1903 on the DR extension from Ealing Common. Services were transferred to the Piccadilly Line from 4 July 1932 but trains served the station for just two days before moving to a new station, which had been built around 600m to the south. Although opened as 'Park Royal', its buildings were not completed for several years and it was renamed 'Park Royal (Hanger Hill)' on 1 March 1936, before reverting to its current title in 1947.

Design: Park Royal is undoubtedly a Holden-inspired station but is somewhat different from the 'Sudbury box' form used elsewhere on this branch. Designed by consultant architects, Welch and Lander, the circular ticket hall and tall square tower remind one of Chiswick Park but the building differs in important respects, most obviously at platform level. The ticket hall is accessed by two entrances – one of which serves as a small shopping arcade – and features clerestory windows at high level, red brick wall finishes and the original passimeter (now disused). The platforms are entirely exposed except for brick seating enclosures and a small wooden shelter on the westbound platform. A good view of the station's architecture may be observed from the eastbound platform, with the stepped roofs over the staircases being most noticeable.

Features: Several original enamel signs survive in the ticket hall and overbridge, while much of the early ticket office equipment, including the ticket issuing machine itself, can still be seen inside the passimeter. The original building was located on the south side of Twyford Abbey Road but no signs of its existence are now visible.

Parsons Green

District 4.1m Surface

Layout: Street level ticket hall leading up to two single platforms via staircases.

History: Opened on 1 March 1880 on the DR extension from West Brompton to Putney Bridge & Fulham.

Design: The station was originally entered through the entrance in Parsons Green Lane only. This is built into the side of the viaduct carrying the railway and remains almost unaltered, with the exception of lighting brackets and bronzed poster frames installed by the early 1930s. An additional entrance from the adjacent footpath was created around 1934. The ticket hall features a fine arched ceiling and a brick UTS suite which has attempted to fit in with the style of the station. Early timber panelled staircases lead up to the platforms, which retain their original canopies, although the rear walls have been covered over with boarding. The key redeeming factor at this level is the potentially attractive, yellow brick signalbox, which occupies a site just off the eastern end of the eastbound platform and is best viewed from Beaconsfield Walk.

Perivale

Central 1.0m Surface

Layout: Street level ticket hall leading up to one island platform via a staircase.

History: Opened on 2 May 1904 as a halt on the GWR and indeed was referred to as 'Perivale Halt' until 10 July 1922. The station was closed between 2 February 1915 and 28 March 1920, and rebuilt completely for the inauguration of Central Line services on 30 June 1947, although construction of the new station was not completed for over a year. Ownership transferred from the GWR to London Transport on 1 January 1948.

Below:
The crescent-shaped front of Perivale.

Design: Designed by Lewis, the street building has a distinctive, concave brick frontage, dominated by a large ribbed window. Part of the canopy was not constructed as Curtis intended, resulting in it having a rather abrupt end section. The ticket hall has a very high ceiling and retains many of its original fittings and finishes. These include the recessed telephone kiosks and integrated poster display panels. Little of significance exists on the platform, especially as the concrete canopy form used on the majority of stations on the West Ruislip extension was not deployed at this site. The angular metal version which exists instead is identical to that found also at Hanger Lane.

Piccadilly Circus

Bak/Picc 31.7m 5.0m Tube Grade II

Layout: Sub-surface ticket hall leading down to four single platforms via two flights of escalators, low level passageways and staircases.

History: Opened on 10 March 1906 by the BS&WR, with GNP&BR platforms being opened on 15 December of the same year. The surface booking hall and lifts soon proved to have too small a capacity to cope with the heavy flow through the station and plans were prepared to create a new hall beneath the Circus itself, with access gained by means of open staircases and from the original building. This facility, complete with five escalators leading down to lower concourse level, was opened on 10 December 1928, with the old ticket hall closing on 21 July the following year. A modernisation scheme, completed in 1987, resulted in the installation of new finishes in the low level areas of the station and the restoration of the 1920s ticket hall, completed in 1989.

Design: The main, circular ticket hall is rightly regarded as one of the most impressive architectural structures on the Underground. Designed by Holden, it makes ample use of bronze and marble, with notable decorative features including the fluted columns and panelled false ceiling. The lower concourses and platforms have been clad with cream wall and floor tiling. The former includes a distinctive red and green pattern throughout, with blue and brown edging applied in Piccadilly and Bakerloo Line areas respectively. Standard line colour co-ordinated fittings, such as trunking and seating, have been installed on the platforms.

Features: Entrances contained within the three original Green facades were still in use for access to the station as recently as 1990 when the entire block was demolished to make way for the construction of the new Criterion building. The ornate cast iron railings and distinctive lamp-post portals at the head of the access staircases date from the circular ticket hall's reconstruction in the late 1920s and were provided by the local council.

Pimlico

Victoria 6.6m Tube

Layout: Sub-surface ticket hall leading down to two single platforms via escalators and a low level concourse.

History: Opened on 14 September 1972 although trains on the Brixton extension of the Victoria Line had been in service since 23 July of the previous year.

Design: The ticket hall is accessed by means of staircases from street level and is finished in a variety of wall tiling, ranging from a dull olive green by the exits to a lurid orange on the ticket office facade. A panelled false ceiling, with integrated fluorescent light fittings, and speckled terrazzo floor tiling complete the finishes found in this area. Prominent use is made at platform level of dark and light grey tiling – the former in the lower concourse and on the trackside walls, the latter on the platform side. As with elsewhere on the Victoria Line, some of this wall tiling is failing quite badly. The seating recess tiling features one of the least imaginative designs on the line; the pattern consisting of variously sized yellow dots on a white background.

Pinner

Metropolitan 1.5m Surface

Layout: Street level ticket hall leading directly on to two single platforms linked by subway.

History: Opened on 25 May 1885 as the temporary terminus of the MR extension from Harrow (later Harrow-on-the-Hill). Services were extended further to Rickmansworth on 1 September 1887. An additional entrance for use by residents of the local Cecil Park estate was opened *circa* 1912.

Design: The broad, low ticket hall building is typical of the type constructed by the MR during its expansion to the northwest of London in the latter decades of the 19th century. Its red-brick form has remained largely unchanged except for well-disguised modifications to the entrance (which moved slightly to the left to take over an adjacent window) during the installation of the UTS ticket office in the mid-1980s. Much of the early timber wall panelling survives in the ticket hall, although the space is spoilt by insensitive lighting and general visual clutter. The southbound platform has retained its standard MR canopy, with associated decorative cast ironwork and fretted valance. In contrast, the canopy on the northbound platform was rebuilt around 1960/61 in connection with four-tracking to Moor Park and is rather more functional in appearance.

Plaistow

Dist/H&C 5.0m Surface Local

Layout: Street level ticket hall leading down to two single platforms (plus one reversing bay on the eastbound side) via an overbridge and staircases.

History: Opened on 31 March 1858 by the LTSR, with DR services commencing on 2 June 1902. The station was rebuilt around 1903-05 and Metropolitan (now H&C) Line trains started using the facilities from 30 March 1936.

Design: The street level building has an imposing presence and though constructed from the same dark brick as its fellow stations at East Ham and Upton Park, its design is rather different. It consists of three sections, with an entrance block each side of, and slightly set back from, the main facade. This contains a tall arched window feature, which has been partially bricked-in by a retail unit facing on to the ticket hall. A

multiple-hoop patterned parapet wall once adorned the building above cornice level and this survived until the mid-1950s. Despite the loss of this feature, the main station building, along with an adjacent brick elevation containing a secondary entrance, remains largely as built and with sensitive restoration its appearance could be most pleasing.

The symmetry of the large rectangular ticket hall is ruined by the intrusion of the UTS ticket office and two ungainly shop units. This area's only redeeming feature is the high, timber planked ceiling with its unusual patterning, illuminated by an array of uplighters. The overbridge and staircases are most attractive because of the retention of the 1900s brown and white brickwork and their glazed, arcade-like roofs. At platform level, this station is perhaps the best preserved of any on this stretch of line, although much redecoration, rationalisation and restoration work – especially of the yellow brickwork – is required if these areas are to reflect their true potential. Whereas the westbound platform retains its LTSR decorative bracketry, the canopy at the western end of the eastbound was added when the reversing bay was created in 1959, and is notable for its closely-spaced, twin line of supporting columns.

Features: Three beautifully restored cast iron-framed timber benches, dating from the late 19th century and incorporating the letters LTSR within their metalwork, exist on each platform. The LTSR platforms and access staircase – disused since around 1960 – have survived on the far side of the District Line westbound platform.

Preston Road

Metropolitan 2.2m Surface

Layout: Street level ticket hall leading down to one island platform via a staircase.

History: Opened on 21 May 1908 as a halt on a section of the MR which had commenced services on 2 August 1880. It was constructed at the request of the nearby Uxendon Shooting Club, which was to host the shooting tournament of the 1908 Olympic Games being held at White City. The timber single platforms were built on the eastern side of the road bridge and originally served as a request stop only. The station was reconstructed in its present form in the early 1930s in connection with road bridge widening, with the resited northbound and southbound faces of the island platform being opened on 21 November 1931 and 3 January 1932 respectively. All work to the station was completed by February 1932.

Design: The main brick building is very similar to that designed by C. W. Clark for Kingsbury, opened by the MR less than a year later. The station's entrance is incorporated into a parade of shops with flats above. Its small ticket hall is spoilt by the intrusive nature of the UTS suite and the use of unattractive square light fittings. However, at platform level, the station retains the wooden canopy and timber-clad buildings from its 1930s reconstruction, with the open area being enhanced by the presence of large, well-maintained flower beds.

Putney Bridge

District 3.8m Surface

Layout: Street level ticket hall leading up to one island and one single platform via staircases.

History: Opened as 'Putney Bridge & Fulham' on 1 March 1880 as the terminus of the DR extension from West Brompton. The station's name was changed to 'Putney Bridge & Hurlingham' on 1 September 1902, with its suffix omitted around 1932.

Design: The street building has one of the largest main elevations of any Underground station. Constructed of yellow brick, it features a painted arch above the two entrance doors which once contained signage spelt out in individual letters. Each side of the doors are bronze notice cases installed around 1930. The ticket hall has a high, arched ceiling and was modernised at the time of UTS installation, resulting in the use of brown wall and floor tiles. Unusually, the old ticket office was not incorporated into the UTS scheme and its fine timber frontage still survives. Timber staircases lead up to the platforms which were substantially altered around 1910 for track electrification when the original single west-

bound platform was converted into an island.

Queensbury

Jubilee 1.7m Surface

Layout: Street level ticket hall leading up to two single platforms via a subway and staircases.

History: Opened on 16 December 1934, although trains had first served this branch of the MR on 10 December 1932. Services were transferred to the Bakerloo Line on 20 November 1939 and then in turn to the Jubilee Line on 1 May 1979.

Design: The temporary station building with which the station opened was replaced in 1936 by a subdued entrance contained within a large three-storey apartment block, flanked by three shop units on either side. Dark brown tiles line the walls of the pleasant ticket hall, which features a curved clerestory window and several original shop fronts. This tiling extends along much of the access corridor, although the subway and staircases have plain brickwork finishes. The walls of the simple platform buildings are also constructed of brick, with unobtrusive concrete canopies above. Most of the platform areas are uncovered and are bounded by painted palisade fencing.

Features: Queensbury is one of the very few stations which is not identified by means of a roundel on the main frontage but instead by two protruding blue name bars. Knightsbridge is the only other site to have retained these features. A small brick building which once served as a bomb shelter during World War 2 may be found to the rear of the station next to the car park. The name 'Queensbury' has no historical basis whatsoever and was coined by a local property developer to match the adjacent suburb at Kingsbury.

Queensway

Central 5.6m Tube Grade II (prop.)

Layout: Street level ticket hall leading down to two single platforms via lifts, low level passageways and staircases.

History: Opened as 'Queen's Road' on 30 July 1900 on the original section of the CLR. The station's name was changed to 'Queensway' on 1 September 1946.

Design: The surface building is one of the few original CLR structures to remain largely intact. Although the brown terracotta tiling has been painted a dull shade of red, the basic features of a Measures design are clearly discernible. Unlike many other stations which have been built above, the Coburg Hotel tends to enhance, rather than detract from, the overall appearance of the block, having been designed by the eminent architect, Delissa Joseph. The ticket hall was extensively rebuilt as part of UTS installation and lift replacement projects in the late 1980s. The former resulted in the blocking in of the original entrance facing Bayswater Road. Despite the elimination of almost all original features, it remains an impressive sight, dominated by the two fluted metal columns supporting the high, black-painted ceiling. The low level passageways were refurbished at the same time as the ticket hall and have been clad with high quality wall and floor tiled finishes. Original white tiling on the platform walls has been later overlaid with square beige tiles.

Ravenscourt Park

District 1.8m Surface

Layout: Street level ticket hall leading up to two island platforms via a subway and staircases.

History: Opened as 'Shaftesbury Road' on 1 April 1873 by the LSWR. DR and MR services commenced on 1 June and 1 October 1877 respectively. The station was renamed 'Ravenscourt Park' on 1 March 1888 and MR services suspended on 31 December 1906. As at Turnham Green, the original island platform was supplemented by a second identical platform (opened on 3 December 1911) to the north to serve LSWR trains. On the suspension of these services on 5 June 1916, this platform was taken out of regular service until 1932 when the Piccadilly Line extension from Hammersmith to Acton Town and beyond resulted in the adoption of the current layout.

Design: The layout of this station at street level is most peculiar, with the original red brick building facing Ravenscourt Place linked to another entrance adjacent to the railway bridge over Ravenscourt Road by means of a poorly-matched brick retaining wall. The latter entrance resembles a stone 'Triumphal' arch with an ornate metal grille (incorporating a heraldic shield) above the collapsible gates and tall bronzed frames on either side. The effect is spoilt only by the crude canopy which cuts across the top of the arch itself. A small garden area, fronted by a series of four stone plinths, was removed from in front of the Ravenscourt Road entrance in the early 1930s. The two ends of the Ravenscourt Place building are clad in matching style, although lacking the canopy. Internally, the building presents an impressive space, mainly because of the height of the ceiling. However, as with many other stations, the UTS ticket office has been crudely installed and diminishes the open nature of the hall. Accessed by means of standard balustraded staircases, the two platforms retain their 1911 vintage canopies, made distinctive by the highly ornate nature of the valances and the lattice girder form taken by the pillars. One of the original timber-screened seating units survives on each platform along with metal railings around the staircases, although the latter have been partially obscured by visually intrusive advertising panels. The overall impressive appearance of the platforms is spoilt by the fibreglass waiting rooms which were installed in the mid-1980s.

Rayners Lane

Met/Picc 2.6m 1.2m Surface Grade II (prop.)

Layout: Street level ticket hall leading down to two single platforms via staircases.

History: Opened on 26 May 1906 as a halt on the MR, although services on the Uxbridge branch had started on 4 July 1904. DR trains were extended from South Harrow to serve Rayners Lane and beyond from 1 March 1910. The platforms were lengthened to cater for seven-car trains in 1918 and for eight-car trains in 1927. Piccadilly line services commenced on 23 October 1933.

Above:
Rayners Lane exterior.

Design: When first opened, the station was served by a very small wooden structure, used as a ticket office. This was replaced from 8 August 1938 by the current building, designed by Reginald H. Uren but very much in the style used by Holden at Sudbury Town and others earlier in the decade. As well as being a superb example of this architecture, the station is particularly notable for the way it dominates the street scene, because its lobby has been located forward of the main building line and over much of the pavement. When first built, this allowed passengers to enter from either side. However, the installation of the UTS suite within the right hand entrance in the mid-1980s now prevents this, thus diminishing the design's integrity. Nevertheless, many of the original features remain, including the rounded shop units in the style of Eastcote and the pole-mounted silhouette roundels on each roof. The ticket hall is smaller in scale compared with many others of the same style and has been disfigured by the construction of the ticket office as mentioned above. It is redeemed by the usage of the black glazed brick deployed to such good effect at Oakwood and Northfields. The platforms are func-

tional in design, with red brick retaining walls under the concrete canopy, integrated waiting rooms and retail units. Concrete fencing and lamp standards in the open sections are in keeping with the remainder of the station but have in fact been replicated in recent years, The metal-framed bench seats all date from the 1930s but do not originate from this station.

Redbridge

Central 1.4m Sub-Surface

Layout: Street level ticket hall leading down to one island platform via a staircase.

History: Opened on 14 December 1947 on the Central Line extension from Leytonstone to Newbury Park, although the main station building was not completed until the following year.

Design: The design of Redbridge station was amongst the last to involve Charles Holden and, as such, acts as the final stage of a development process that stretched back for more than two decades. Its surface building incorporates various elements used on earlier stations, most noticeably the low, circular ticket hall form of Southgate and the prominent brick tower of Chiswick Park – although both features are on a considerably smaller scale at this site. The ticket hall has had one of its three entrances infilled for the inclusion of the ticket office suite (again similar to Southgate) but nevertheless retains much of its charm. This area is most notable for two features unique to this station – a stunning circular skylight consisting of 12 recessed sections, with original 'torpedo' light fittings between in radial form; and bronze sign boxes throughout incorporating embossed roundels within their design. A wide, L-shaped staircase leads down to the platform, which was built by the 'cut and cover' method of construction, because of its proximity to the surface. Originally clad throughout with standard square, yellow tiling, the walls of the staircase and signage/seating panels have been refinished using a mottled pink tile, which is inappropriate to this location. Although the atmosphere is somewhat gloomy because of the retention of the original fluorescent light fittings, this platform exemplifies how an architect can create a spacious, well-designed environment when not constrained by the limitations imposed by bored tunnels.

Features: Redbridge has the shallowest 'sub-surface' platforms on the 'tube' sections of the system at only 16ft (4.87m) below ground level.

Regent's Park

Bakerloo 2.5m Tube

Layout: Sub-surface ticket hall leading down to two single platforms via lifts and low level passageways and staircases.

History: Opened on 10 March 1906 on the original section of the BS&WR.

Design: This station has no street level buildings and is accessed by means of two open staircases and twin sloping subways leading to the ticket hall. The latter retains

some fine, green moulded tiling at dado height. Until the installation of UTS equipment and replacement of lifts around 1986, the ticket hall had kept its original finishes including the ornate ticket office windows, but these have now been replaced by a totally inappropriate, grey and red tiling scheme; the only redeeming features being attractive wooden panelling and original ornamental iron grille on the lift frontage and pendant light fittings. The brown and cream wall tiling at platform level remains largely as original, although its height was extended during a minor modernisation scheme completed in 1992. New lighting, trunking, signage and floor tiling were also installed as part of this project.

Rickmansworth

Metropolitan 1.4m Surface

Layout: Street level ticket hall leading to two single platforms via subway.

History: Opened on 1 September 1887 as the temporary terminus of the MR following its extension from Pinner. The platforms underwent substantial reconstruction during the 1980s owing to problems with subsidence.

Design: The main building is very similar to those of other stations on this stretch of the MR, although it is most notable for a distinctive, metal-framed canopy above the main entrance. The ticket hall displays little of interest, except for the unusual feature of a café frontage directly opposite the ticket office. Both original platforms had typical MR canopies, with a circular pattern within the supporting bracketry – identical to that under the entrance canopy. The new canopies and pillars are of a simple yet pleasing design and are complemented on the northbound platform by the replacement of the earlier timber buildings by a light brown brick structure. The subway under the tracks was enlarged at this time and the platform-side wall of its southbound staircase features particularly noticeable circular, unglazed openings within the yellow brickwork. An original brick water storage tower survives at the northern end of the London-bound platform.

Roding Valley

Central 0.1m Surface

Layout: Street level ticket hall leading to two single platforms via a footbridge.

History: Opened on 3 February 1936 by the LNER. Services on the Central Line were extended to here on 21 November 1948, although the station building's reconstruction was not completed until the following year.

Design: The small brick entrance building is set back a considerable distance from the main road and is preceded by a slip road surrounding a pleasantly vegetated island. It contains a ticket hall that is perhaps the least substantial of any on the system, in terms of size and facilities, and which leads directly on to the Hainault-bound platform. The platforms themselves are rather different from the heavy, red brick structures found elsewhere on this branch line and have an agreeably open appearance, enhanced by the use of tubular metal railings at the back edges and the presence of a particularly fine example of an unroofed latticework footbridge.

Rotherhithe

East London 1.5m Sub-Surface

Layout: Street level ticket hall leading down to two single platforms via escalators and staircases.

History: Opened on 7 December 1869 by the East London Railway. MR and DR services commenced over this line on 1 October 1884 but were suspended on 31 July 1905 and 2 December 1906 respectively. The line was reopened to MR traffic from 31 March 1913. Escalators were installed in 1982/83, access to the platforms previously being solely via staircase.

Design: Although the exterior of the station appears to date from the 1860s, the entire street-facing facade was in fact added around 1905, in order to bring out the building into line with others facing Brunel Road. The attractive yellow brick facade is not dis-

Below:
The 1905 station entrance at Rotherhithe.

115

similar to that of West Brompton as it was when first built, with three windows each side of the entrance doors; the arches of each picked out in red brick. The raised parapet wall above the entrance, with decorative scrolled features on either side, originally had station name lettering on the rendered panel. Modernisation work to the ticket hall in the early 1980s was carried out in conjunction with the installation of the escalators, which are covered by an overall glazed vaulted soffit and lead down to a landing over the tracks. This has resulted in the rafting over of much of the platforms' length, diminishing the effect of the high, brick vaulted ceiling still to be found at Shadwell and Wapping. The resulting composite of orange melamine wall panels, corrugated metal canopies, and concrete and brick finishes creates a disjointed and rather unattractive appearance, especially in contrast to that of the areas at ticket hall level. The environment is further diminished through the intrusion of a metal girder bridge at the southern end of the platforms, which carries the approach to the Rotherhithe Road Tunnel, opened by the London County Council in 1908.

Royal Oak

Hammersmith & City 1.3m Surface

Layout: Street level ticket hall leading down to one island platform via a staircase.

History: Opened on 30 October 1871, served by both GWR and MR trains, although this section of line had been opened in 13 June 1864 by the semi-independent H&CR. The original single platforms were replaced by an island in 1904. GWR services stopped using the station from 1 October 1934 and it transferred to London Transport ownership on 1 January 1970.

Design: Although the small, red brick street building is quite attractive, its appearance has been greatly diminished through the construction of massive bridge girders in front of its main elevation and the addition of a crude metal canopy which covers half of the facade. The great girdered bridge over the railway tracks was given a new lease of life in 1992, when it was painted in

a stunning red/light grey/green colour scheme. A plaque on the bridge outside the station commemorates this work. The building is largely hidden from view behind these features and consequently this station has a lower street profile than almost any other. At platform level, little of note remains, the original canopy and supports having been replaced by a crude recent design.

Ruislip

Met/Picc 1.3m Surface Local

Layout: Street level ticket hall leading to two single platforms via a footbridge.

History: Opened on 4 July 1904 as the only intermediate stop on the MR branch from Harrow-on-the-Hill to Uxbridge. DR services commences on 1 March 1910 and were transferred to the Piccadilly Line on 23 October 1933.

Design: This large, red brick building displays many of the stylistic traits of its later counterparts on the Watford and Stanmore branch lines, and is the only one of the first three stations (including Harrow-on-the-Hill) on this branch to have survived. Although superficially similar to the stations on the northern extensions of the railway, the design is more advanced and without doubt, has more visual impact. This is mainly owing to the large porch feature in front of the entrance and the contrasting render and brick patterns above the windows. The building has remained largely unaltered, except for modifications to the original chimney stacks. The ticket hall features a very high, pitched timber roof and green-painted timber panelling on the walls to dado height. The eastbound platform has changed little since the station's opening, retaining its original valanced canopies and fluted metal columns – the detail contained on the latter being well picked-out during a recent redecoration project. It is joined to the westbound platform by a superb latticed footbridge, which had a pitched timber roof added in the 1920s.

Features: An original signalbox survives in good condition at the eastern end of the westbound platform.

Above:
The Metropolitan Railway building at Ruislip.

Ruislip Gardens

Central 0.5m Surface

Layout: Street level ticket hall leading up to one island platform via a staircase.

History: Opened on 9 July 1934 by the GWR and GCR. Central Line trains first used the station on 21 November 1948 when the line was extended from Greenford to West Ruislip, although rebuilding work at street level was not completed until around 1962.

Design: The original proposal by Curtis for the ticket hall building resembled a 'Sudbury box' in appearance but this was never constructed. Instead, one of the least impressive entrances on the system was built, consisting merely of a low concrete structure, masked by a brick box to the left of the entrance and a dull grey retail unit to the right. The only point of interest is the large concrete canopy which extends out from the main wall at roof level. In contrast, the ticket hall is quite attractive, making good use of plain brick and St James's tile finishes. Platform areas are amongst the most attractive on this section of line, as they retain their original curved, concrete canopy and some 1940s signage.

Features: The wooden door on the half-landing on the staircase leads to the derelict remains of a subway, which once ran beneath the tracks and gave access to the main line platforms, which were closed on 21 July 1958.

Ruislip Manor

Met/Picc 1.3m Surface Local

Layout: Street level ticket hall leading up to two single platforms via staircases.

History: Opened on 5 August 1912 although services on this section of line by the MR and DR had started on 4 July 1904 and 1 March 1910 respectively. The station was temporarily closed between 12 February 1917 and 31 March 1919. DR services transferred to the Piccadilly Line on 23 October 1933, with associated reconstruction work being completed on 26 June 1938.

Design: The 1930s street building contains a ticket hall located directly under the tracks, with access gained from matching brick entrances on either side. The ticket hall makes use of attractive tiled materials but has been spoilt by the construction of a UTS ticket office, which ruins the hall's symmetry. However, the situation is redeemed by a unique clock and individually lettered signs on the headwall. The recent retiling of the ticket office frontage to match that of the remainder of the hall has also helped. Brick faced staircases lead up into standard 1930s platform buildings – not unattractive but somewhat soulless, especially since ugly metal palisade fencing has been installed in place of the original tubular railings. The original 1912 vintage timber waiting rooms located mid-way along each platform contrast sharply with the brick and concrete building materials used elsewhere on the station.

Russell Square

Piccadilly 9.4m Tube Grade II (prop.)

Layout: Street level ticket hall leading down to two single platforms via lifts and low level passageways and staircases.

History: Opened on 15 December 1906 on the original section of the GNP&BR.

Design: This Leslie Green station is one of the few in central London to survive largely in its original form at low level. The wide, red terracotta elevation is in generally good condition, although changes were made to the areas beneath two of the arches during lift replacement and ticket hall modernisation works in the 1980s. None of the original ticket hall finishes survive but modernisation has been well carried out, and this area presents a very bright, modern appearance. The low level areas of the station retain almost all of their original green and black bordered tiling, with the platforms displaying a distinctive multiple chevron pattern. Most of the numerous name and directional signs within the tiling have also survived, although some have been partially hidden by injudiciously sited switchrooms.

Seven Sisters

Victoria 10.4m Tube

Layout: Two sub-surface ticket halls leading down to three single platforms via escalators.

History: Opened on 1 September 1968 on the initial section of the Victoria Line, between Walthamstow Central and Highbury & Islington, although the secondary ticket hall in Seven Sisters Road was not opened for a further three months.

Design: The station has no street level buildings and its two separate ticket halls are accessed by means of open staircases. Standard Victoria Line finishes have been deployed throughout and this is one of the few stations on the line not to feature more than one tone of grey within the wall tiling. The pattern within the seat recesses portrays the seven trees which give the area, and the station, its name.

Shadwell

East London 1.3m Sub-Surface

Layout: Street level ticket hall leading down to two single platforms via lifts and low level staircases.

History: The original station was opened by the East London Railway on 10 April 1876, although an earlier station, located on a viaduct, had been opened on the London & Blackwall Railway on 1 October 1840. DR and MR services commenced over the line on 1 October 1884 but were suspended on 31 July 1905 and 2 December 1906 respectively. The line was reopened to MR traffic from 31 March 1913. The station's name changed to 'Shadwell & St George-in-the-East' on 1 July 1900 but reverted to 'Shadwell' in 1918. A new street level building facing Cable Street was brought into service, along with lifts leading to mezzanine level, around 1983.

Design: Dominated by a massive pitched roof of tinted glass, the station has a very modern appearance. Its ticket hall is brightly illuminated because of the high

Above:
The cavernous interior of Shadwell station. *Hugh Madgin*

degree of natural light and makes ample use of brown brickwork and floor tiling. The platforms are contained under a massive, arched, brick roof which runs for almost their entire length. Their narrow width is restricted further by orange melamine panels which were installed in the early 1980s to hide the worst of the water seepage problems which afflict all the sub-surface stations on this line. The area beyond the roof at the northern end of the platforms has tall brick retaining walls spanned by large metal Victorian buttresses and grilles. The poor state of the ceiling and the garish nature of the panels have combined to give these areas a most unpleasant atmosphere, although the potential for dramatic improvement is considerable.

Features: The original station building still exists, located in Watney Street alongside the viaduct that now carried the Docklands Light Railway. Although disused, its basic form remains largely intact and the portals to the entrance/exit staircases leading to street level may be observed towards the northern end of each platform. The remains of the staircase link between the ELR and L&BR stations (which was in use between 1 August 1895 and 7 July 1941, when the latter station closed) still survive, with the entrance building visible on the south side of Chapman Street.

Shepherd's Bush (Cent)

Central 6.5m Tube

Layout: Street level ticket hall leading down to two single platforms via escalators, low level passageways and staircases.

History: Opened on 30 July 1900 as the western terminus of the original section of the CLR. Heavier than expected usage of the station within months of opening led to the need for additional lift capacity and two additional shafts – each containing two electro-hydraulic lifts – were installed to the rear of the ticket hall. These came into service in December 1902 and February 1903 respectively. Services were extended to Wood Lane on 14 May 1908. Reconstruction work resulted in the provision of escalators in place of the lifts from 5 November 1924 and a much enlarged ticket hall on

23 January 1925. The platforms were lengthened at their eastern end in the late 1930s to allow for the introduction of eight-car trains in connection with the proposed Central Line extensions. An extensive modernisation project covering the replacement of most station finishes was completed in May 1985.

Design: The exterior of the original Harry Measures building survives largely in its original form, faced with attractive beige terracotta. Its appearance is marred by an ugly metal canopy added by the 1930s and uncontrolled advertising around the retail units. The ticket hall has been extensively remodelled twice during its history, the two tone brown tiling facing the ticket office being the only area where the original finishes have survived. A stunning chequered green and red tile pattern has been applied to the ticket office frontage but unfortunately this contrasts too sharply with the remainder of the station at street level. The large concourse to the rear was constructed at the time of escalator installation and features a very high ceiling and an unusual painted mural on the headwall above the escalator shaft, added in the mid-1980s. The platform walls are faced with the same pattern as used on the ticket office and this is complemented by the use of brown floor tiles. Unfortunately, the overall effect is spoilt by the use of a particularly unreflectant textured ceiling paint.

Features: The entrances to some of the lift shafts can still be seen at the far end of the passageway leading to the base of the spiral staircase. The platforms are unusual in that they converge to form an island at their eastern end.

Shepherd's Bush (H&C)

Hammersmith & City 3.6m Surface

Layout: Street level ticket hall leading up to two single platforms via staircases.

History: Opened on 13 June 1864 as part of the semi-independent H&CR, with services provided by the GWR from Farringdon Street. MR trains first served the station on 1 April 1865 and the line became the joint responsibility of the MR and GWR from

Above:
Inside the booking hall at Shoreditch.

1 July 1867. As the station was positioned awkwardly between Uxbridge Road and Goldhawk Road, it was resited around 250m to the north, at the junction with the former. Trains first served the new platforms from 1 April 1914.

Design: Accessed by means of small, drab entrances either side of the bridge carrying the railway over Uxbridge Road, the ticket hall is contained within one of the bridge arches and therefore has a potentially attractive curved brick soffit, but unfortunately this has been covered by paint. The blue tiled finishes were installed at the time of UTS installation in the mid-1980s. Panelled access staircases lead up to the platforms which resemble several others on this stretch of line, with their timber-panelled rear walls and simple metal canopies. Once amongst the most depressing of stations at this level, the environment has been significantly improved through the installation of glazed waiting areas, a new signage scheme and standardised seating, along with a bright painting scheme.

Features: The approach roads to the original station, along with the brick arches underneath the railway viaduct, were converted into what is now known as 'Shep-

herd's Bush Market', opened just months after the station's closure, on 29 June 1914.

Shoreditch

East London 0.3m Surface Grade II (prop.)

Layout: Street level ticket hall leading down to one single platform via a staircase.

History: Opened on 10 April 1876 by the East London Railway, although the station was not served by MR trains until 31 March 1913.

Design: Possibly the least known Underground station in inner London, Shoreditch retains a certain charm. Very similar in style to the old station building at Shadwell, it has remained largely intact at street level, although reroofing has led to the removal of the chimneys that once adorned the ends. The ticket hall has been extensively altered over the years and has kept few of its original features, although a splendid timber-planked floor adds considerably to its character. The access staircase and platform remain largely as first built; the latter boasting a fine brick retaining wall and a valanced canopy. The remains of the original southbound platform, which was taken out of operational use by the late 1940s, can be observed on the opposite side of the track.

of the platforms and carries the Ranelagh sewer, which once flowed on the surface as the River Westbourne.

Sloane Square

Circ/Dist 12.2m Sub-Surface

Layout: Street level ticket hall leading down to two single platforms via staircases. Access by escalator in up direction only.

History: Opened on 24 December 1868 on the DR extension from South Kensington to Westminster Bridge. The building was extensively reconstructed in the late 1930s to allow for the provision of escalators and a new ticket hall, the new facilities becoming operational on 27 March 1940. Bomb damage caused by a direct hit on 12 November of the same year resulted in further rebuilding after the war and this was completed on 3 May 1951.

Design: The original street building was very similar to those built by Fowler for other stations on the early MR and DR extensions, such as Baywater. However, its appearance was substantially altered around the turn of the century through the construction of shop units in the forecourt, thereby screening off much of the facade. The current building is bland in comparison, making use of flat concrete panels at first floor level, and was modified when an office development was added above in the 1960s. Internally, the ticket hall has been attractively tiled and presents a pleasant environment to the station's users. An arched overall roof once covered the platforms, similar to those that still exist at Paddington and Notting Hill Gate, but this was dismantled at the time of the station's first reconstruction. The current canopies date from the 1950s rebuilding, while the green wall tiling, with its lattice-arched pattern, was installed during a modernisation scheme completed in 1985.

Features: Remains of the brick retaining walls and the metal brackets which supported the overall roof may be observed above canopy level. A large metal conduit spans the tracks towards the western end

Snaresbrook

Central 1.2m Surface

Layout: Street level ticket hall leading to two single platforms, which are linked by a footbridge.

History: Opened as 'Snaresbrook & Wanstead' on 22 August 1856 by the ECR, which became part of the GER in 1862. The station was reconstructed in 1893 and became known as 'Snaresbrook for Wanstead' from 1929. Services transferred to Central Line operation on 14 December 1947, the name changing to 'Snaresbrook' at this time to avoid confusion with the newly opened tube station at Wanstead.

Design: The main station building was constructed by the ECR and is very similar to those surviving at Leyton and Woodford. Its simple, red brick construction is marred by several of its windows having been blocked in (although this may have been an original design feature) and the construction of an entrance lobby to the left-hand side in October 1948. The ticket hall retains none of its original features and has modern tiled finishes throughout. The platforms are amongst the most attractive at this end of the Central Line, as the canopies retain many decorative metal support brackets and valanced edges of different designs, the earliest dating from the 1890s. Arched windows within the brick wall on the westbound side are a particularly unusual feature, as are the three types of canopy as one progresses down the platform. The footbridge connecting the platforms was installed in 1947 in place of a previous 'covered way' and the concrete roundel/advert display panels date from the same era.

Features: The eastbound (the northernmost) platform once served two sets of tracks, acting as a bay platform between 1893 and 1950. The bay area is now partially used as the station car park.

Above:
South Ealing from the western end.

South Ealing

Piccadilly 2.8m Surface

Layout: Street level ticket hall leading down to two island platforms via an overbridge and staircases.

History: Opened on 1 May 1883 on the DR extension from Mill Hill Park (later Acton Town) to Hounslow. A second island platform was added to allow for Piccadilly Line services, which commenced on 9 January 1933. District Line trains stopped using this branch on 9 October 1964.

Design: The original brick DR building was substituted around 1932 by a temporary ticket hall structure – similar in style to the Embankment entrance to Westminster station – to the south of the railway bridge. A temporary covered walkway led from this structure to the newly constructed island platforms. A new permanent building was opened on the site of the original ticket hall in 1988 and features a small brick tower with a roundel on each side, which harks back to Holden's designs further down the line at Osterley and Boston Manor. The simple yet effective ticket hall has the same atmosphere as the example at Surrey Docks (now Surrey

Quays) opened several years earlier, with its two-tone brick walls, quarry tiled floor and wide expanses of glass. A new, extensively glazed footbridge incorporates the steelwork of the previous temporary structure and leads down to the two island platforms. The eastbound platform has a long concrete canopy with a rounded waiting room at its western extremity. Dating from around 1936, it pioneered the style that would be used elsewhere on the system a few years later, most notably on rebuilt stations on the Metropolitan Line between Finchley Road and Harrow-on-the-Hill. The canopy on the westbound platform is similar in design to its counterpart but is substantially shorter and dates only from the late 1980s. An original 1883 timber waiting room survives in the open section.

South Harrow

Piccadilly 1.3m Surface

Layout: Street level ticket hall leading up to two single platforms via staircases.

History: Opened on 28 June 1903 as the terminus of the DR extension from just north of Ealing Common (although services had started to Park Royal & Twyford Abbey five days earlier). The line was extended to Rayners Lane and beyond from 1 March 1910. Services were transferred to the Piccadilly Line on 4 July 1932. A new station building, resited less than 200m to the north of the original, was brought into use on 5 July 1935.

Design: This station is typical of the style adopted by Holden and his colleagues in the mid-1930s, especially at locations where the ticket hall straddles the railway bridge over the main road. Like Ruislip Manor, the hall is entered by means of small brick entrances either side of the bridge and is clad with the usual beige faience and St James's tiles on the walls and floor respectively. An attractive clock and built-in bronze train indicator panel are notable features of this area. The brick staircases leading up to platform level feature seating recesses, again in common with Ruislip Manor. The platforms themselves are fairly functional in nature, the concrete canopies being supported by brown tiled columns and brick retaining walls. Three of the 1930s concrete publicity panels survive on the open ends of the platforms.

Features: The original station building, as well as the remains of the old platform surfaces and lamp-posts, still exists at the end of the eastbound platform and is now used as staff accommodation. It is perhaps best viewed from the adjacent car park and notable for its similarity to the station building still in use at North Ealing. Other than the removal of the entrance doors, the building has survived remarkably intact.

South Kensington

`Circ/Dist/Picc  19.4m  3.8m  Misc`

Layout: Sub-surface ticket hall leading to one island sub-surface platform (plus one disused single platform) via a staircase and to two tube platforms (serving the Piccadilly Line) via two flights of escalators, low level passageways and staircases.

History: Opened on 24 December 1868 as the terminus of the branch line of the MR from just west of Edgware Road (although services had commenced to Brompton [Gloucester Road] – later Gloucester Road –

on 1 October of the same year). On the same day, the MR provided services between Brompton (Gloucester Road) and Westminster Bridge (later Westminster), on behalf of the DR to the east of South Kensington. In July 1871, the DR started operating its own trains and station facilities after a dispute with the Metropolitan, resulting in a layout consisting of one single and three island platforms with separate facilities for the two companies. In July 1871, the DR started using its own station building and tracks after a dispute with the Metropolitan, resulting in a layout consisting of two island and two single platforms with separate facilities for the two companies.

The subway linking the ticket hall to the museums in Exhibition Road was opened on 4 May 1885, closed at the end of the Inventions Exhibition on 10 November 1886 and opened permanently to the public on 21 December 1908.

Much of the station was rebuilt in the late 1880s in conjunction with further track layout modifications. This was simplified in 1957 with the combining of the two islands through the closure of the central reversing bay. The tracks to the single eastbound and westbound platforms were taken out of service from 8 January 1967 and 30 March 1969 respectively.

Trains on the GNP&BR first stopped at this station on 8 January 1907, although the line had commenced operations 24 days earlier. Escalators between Piccadilly Line platform level and a new intermediate concourse were brought into service on 30 September 1973, and between the concourse and the new combined ticket hall on 20 January 1974, along with direct access to and from the District Line platforms.

Design: The original standard Fowler-designed building was demolished around 1907 and replaced by white terracotta entrances at each end of a small shopping arcade designed by George Sherrin, which gave access to a new sub-surface ticket hall. These are notable for the beautifully ornate wrought ironwork above each set of gates, which incorporates station and line name lettering. Further lettering is contained within the faience at high level, although this has been largely obliterated by a standard 1920s canopy above the southern entrance. The sub-surface platforms were originally covered by a glazed roof but this was removed around 1903. The island platform had a bay road down the centre until 1957, which explains why it is so wide and has two matching glazed canopies. This area was subsequently used to provide direct staircase access to the Piccadilly Line areas. Yellow brick retaining walls may be observed on the far side of the tracks, especially on the eastbound side. Few signs of the single westbound platform survive, other than some canopy support-columns, and the area is currently occupied by a profusion of temporary accom-modation buildings.

The original blue and cream tiling scheme on the Piccadilly Line platforms survived until the mid-1980s when it was replaced by possibly the most attractive design deployed at any station under the 1980s modernisation programme. The pre-dominantly white wall tiling features animal murals in relief on a beige background at low level, with a random chequered pattern above the name frieze. A dark grey tiled floor finish complements the walls' design perfectly, while the original tile bands and entrance/exit portals survive on both plat-forms.

Features: The facade of the original Leslie Green GNP&BR building still survives adjacent to the southern arcade entrance, although it has not provided access to the station for passengers since the replace-ment of lifts by escalators.

The GNP&BR platforms were con-structed above each other so as to afford level interchange with a proposed DR 'express' tube service. This resulted in the need for the lifts (the shafts of which are still visible at platform level) to stop twice at depths of 60ft and 78ft – a feature unique to this station. A 120ft section of the westbound tunnel of the 'express' tube was built and clad to match the fin-ishes of adjacent GNP&BR platform but was never served by trains.

South Ruislip

Central 0.9m Surface

Layout: Street level ticket hall leading up to one island platform via a subway and a staircase.

Below:
The glazed drum at South Ruislip.

Above:
The frontage of South Wimbledon station. *Hugh Madgin*

History: Opened as 'Northolt Junction' on 1 May 1908 by the GWR and GCR. The station was renamed 'South Ruislip & Northolt Junction' on 12 September 1932 and 'South Ruislip' on 30 June 1947. It was rebuilt in advance of the inauguration of Central Line services on 21 November 1948, although the street building was not completed until around 1962 owing to financial problems.

Design: The street level building is one of the most unusual on the entire system, for it has a 16-sided glazed drum structure above canopy level, faced with obscured glass. Inside the ticket hall, the frieze wall boasts a unique abstract mural, while the floor space is dominated by a circular free-standing publicity frame. The subway under the tracks and staircase leading to the platform are faced with dull grey wall tiling and contrast poorly with the ticket hall. The gracefully curved concrete canopy on the platform is very similar to those at Northolt and Ruislip Gardens, and retains some interesting 1940s concrete/timber bench seats.

South Wimbledon

Northern 1.9m Tube Grade II

Layout: Street level ticket hall leading down to two single platforms via escalators and a low level concourse.

History: Opened as 'South Wimbledon (Merton)' on 13 September 1926 on the Northern Line extension from Clapham Common to Morden. The suffix has been gradually dropped over time.

Design: Unlike at many of the other stations on the Morden extension designed by Holden, South Wimbledon has a smoothly curved, convex facade, joining High Street Merton with Morden Road. However, it does make use of the standard building material (ie Portland stone) and design features (eg a large roundel incorporated within the glazing above the entrance). The ticket hall has survived in better condition than many of its contemporaries, helped by the recreation of the green and black bordered tile pattern on the ticket office frontage. Almost all the retail units both inside and outside the station retain their original shop fronts, including superb moulded timber frames. Likewise, the low level concourse and platforms have retained almost all of their original finishes and fittings.

Features: The suffix of the original name of the station may be discerned on many of the platform roundels.

South Woodford

Central 3.0m Surface

Layout: Two street level ticket halls leading to two single platforms, which are linked by a footbridge.

History: Opened as 'George Lane' on 22 August 1856 by the ECR, which became part of the GER in 1862. The station was resited to its current location around 1883 and renamed 'South Woodford (George Lane)' on 5 July 1937. It was first used by Underground trains on the newly extended Central Line on 14 December 1947 and its name changed to 'South Woodford' in 1950.

Design: In common with other stations built around this time, South Woodford has separate ticket offices on either side of the tracks. The more substantial building, found on the eastbound side, dates from the 1883 resiting and is of red brick construction, with an attractive glazed canopy cantilevered from the frontage across its full width. The other entrance was opened as recently as March 1948 and gives immediate access to the ticket hall. A subway underneath George Lane was also constructed at this time. Both ticket halls lead directly on to their respective platforms, which are linked by means of a plain metal footbridge at their northern end. This originally gave direct access to the forecourt in front of the main ticket hall building but was modified for the introduction of Central Line services, which also resulted in the closure of two nearby level crossings. The eastbound platform retains its attractive valanced 1883 canopy, supported by ornate brackets and columns for much of

its length. In contrast, the westbound platform has been extensively modified, through the construction of a long canopy extension, supported by timber pillars, around 1905 and rebuilding at the northern end in the late 1940s. Little of the original fabric, other than the painted brick retaining wall, has survived.

Features: Some of the original silhouette roundels installed when the station was first served by Underground services survive on the platform walls and retain the 'George Lane' suffix. An unusual pane of etched glass survives within the window in the ladies' waiting room on the eastbound platform.

Southgate

Piccadilly 3.1m Tube Grade II

Layout: Street level ticket hall leading down to two single platforms via escalators and a low level concourse.

History: Opened on 13 March 1933 on the Piccadilly Line extension from Arnos Grove to Enfield West (later Oakwood).

Design: Southgate is widely regarded as one of the finest pieces of work carried out by Charles Holden on the Piccadilly Line extensions and consequently ranks highly in the list of the most important 1930s public buildings in London. Its appearance is dissimilar to any other on the system, with the possible exception of Hanger Lane. It occupies an elliptical island site, separated from the matching shopping arcade by a bus slip road, with the whole being designed as an integrated development. Two lighting-cum-seating units, which once adorned the pavements of several stations at this end of the line, survive at the island's extremities. The circular ticket hall has clerestory windows around the perimeter and distinctive metal panels on the exterior of the shop units and ticket office. The latter occupies the site of one of the original entrances into the ticket hall but has been well matched in. One of the few surviving passimeters on the system has recently been restored and converted into a ticket collecting facility after years of disuse. The escalators were replaced in the late 1980s, with particular care being taken to retain the balustrade uplighters and to give the metal panels a bronzed finish so as to be in keeping with the rest of the station. The low level concourse retains both of its original bronze uplighters in full working order. Finishes at platform level are very similar to those found at its sister stations, with the beige wall tiling bordered by an orange trim in this particular case.

Features: Southgate is the only tube station from which natural daylight can be seen by looking down the running tunnels at the eastern end. The troughs which line each side of the platforms at high level once contained light fittings, which served as the primary source of illumination until a central run of fluorescent tubes was installed in the 1950s.

St James's Park

Circ/Dist 12.5m Sub-Surface Grade II

Layout: Two street level ticket halls leading down to two single platforms via staircases.

History: Opened on 24 December 1868 on the DR extension from South Kensington to Westminster Bridge (later renamed Westminster). It was substantially rebuilt in the late 1900s, culminating in the opening of Electric Railway House – the headquarters building of both DR and UERL – in 1909. The platforms were rafted over for the construction of a new office block now known as 'Wing over Station', opened in 1923. Work on the construction of 55 Broadway (see Features) was substantially complete by 1928, although the complex was not opened officially until 1 December the following year.

Design: The original building designed by Fowler was rebuilt in the late 1900s, at the same time as the removal of the glazed overall roof which once spanned the brick retaining walls. The ticket hall was later incorporated within the ground floor of 55 Broadway (see below) and now forms part of the entrance into a shopping arcade development. An impressive skylight and attractive timber panelling may be observed above the half-landing on the staircases leading down to the platforms. The platforms are almost unchanged since they were modernised in the early 1920s, the

walls being clad with the predominantly white, metal tiles which were in common use at that time. The Palmer Street entrance was constructed in the early 1900s but was substantially rebuilt around 1962.

Features: The massive, white stone building above the entrances to the shopping arcade is known as '55 Broadway' and has acted as the headquarters of London Transport (and some of its predecessors) since it was completed in 1929. Designed by Holden, it was reputedly the largest office block in London when first constructed and is rightly regarded as one of the most important buildings of its decade, especially as one considers that the exterior is adorned by sculptures by such luminaries as Moore, Gill and Epstein.

St John's Wood

Jubilee 3.7m Tube Grade II (prop.)

Layout: Street level ticket hall leading down to two single platforms via escalators and a low level concourse.

History: Opened on 20 November 1939 on the new section of the Bakerloo Line linking Baker Street and the Stanmore branch of the Metropolitan Line. The station was known as 'Acacia Road' prior to opening. Services were transferred to the Jubilee Line on 1 May 1979.

Design: The surface building occupies a corner site and is fronted by an extensive garden area. Although the drum-like form of the ticket hall still exists, the effect has been diminished by the building of an apartment block above in 1963. The walls of the ticket hall are clad with beige faience tiles and this is in generally good condition. Some of the original shop fronts, which had been crudely ripped out in the late 1980s, have recently been reinstated. The escalator shaft retains its original bronze uplighters on the balustrades, while the low level concourse and platforms are very similar to those of other stations designed in the late 1930s. Extensive use is made of cream wall tiling with a yellow trim and featuring moulded patterns by Stabler including representations of St Paul's Cathedral, the Palace of Westminster and the head of Thomas Lord (of cricket ground fame) on

Above:
The entrance to St John's Wood station.

selected tiles. The tiled name frieze on the platforms is also a key feature of stations of this vintage.

St Paul's

Central 6.9m Tube

Layout: Sub-surface ticket hall leading down via two banks of escalators to a mid-level concourse and a single eastbound platform, linked to the westbound platform by a single bank of escalators.

History: Opened as 'Post Office' on 30 July 1900 on the original section of the CLR. At early stages of planning, the station was referred to as 'Newgate Street' (in 1891) and 'General Post Office' (in 1895). The ticket hall was rebuilt in 1929 and was later resited to allow for the provision of escalators in place of lifts. The station used the title 'St Paul's' from 1 February 1937, with the new ticket hall and escalators brought into service from 1 January 1939. The entrance was rebuilt again around 1965 in conjunction with the Paternoster Square development and yet again in 1973 for road widening.

Design: The ticket hall is accessed by means of staircases, one of which is covered by a particularly nondescript metal canopy. The two staircases on the opposite side of Cheapside retain the standard metal railings common to stations modernised in the 1930s. Finishes to the subway link and the ticket hall itself were upgraded in the mid-1980s through the installation of a granite-like floor finish and large white faience wall tiles. The yellow wall tiling on the walls of the middle and low level concourses dates from the installation of escalators and once extended on to the platforms. It contains many decorative tiles by Harold Stabler, similar to those at St John's Wood, and portrays a variety of images, including the Palace of Westminster and the London Transport headquarters at 55 Broadway. The platforms retain their original CLR white tiling over the soffits but have been retiled in a similar style to the original on the main walls, with granite-like slabs used as the flooring material. In common with many schemes under the 1980s modernisation programme, colour co-ordinated trunking and seating have been deployed throughout.

Features: A bronze 'Way Out' roundel at the base of the lower flight of escalators is the only reminder of the related uplighter fittings that once adorned these escalators and still survive at only four sites. The original station building was located on the western corner of the junction between King Edward Street and Newgate Street, while the Holden-designed entrance of 1929 was severely damaged during an air raid in 1940 and eventually demolished around 20 years later.

Stamford Brook

District 2.1m Surface

Layout: Street level ticket hall leading up to one island and one single platform via a subway and staircases.

History: Opened in conjunction with the LSWR on 1 February 1912, although services had commenced on this section of the DR on 1 June 1877. A new platform was provided on 5 June 1932 to serve eastbound District Line trains, following the extension of the Piccadilly Line from Hammersmith to Acton Town and beyond.

Design: This station's attractive red brick street building is squashed between a house at the end of the parade and the railway viaduct. It features a 'Dutch' gable and an ornate metal grille above the entrance gates, although this is partially obscured by a standard canopy, installed by 1916. The ticket hall has a particularly high ceiling, with a large skylight above the ticket office windows. Extensive improvement work has recently resulted in the installation of new tiled finishes and a more effective lighting scheme. These finishes have been extended throughout the access areas, including the attractive vaulted subway area. The original island platform was designed to fit in with the other stations on this section of line, which were all rebuilt around this time, and retains its serrated valance on the canopy edge. Partially enclosed seating units incorporating station signage are also attractive features but the overall impression is diminished by the provision of an incongruous fibre-glass waiting room in the centre of the platform. The eastbound platform is completely unlike its companion in terms of appearance and construction. Similar to those built by Holden at Chiswick Park, it features a long

concrete canopy supported by buttresses attached to the retaining wall. Exposure to pollution and brake dust over the years have resulted in extensive discolouration and this has led to the wall surfaces being painted over.

Stanmore

Jubilee 1.8m Surface Grade II (prop.)

Layout: Platform level ticket hall (accessed by means of a street level entrance lobby and covered staircase) leading directly to one island platform.

History: Opened on 10 December 1932 as the terminus of the MR branch line from Wembley Park. Services transferred to the Bakerloo Line on 20 November 1939 and to the Jubilee Line on 1 May 1979.

Design: The attractive, cottage-like station building is set back from the main thoroughfare and is fronted by an extensive garden area and a bus slip-road. The entrances to the slip-road are marked by pole-mounted silhouette roundels on top of metal-clad plinths. Much of the facade is taken up with integrated shop units. Passing through the main doors, one enters an area which served as the ticket hall until 1964. It has much in common with the hall at Kingsbury such as the brown wall tiling, high vaulted ceiling and moulded timber surround to the telephone recess. A long staircase leads down to the new ticket office, which was built at the northern end of the platform for the convenience of users of the adjacent station car park. As with the other stations on the branch, the platform's buildings and canopy cover only a small proportion of its length (although lengthened twice during the station's history – most recently by a full car's length in early 1993) and are of little note. However, the large flowerbeds installed on the open section contribute towards this station having a quiet, almost rural atmosphere.

Features: The station was built in a cutting, for it was envisaged that the line could be extended further north at some stage. Provision was thus made by positioning the ticket hall at street level, so that the tracks could proceed beneath.

Stepney Green

Dist/H&C 2.5m Sub-Surface Grade II (prop.)

Layout: Street level ticket hall leading down to two single platforms via an over-bridge and staircases.

History: Opened on 23 June 1902 by the Whitechapel & Bow Railway, although services had commenced on this section of the DR exactly three weeks earlier. Metropolitan (now H&C) Line trains first used the station on 30 March 1936.

Design: Stepney Green is amongst the most interesting and unusual stations on the District Line. Its Ford-designed street level building is similar in style to that of Bow Road, with its red brick construction, wide arched windows and fanlight over the entrance door (a second entrance into the ticket hall from Globe Road was closed off when the UTS suite was installed). The ticket hall retains almost none of its original features, although its basic form remains. Brick finishes to the overbridge and staircases to the platforms are currently painted over. The platforms were originally much wider than they are today but brick false walls were built around 1980 and these largely obscure the earlier finishes. Nevertheless, some of the sturdy metal pillars which once ran down the centre of each platform may still be observed on the eastbound side. A recently completed refurbishment project resulted in the installation of panels along the rear wall of the eastbound platform to screen off unattractive non-public areas behind and the cleaning of the vaulted brickwork above the platforms.

Features: An early sign survives on the staircase well at ticket hall level.

Stockwell

North/Vict 6.1m 15.8m Tube

Layout: Sub-surface ticket hall leading down to four single platforms via escalators, staircases and low level passageways.

History: Opened on 18 December 1890 as the southern terminus of the C&SLR. The line was extended to Clapham Common on

Below:
The vaulted roof at Stepney Green.

3 June 1900. Closed between 29 November 1923 and 30 November 1924 to allow for the enlargement of the running tunnels and the provision of escalators, the station's original island platform was abandoned at this time and two new single platforms provided 50m to the south. The station was substantially rebuilt again in the late 1960s prior to the commencement of Victoria Line services on 23 July 1971, when two new platforms were brought into use.

Design: The current street building, constructed for the inauguration of the Victoria Line, replaced the earlier C&SLR building, which had itself been modernised by Holden in the mid-1920s. It has a rather nondescript appearance and is notable only for the fact that it is one of the very few surface buildings constructed for the Victoria Line. The dark brick sections either side of the ventilation tower were added at a later date. The finishes to the lower concourses and platforms are typical of others found on the Brixton extension and these materials have also been used on the Northern Line platforms. Seat recesses feature a stunning angular wave pattern using two-tone blue and white tiling.

Sudbury Hill

Piccadilly 1.7m Surface Grade II (prop.)

Layout: Street level ticket hall leading down to two single platforms via an overbridge and staircases.

History: Opened on 28 June 1903 on the DR extension from north of Ealing Common to South Harrow. It was rebuilt in preparation for the transfer of services to the Piccadilly Line on 4 July 1932, although reconstruction was not completed until the following year.

Design: Sudbury Hill was the first, fully developed example of the format and style Holden was to devise for the majority of buildings on line extensions during the 1930s. The main structure consists of a brick 'box' containing a large vertical window within each facade and topped by a concrete roof. It is preceded by a low enclosed canopy which forms an entrance lobby with retail units on either side. The

building is set back from the road and the station's presence is marked by a large pole-mounted silhouette roundel on top of the side wall of the forecourt. Encroachment of the UTS suite spoils the ticket hall but its general atmosphere remains undiminished. The outline of the original passimeter (removed around 1985) can still be discerned on the St James's tiled floor. At platform level, the station is less impressive and presents a somewhat unco-ordinated appearance. Nevertheless, it is interesting to observe features in the design which were to be developed elsewhere, eg the stepped roof of the staircases and recessed waiting areas, which were both used most noticeably at Park Royal.

Sudbury Town

Piccadilly 1.4m Surface Grade II

Layout: Street level ticket hall leading to two single platforms with an overbridge (also a subsidiary entrance from Orchard Gate).

History: Opened on 28 June 1903 on the DR extension from north of Ealing Common to South Harrow. In preparation for the transfer of services to the Piccadilly Line on 4 July 1932, the station was completely rebuilt; opening in its new form during July the previous year.

Design: Although its sister station at Sudbury Hill was the first fully developed example of Holden's new style of building for the Piccadilly Line extensions, Sudbury Town was completed over a year earlier and is in many ways more interesting because of its experimental nature. The magnificent facade features bronze lettering spelling out the station's name on the concrete band at roof level and a large silhouette roundel on the brickwork directly beneath (although neither is original). The main area of the ticket hall is notable for its sheer volume, although the decorative ceiling, integrated retail unit and distinctive clock and barometer dials at high level are also key features. Opposite the ticket office, the hall has a much lower ceiling and retains its original wooden passimeter. The original bicycle storage area was converted into a new ticket office and associated staff accommodation around 1985. Direct access is gained on to the eastbound platform, which along with its companion displays more integrity and charm than almost any others designed subsequently by Holden. The neat concrete canopies extend along for around a third of the platforms' total length and concrete paving has been laid on the floor surfaces below. Two roundels incorporated into the window frames are features unique to this station, as are the large timber advertising panels behind the attractive flowerbeds on the open sections. The platforms are connected by means of a concrete footbridge which also acts as a public right of way over the tracks.

Features: When first opened, the station was identified by means of neon signs on either side of the building in the positions currently occupied by bronze lettering. These survived until 1939 at the earliest. The hooped lamp standards around the forecourt are modern copies of the original versions and were installed around 1990. However, many examples of the original fittings remain, including the signs on the entrances to the overbridge. The main area of the ticket hall once acted as a testing area for various uplighter prototypes and the two mismatching white floor tiles in line with the end of the shop unit mark their positions.

Surrey Quays

East London 2.4m Surface

Layout: Street level ticket hall leading down to two single platforms via an overbridge and staircases.

History: Opened as 'Deptford Road' on 7 December 1869 by the East London Railway. MDR and MR services commenced over this line on 1 October 1884 but were suspended on 31 July 1905 and 2 December 1906 respectively. The station was renamed 'Surrey Docks' on 17 July 1911 and the line was reopened to MR traffic from 31 March 1913. The main street level building was completely reconstructed between 1979 and 1982 as part of a programme to upgrade all stations on the East London Line. The station's name was changed to 'Surrey Quays' from 24 October 1989 to coincide with the opening of a nearby shopping centre of the same name.

Design: The street level building is one of the most unusual pieces of architecture at any Underground station. Constructed from beige coloured bricks, its strangely curved form is at its most dramatic when viewed from the west. An attractive ticket hall makes use of simple materials and fittings, enhanced by the large expanse of glazing on the eastern side and the flower baskets that adorn the ceiling. The overbridge that gives access to the southbound platform uses the same materials and construction methods as the ticket hall and again presents a bright, attractive travelling environment. Under the bridge raft, the platforms' appearance is rather dingy, although the yellow brickwork on the northbound side was given a thorough clean in preparation for the station's most recent renaming. The distinctive cast iron columns between the tracks have decorative capitals and once supported the original timber street level building. The remains of an old bay road, for which tracks were never provided, may be observed next to the retaining wall on the southbound side.

Swiss Cottage

Jubilee 4.5m Tube

Layout: Sub-surface ticket hall leading down to two single platforms via escalators and a low level concourse.

History: Opened on 13 April 1868 as the terminus of the M&SJWR from Baker Street. The M&SJWR was taken over fully by the MR in 1882. New tube platforms were brought into service on 20 November 1939 on the new section of the Bakerloo Line linking Baker Street and the Stanmore branch of the Metropolitan Line, with use of the Metropolitan Line platforms ceasing on 17 August 1940. Responsibility for the station transferred to the Jubilee Line on 1 May 1979.

Design: The original street building was typical of the style used for inner urban stations in the late 1860s and resembled closely its sister station at Marlborough Road, which still stands at the junction of Finchley Road and Queen's Grove. This was replaced in the late 1920s by a standard C. W. Clark-designed building, which continued to act as the station's entrance until replaced by staircase access by the early 1960s. The entrance was resited within a development on the west side pf Finchley Road around 1980, when the entire site on the west side of Finchley Road was redeveloped. The ticket hall is now accessed by means of staircases and subways from various locations around this busy road junction; the only substantial surface structure being a tall brick ventilation tower, built for the inauguration of the Jubilee Line. The hall takes an unusual form, with its curved upper level linked to the main floor by a wide flight of steps and the floor of the upper landing making use of distinctive green speckled tiles. Low level areas of the station are very similar to those of St John's Wood although in this case, a green and brown border to the tiling is utilised.

Features: The concourse is noticeable for the retention of two of the massive steel floodgates which were provided as a wartime contingency measure. The timber door on the left-hand side of the corridor leading from the ticket hall to the exit on the west side of Finchley Road gives access to the old MR northbound platform.

Temple

Circ/Dist 6.9m Sub-Surface Grade II (prop.)

Layout: Street level ticket hall leading down to two single platforms via staircases.

History: Opened as 'The Temple' on 30 May 1870 on the DR extension from Westminster Bridge (now Westminster) to Blackfriars. The station was originally to have been called 'Norfolk Street'. Its name changed to just 'Temple' over a matter of time.

Design: This station was constructed as part of the Thames Embankment project and, like most of the original DR stations, had an overall glazed roof, although it was required to have an especially flat profile at the insistence of the Duke of Norfolk who owned the land across which the railway passes. The original small brick building was replaced around 1911 by the typical Harry Ford design that exists today, which makes use of the simple, neo-Georgian Renaissance style he also deployed for other DR station reconstruction projects.

Access to the station is now solely from the main elevation at right-angles to Temple Place, although a second entrance was to be found on the Embankment facade until 1984. This has been particularly crudely infilled and this elevation is redeemed only by the presence of fine examples of 1920s notice cases and signs. Windows above the staircases in the attractively upgraded ticket hall once offered a view over the platforms, but this was eliminated when the overall roof was replaced by a plain girdered soffit. Original balustraded staircases lead down to the platforms which were subject to a partial modernisation scheme in the mid-1980s, resulting in the installation of attractive green and cream wall tiling. Ornate metal columns dating from 1911 also adorn the platforms, which are amongst the most impressive on this stretch of line.

Features: A poster Underground map dating from 1932 was discovered in 1991 beneath an advertising frame outside the station. This has been restored and reinstated to the right of the entrance.

Theydon Bois

Central 0.4m Surface

Layout: Street level ticket hall leading to two single platforms with a footbridge.

History: Opened as 'Theydon' on 24 April 1865 by the GER and was renamed 'Theydon Bois' on 1 December of the same year. The station was partially rebuilt in 1885/86 and again around 1893 in connection with the doubling of the tracks. It was further modified in advance of the commencement of Central Line services on 25 September 1949.

Design: Substantially of red brick construction, the external appearance of the main street level building is somewhat confused. The entrance to the ticket hall appears as a low brick structure attached to the side of a two-storey, house-like building which serves as station staff residential accommodation. Overall, it is very similar in design to its contemporary at Epping. A small, plainly decorated ticket hall gives directly access on to the westbound platform, the construction of which dates from the station's opening. Sections of canopy

Above:
A Circle Line train on the inner rail departs from Temple station. *Hugh Madgin*

Below:
Four decades of Central Line operation have left the Great Eastern character of Theydon Bois largely intact. *Hugh Madgin*

either side of the waiting room on each platform probably date from the 1940s. The two platforms are linked by an attractive latticed iron footbridge, built in 1885 and marked by an identification plaque.

Tooting Bec

Northern 4.8m Tube Grade II

Layout: Sub-surface ticket hall (accessed from two entrance buildings) leading down to two single platforms via escalators and a low level concourse.

History: Opened as 'Trinity Road (Tooting Bec)' on 13 September 1926 on the Northern Line extension from Clapham Common to Morden. The station was renamed 'Tooting Bec' on 1 October 1950.

Design: Like Balham, Tooting Bec has surface buildings on opposite sides of a major road junction, although in this case their appearance is noticeably different. Whilst in terms of materials and basic format they conform with Holden's design principles for all the stations on the extension, the building on the corner of Balham High Road and Tooting Bec Road has its side facades swept back so far, they are almost at right-angles to the main elevation, therefore warranting their own roundels within the glazing. Both buildings contain entrance lobbies – illuminated by large round chandeliers – which lead down to the sub-surface ticket hall. Although most of the original green and white tiled finishes remain in good condition, the appearance of this large area appears disjointed and is marred by unco-ordinated advertising, poor floor finishes, mismatching tiling on the ticket office facade and inadequate lighting. The lower levels are typical of the other stations on the Morden extension.

Features: The headwalls above the staircases leading down to the ticket hall each feature an original 1926 roundel, distinguishable by dashes above and below the lettering.

Tooting Broadway

Northern 8.5m Tube Grade II

Layout: Street level ticket hall leading down to two single platforms via escalators and a low level concourse.

History: Opened on 13 September 1926 on the Northern Line extension from Clapham Common to Morden.

Design: The design of the exterior is almost identical to that of South Wimbledon, ie a broad, gently curved facade constructed from Portland stone and featuring large windows above the entrances. The ticket hall has a fine corniced ceiling, containing two lovely octagonal skylights, and featuring decorative latticework within the windows. At lower concourse level, the station is rather different compared to other stations on the Morden extension, for the escalators descend at right-angles, rather than parallel, to the orientation of the platforms. These areas are also notable for the existence of four floodgates and some particularly fine directional signs. In contrast, the platforms are typical of the Northern Line stations of this vintage.

Tottenham Court Road

Cent/North 25.4m 9.2m Tube Grade II (prop.)

Layout: Sub-surface ticket hall leading down to four single platforms via two flights of escalators, and low level passageways and staircases.

History: Opened on 30 July 1900 on the original section of the CLR. A separate station named 'Oxford Street' was opened on 22 June 1907 by the CCE&HR, with interchange with the CLR provided at low level. Its name was changed to 'Tottenham Court Road' on 9 March 1908, the CCE&HR station of the same title being renamed 'Goodge Street' on the same day so as to avoid confusion. An expanded sub-surface ticket hall was completed on 16 August 1925 allowing it to serve traffic on both lines. Access to the new lower concourse was facilitated by the provision of three escalators, which started in operational use on 29 September 1925. A further two escalators leading down to the Northern Line areas were brought into service on 3 February the following year. An additional single escalator, extending down from a long connecting subway to between the Northern Line platforms, was first used on 27 April 1933. The Central Line platforms were length-

Above:
Paolozzi tiling at Tottenham Court Road.

ened to accommodate the longer trains planned for the line's extensions, with retiling of finishes taking place at the same time. The ticket hall was rebuilt again around 1965, and the entire station was subject to an extensive modernisation project between 1982 and 1986.

Design: The ticket hall is accessed by means of three open staircases on the corners of the road junction and also via the original CLR building on Oxford Street. The latter retains its brown terracotta facade and attractive Delissa Joseph building above, but its appearance has been substantially altered by the addition of a garish barrel-vaulted canopy as part of the modernisation project. The CCE&HR station was unusual in that it did not have a standard Leslie Green-designed surface building and was instead accessed by means of staircases, the original wrought iron railings of which still survive. Despite having been extensively rebuilt over the years, the ticket hall located under the road does not have any of the elegance or spaciousness displayed by the circular halls at Oxford Circus or Piccadilly Circus, At low level, the finishes were amongst the first to be mod-

ernised during the 1980s and are somewhat more lavish than projects developed later in the decade. A standard cream coloured tile is used on wall and floor finishes throughout, except where highly patterned mosaic (designed by the eminent sculptor and artist, Eduardo Paolozzi) has been incorporated. This is located primarily in distinctive circular areas at concourse level (which occupy the lift shafts that once extended down from the CLR ticket hall) and on the central portion of each platform. These murals have proved to be highly controversial but whether liked or disliked, no one can doubt the impact they make on the appearance of the station.

Tottenham Hale

Victoria 3.1m Tube

Layout: Street level ticket hall leading down to two single platforms via escalators and a low level concourse.

History: Opened on 1 September 1968 on the initial section of the Victoria Line.

Design: The station has a small, plain surface building which it shares with the adjacent British Rail station. Although the ticket hall was partially upgraded in connection with the reconstruction of the main line platforms for the inauguration of Stansted Express services in 1991, the basic Victoria Line finishes remain in this area and throughout the rest of the station. The platforms have bare tunnel irons exposed over the tracks, while the tiling within the seat recesses is one of the most attractive in the series, depicting an ancient local ferry service.

Totteridge & Whetstone

Northern 1.0m Surface

Layout: Street level ticket hall leading down to two single platforms via staircases.

History: Opened as 'Totteridge' on 1 April 1872 by the GNR and renamed 'Totteridge & Whetstone' exactly two years later. Services on the Northern Line were extended to High Barnet from East Finchley on 14 April 1940.

Design: The basic structure of the original GNR building survives, although its appearance has been extensively modified over the years. It consists of two steeply gabled wings either side of the central entrance area, which was rebuilt and brought forward to the pavement line during the early 1960s. The small ticket hall retains none of its original finishes or features, with the exception of a stone fireplace beneath the windows. The platforms, however, remain largely as built and have a distinctly rural feel to them, owing partly to the extensive vegetation on either side. Valanced canopies, yellow brick buildings and unusual railings on the gates at the base of the staircases contribute towards making these station areas some of the most pleasing on the line. Several attractive iron-framed seating units, dating from around the turn of the century, add further to its character.

Tower Hill

Circ/Dist 14.1m 0.4m Sub-Surface

Layout: Sub-surface entrance ticket hall leading down to one island and one single platform via staircases. Exit from station by means of separate staircases and hall.

History: Opened as 'Tower of London' on 25 September 1882 when the MR extended its services from Aldgate. The station was designed as a temporary halt and was in operation for only two years before being replaced by a new station known as 'Mark Lane', sited less than 100m to the west. Built in conjunction with the DR as part of its extension from Mansion House to Whitechapel, the new station was opened on 6 October 1884, although the old facilities were not taken out of use for a further six days. Mark Lane was renamed 'Tower Hill' on 1 September 1946 and was closed on 4 February 1967 when its facilities were relocated on to the site of the old 'Tower of London' station, although terminal and reversing facilities for trains were not fully operational until 21 January the following year. A new entrance and ticket hall was opened in 1988.

Design: Access to the new ticket hall is by means of a short flight of steps and the area makes use of high quality finishes throughout. The old hall is incorporated within the ground floor of a drab office development and functions solely as a means of exiting the station. The platforms make extensive use of the grey wall tiling which acted as the basic cladding material in the late 1960s.

Features: Extensive remains of the eastbound platform of Mark Lane station may be observed as one approaches by train from Monument. The entrance at street level to the sub-surface ticket hall was designed by Harry Ford and constructed around 1911 to replace an earlier brick structure at the junction with Seething Lane. It still exists as the access to a pedestrian subway on the northern side of Byward Street. The original street level building of 'Tower of London' station survived until as recently as September 1940, latterly in use as a tea warehouse. A small portion of the City of London's Roman wall may be observed inset into the trackside wall opposite the eastern end of the westbound platform. A sundial, designed by sculptor Edwin Russell, was added to the roof of the new ticket hall. This incorporates a bronze frieze charting the history of London.

Tufnell Park

Northern 2.7m Tube Grade II (prop.)

Layout: Street level ticket hall leading down to two single platforms via lifts and low level passageways and staircases.

History: Opened on 22 June 1907 on the original section of the CCE&HR. The layout at street level was altered in the mid-1980s to allow for the installation of the UTS suite.

Design: The surface building is typical of the style developed by Green for all the stations on the initial sections of the tube railways and retains four of the original 'Tiffany' cantilevered lamp fittings on its exterior. A retail unit once occupied its apex, with windows facing in three directions. However, the entire layout at street level was radically altered in the mid-1980s in conjunction with lift replacement and UTS installation. This resulted in the window facing Tufnell Park Road, along with one of the exit bays from the lifts, being blocked in and faced with matching red terracotta, while the window facing Brecknock Road was removed completely and now forms part of the station entrance. The ticket hall has been largely retiled so as to be in keeping with the original finishes that remain, such as the dark green moulded tiles around the emergency staircase. This potentially attractive area is spoilt by the existence of an unsympathetic lighting scheme. The low level passageways and platforms remain largely unaltered. Here, Green made use of an orange and cream tiling scheme not dissimilar to the one deployed at Covent Garden, although it is now largely covered with an ugly mixture of paint and advertising.

Features: As with many Leslie Green stations an UNDERGROUND tiled sign was added to the facade c1908, although in the case of Tufnell Park, this was usually positioned at *high* level above the original retail unit. When opened, the ticket office was sited on the wall where telephones are now located.

Below:
The delightfully-named Turnham Green.

Turnham Green

Layout: Street level ticket hall leading up to two island platforms via a subway and staircases.

History: Opened on 1 January 1869 by the LSWR. The MR and DR extended their services to the station on 1 June and 1 October 1877 respectively (the former being suspended on 31 December 1906). The original single island platform was supplemented by a second platform to the north for the use of LSWR services only, the entire station being inaugurated in reconstructed form on 3 December 1911. LSWR services ceased on 5 June 1916 and the track layout was substantially altered for the introduction of Piccadilly Line services through the station from 4 July 1932. Piccadilly Line trains started serving the platforms early morning, late evening and on Sundays from 23 June 1963.

Design: The rebuilt street level building is overshadowed by the adjacent railway viaduct and presents a rather plain, uninteresting appearance. Likewise, the ticket hall has little to commend it, having been considerably rebuilt over the years, most recently in connection with UTS installation. The subway under the tracks is of far more interest as it features white, glazed brickwork and a high, vaulted ceiling dating from the station's reconstruction. The canopies also date from this time and extend almost the full length of the platforms. Their serrated valances and the timber seating enclosures beneath contribute towards making these areas particularly attractive. The station was often known as 'Turnham Green (Bedford Park)' from 1892 and this is reflected in some of the signage which remains at platform level.

Turnpike Lane

Layout: Sub-surface ticket hall leading down to two single platforms via escalators and a low level concourse.

History: Opened on 19 September 1932 on the Piccadilly Line extension from Finsbury Park to Arnos Grove.

Design: Holden designed this station as an integrated bus-train interchange point, with a complete bus forecourt created to the rear of the main building rather than the slip-road built at Southgate. The building itself is a development of the style pioneered at Sudbury Town, with the basic brick box complemented by two ventilation towers and a low canopy extending over the staircases leading to ticket hall level. Access is also by means of staircases located on the opposite sides of the nearby road junction, linked to the ticket hall via tiled passageways. The hall itself is massive and its size is exaggerated by the fact that its floor is several metres below pavement level. Dark brown tiling lines the walls, while the floor space is dominated by one of the original bronze uplighters. The lower concourse and platforms are very similar to those at other tube stations on the extension; the cream tiling having a yellow border in this particular case.

Features: The 'Tickets & Trains' sign at the top of the staircase at Duckett's Corner is the only original sign to remain above platform level.

When first opened, staircases led up to two islands in the middle of Turnpike Lane, used as tram boarding positions. Although closed c1951, the points where these staircases entered the station may be identified by areas of mismatching yellow tiling on the wall of the subway junction facing the ticket hall.

The advertising column on the pavement adjacent to the main building is on the site of a lighting/signage unit (similar to those at Southgate and Oakwood) which survived until at least 1968.

Upminster Bridge

Layout: Street level ticket hall leading up to one island platform via a subway and staircase.

History: Opened on 17 December 1934 by the LMS, although services on this section of the District Line had recommenced on 12 September 1932 following the suspension of services on this section of line from 1905.

Design: Although of different scale and materials, the surface building is similar in style to those of Hounslow West and Ealing Common stations – opened several years earlier. A standard LMS red brick structure forms the base of the building but is distinguishable from others owing to the octagonal roof section set back from the main walls. This feature causes the ticket hall to resemble that of Bounds Green, although it is somewhat smaller and less prominently glazed. The tiled floor finish features a distinctive black and purple pattern against a brown terrazzo background and this extends to the subway leading to the access staircase. The simple, airy platform has minimal buildings to spoil the view towards the west, and recent redecoration and installation of concrete paving have further enhanced this already attractive area.

Features: Three green painted, timber seating units with distinctive rounded ends and dating from the 1930s survive at the eastern end of the platform. These benches are found at this station and Elm Park only. The restored K4 red telephone box in the ticket hall is thought to be the only example on an Underground station.

Upney

Layout: Street level ticket hall leading down to one island platform via a long ramp.

History: Opened on 12 September 1932 by the LMS to coincide with the electrification of the tracks and the recommencement of District Line services, which had been suspended on 30 September 1905.

Design: This station is identical in almost every way to its sister station at Dagenham Heathway. The street level building is generally intact but is marred by the insensitive bricking-in of one of the windows. The platform is accessed by a long, timber-panelled ramp and has a canopy profile not dissimilar to that installed at Watford several years earlier. Original nosing stones survive along both edges and concrete paving slabs have been installed for the platform's full extent.

Upton Park

Layout: Street level ticket hall leading down to two single platforms via staircases.

History: Opened in 1877 by the LTSR. Much of the station, including the street level building, was rebuilt to coincide with the extension of DR services from Whitechapel to Upminster on 2 June 1902, although work was not completed until July the following year. Metropolitan Line services started on 30 March 1936 and the station transferred to LTB ownership on 1 January 1969.

Design: This station's impressive street level building is located directly above the tracks and is almost identical to the structure at East Ham. The most noticeable difference is caused by the removal of the peculiarly shaped chimney stacks from the plinths either side of the central gable. Internally, the ticket hall has the same barn-like properties caused by an open, raftered ceiling. Other features of interest include two-tone glazed brickwork, decorative iron railings which act as a barrier line, and an early free-standing metal kiosk. The platforms are fairly basic in nature and perhaps reflect their role in transporting football supporters to West Ham's home ground located nearby. Their somewhat run-down appearance is redeemed in part by the heavily serrated canopy valances and potentially attractive brickwork on the 'island' platform.

Features: The central platform was shared with LMS (later BR) services travelling westwards until these were suspended around 1960. Remains of these platforms and the staircases serving them may still be seen.

Uxbridge

Layout: Street level ticket hall leading directly to two island platforms with three bays.

History: Opened on 4 July 1904 as the terminus of the MR branch line from Harrow-on-the-Hill. DR trains used the same tracks from Rayners Lane commencing on 1 March 1910 and these services were transferred to the Piccadilly Line from 23 October 1933. All services were transferred to a completely new station, located on a far more convenient site facing the High Street, on 4 December 1938.

Design: The rebuilt station forms part of a sharply curved shopping parade, with the entrance to the ticket hall sited between two fluted pillars at the apex of the curve, capped by winged wheel carvings by Joseph Armitage. Although Bucknell made a key contribution to the implementation of the project, the basic design of the internal areas reflects on the format devised by Holden for Cockfosters at the other extremity of the Piccadilly Line. Again, there is no clear break between ticket hall and platform – the entire area is enclosed within a massive vaulted roof supported by concrete buttresses and is in some ways even more impressive than Cockfosters because of the greater height needed to accommodate surface as well as tube rolling stock. Illumination is provided by several lines of globe pendant fittings suspended from the roof. The eastern end of the platform area is in the open and trains use three sets of tracks, although the central bay is served by platform 3 only.

Features: A stained glass window depicting various coats of arms in a wide range of vivid colours may be seen within one of the buttress element above the ticket hall area. The original ticket office still exists on the left-hand side as one approaches the platforms but is currently disused.

Vauxhall

Victoria 9.0m Tube

Layout: Sub-surface ticket hall leading down to two single platforms via escalators and a low level concourse.

History: Opened on 23 July 1971 on the extension of the Victoria Line to Brixton.

Design: This station has little street presence as access is gained directly from a public subway. The ticket hall, lower con-

course and platforms are typical of others on the Brixton extension, making extensive use of dark and light grey Victoria Line tiling. The tiling within the seat recesses depicts a floral pattern, reflecting the Vauxhall pleasure gardens, on a green and blue background.

Victoria

Circ/Dist/Vict 63.8m 14.7m Misc

Layout: Two linked sub-surface ticket halls leading to two single sub-surface platforms via staircases and to two tube platforms (serving the Victoria Line) via escalators and low level concourses.

History: Opened on 24 December 1868 on the DR extension from South Kensington to Westminster Bridge (later Westminster). A subway link to the main line station was opened on 12 August 1878 with joint funding with the LB&SCR and LCDR. Extensive modifications were carried out throughout the 1900s, including the rafting-over of the platforms and the construction of a sub-surface ticket hall. A new entrance was created within Terminus Place at around this time, designed by George Sherrin and similar in style to that provided at South Kensington. Further rebuilding was required for the inauguration of Victoria Line services on 7 March 1969, the station serving as the southern terminus of the line until it was extended to Brixton on 23 July 1971. This rebuilding work was not completed until 1972.

Design: Access to the District Line ticket hall can still be gained from Sherrin's splendid arcade. The Victoria and District Line ticket halls are faced with the same finishes, ie beige and blue-green wall tiling, St James's flooring, panelled false ceiling with integrated lighting. The lower levels of the station make extensive use of standard light grey tiling, while the tiling within the seat recesses on the Victoria Line platforms depicts a silhouette of Queen Victoria in white out of blue on a pink background. The District Line platforms were reclad in early 1993 with white wall tiling (replacing the earlier Victoria Line variety) and a vitreous enamel false ceiling. The last remnants of the original DR station may be observed in the form of the footbridge over the District Line tracks and adjacent painted brick arches.

Features: One of the low level concourse features a 'mock' roundel bearing the legend 'Harburg', presented by the Harburg Transport Authority.

Walthamstow Central

Victoria 7.4m Tube

Layout: Access to LUL areas from northbound British Rail platform. Sub-surface concourse leading down to two single platforms via escalators and a low level concourse.

History: The main line station was opened as 'Hoe Street Walthamstow' on 26 April 1870 by the GER and renamed 'Walthamstow Central' on 6 May 1968. The Underground station was opened on 1 September 1968 as the northern terminus of the Victoria Line.

Design: Access to the Underground-owned parts of the station is by means of staircases down from the British Rail platforms. The finishes are almost identical to those used elsewhere north of Seven Sisters, including the exposed tunnel irons above the tracks. The tiling within the seat recesses on the platforms depicts an orange fabric pattern designed by William Morris, who lived in the Walthamstow area.

Wanstead

Central 1.1m Tube

Layout: Street level ticket hall leading down to two single platforms via escalators and a low level concourse.

History: Opened on 14 December 1947 on the Central Line extension from Leytonstone to Newbury Park.

Design: Wanstead proved to be one of the last designs prepared by Holden for the Underground and is markedly different from the stations he had built earlier. The main building and the ventilation tower are finished in bare concrete rather than the usual fair-face brickwork. A glazed silhouette

Below:
A late Holden design at Wanstead.

roundel is set into three of the faces of the tower and these, along with the two pole-mounted versions on the roofs of the side entrance blocks, give this Underground station an unusually high profile in the street environment. An attractive semi-circular flowerbed, illuminated by two distinctively shaped 1940s lamp-posts, is to be found in the forecourt. The ticket hall consists of a simple box structure and presents an impressive sight, with its high panelled ceiling, tall north-facing window and well integrated UTS ticket office. The lower concourse and platforms bear a striking resemblance to those of Swiss Cottage opened eight years earlier, for both make use of the same yellow wall tiling with green borders. The main difference is the presence, in the case of Wanstead, of a curved ceiling panel system over the platforms as well as the access areas. In addition, an early clock with 'bull's-eyes' in place of numerals survives on each platform.

Wapping

East London 0.9m Sub-Surface Grade II

Layout: Street level ticket hall leading down to two single platforms via lifts and staircases.

History: Opened as 'Wapping & Shadwell' on 7 December 1869 by the East London Railway and renamed 'Wapping' on 10 April 1876. DR and MR services commenced over this line on 1 October 1884 but were suspended on 31 July 1905 and 2 December 1906 respectively. The line was reopened to MR traffic from 31 March 1913. The surface building was completely rebuilt to allow for the installation of lifts on 4 October 1915 and again in 1959-60 following bomb damage caused on 11 September 1940. The new building was further modified in 1981-82 during lift replacement.

Design: The original building was similar to that of Shoreditch, but was replaced by 1915 by a timber structure featuring a Classical entrance portico and rectangular windows to either side. The most recent building is considerably less impressive and consists of a polygonal rotunda (housing lift machine room equipment) on the roof of a plain, grey ticket

hall block. The upper lift lobby features considerable areas of wooden panelling, while the lower lobby is marred by the presence of intrusive electrical cabinets and other operational equipment. At platform level, the station is very similar to Shadwell, with its vaulted brick ceiling, melamine wall panels and an open section at the northern end. The main difference is the platform's relatively narrow width which has prevented standard seating units from being installed. The sounds and smells of the nearby River Thames pervade the station at this level, creating an atmosphere that is unique to this section of line.

Features: The East London Line makes use of the Thames Tunnel, constructed under the supervision of Marc and Isambard Kingdom Brunel, and completed in 1843. The first tunnel under the river, it failed to serve any useful purpose until the ELR converted it to rail operation. Contained within the existing lift shaft was the spiral staircase which afforded pedestrians a means of accessing the tunnel, the entrance of which can be seen at the southern end of the platforms. The tunnel entrance and surviving staircases down from lower lobby level now have Grade II listed status.

Warren Street

North/Vict 10.0m 1.3m Tube

Layout: Street level ticket hall leading down to four single platforms via two flights of escalators and low level concourses, passageways and staircases.

History: Opened as 'Euston Road' on 22 June 1907 on the original section of the CCE&HR. The station's name was changed to 'Warren Street' on 7 June 1908. The upper areas were completely rebuilt to allow for the installation of escalators, which started in service on 27 September 1933, although work was not completed until the following year. Further modifications were undertaken in preparation for the inauguration of Victoria Line services on 1 December 1968, including the installation of an additional escalator from ticket hall level. The platforms acted as the terminus of the line until it was extended to Victoria on 7 March 1969.

Design: The original surface building was a standard Leslie Green structure, similar in scale and form to that of Lambeth North but with matching elevations facing Warren Street and Euston Road. When rebuilt in the early 1930s, it assumed a somewhat different appearance, using a design developed by Heaps in conjunction with Holden. Facing on to Tottenham Court Road, it consists of a three-storey, semi-circular structure above the main ticket hall facilities, which is faced with Portland stone and surrounded by a multi-faceted canopy. The ticket hall was substantially refurbished for the start of Victoria Line services and the provision of UTS equipment, the latter resulting in the blocking in of one of the three original entrances. The main lower concourse and Victoria Line platforms are clad with standard grey tiled finishes, with the seating recesses featuring a red and black maze pattern – a visual pun on the station's name. Northern Line areas retain most of their CCE&HR deep blue and cream tiling, although the low level concourse is clad with finishes dating from the 1933 reconstruction. Original screened signage (eg 'Way Out', 'Euston Road') survives within the platform tiling.

Warwick Avenue

Bakerloo 2.7m Tube

Layout: Sub-surface ticket hall leading down to two single platforms via escalators and a low level concourse.

History: Opened on 31 January 1915 on the Bakerloo Line extension from Paddington to Kilburn Park. A substantial modernisation scheme was completed in 1992, following damage caused by a ticket hall fire in 1986.

Design: Warwick Avenue is one of the few early tube stations (others include Regent's Park and Trafalgar Square) that has never had a surface building. Access is by means of covered staircases on either side of the main road, each surrounded by decorative iron railings. The subway leading from the western staircase and the entire ticket hall have been completely modernised in a style matching the original design, making use of green and white wall tiling. The majority of

the green bordered, white wall tiling at platform level has been retained, and complemented by new tiled floor finishes.

Waterloo

Bak/North 28.9m 0.3m Tube

Layout: Two ticket halls (Shell Centre and main line) leading down to four single platforms via escalators, a low level concourse and passageways.

History: The W&CR opened a station on this site on 8 August 1898. Underground services commenced on 10 March 1906 on the original section of the BS&WR, with a small atypical Green entrance building on the eastern side of York Road. The station was substantially rebuilt for the construction of Northern Line platforms; services were extended from Charing Cross (now Embankment) to Kennington on 13 September 1926. This work included the construction of a new sub-surface ticket hall beneath the main line station and a wide low level concourse between the two sets of platforms, connected to the ticket hall by a bank of three escalators which were fully operational on 12 October 1927. The Northern Line platforms were closed between 28 September and 7 October 1938 and again between 1 September and 16 December 1939, to allow the installation of floodgates. A new ticket hall, with associated escalators to lower concourse level, opened on 4 May 1951 in order to serve the nearby Festival of Britain. It was closed between 5 October 1957 and 12 May 1962 (during which finishes were replaced and the direct access through to the South Bank was blocked in), before being incorporated within the Shell Centre office development. The main ticket hall was rebuilt in 1972/73 and again in 1992/93 in preparation for the opening of the Channel Tunnel terminal and planned Jubilee Line extension.

Design: The main ticket hall is accessed from the main line station concourse by an escalator link and passageways. The newly modernised finishes consist of off-white tiling and panelled false ceiling, and are a vast improvement over the drab and confusing environment that existed previously.

Several of the high vaulted arches which support the main line structure above have been exposed and attractively lit, although the brickwork itself is not original. The Shell Centre entrance reflects the stark architectural style prevalent in the early 1960s and features a miscellany of tiled finishes which fails to present a coherent design. Passageways and staircases leading to the Bakerloo Line platforms retain most of the multi-coloured tiling scheme which originally extended along the platforms themselves. In contrast, access areas leading to the Northern Line platforms are clad with standard black-edged white tiling dating from the mid-1920s. Both sets of platforms were extensively modernised in the late 1980s and retain almost none of their original finishes. The predominantly black and white tiling scheme is most notable for the dark decorative features either side of each entrance portal (designed by Christopher Tipping) and the distinctive chequered pattern of the floor tiling. Remnants of the original tile bands over the tracks can still be seen on the Bakerloo Line platforms.

Features: The portals to the old lift shafts still survive in two of the cross-passageways leading to the Bakerloo Line platforms. The Northern Line tracks just to the south of the station are at the deepest point below mean sea level on the Underground system (70ft/21.3m).

Watford

Metropolitan 0.8m Surface Grade II (prop.)

Layout: Street level ticket hall leading down to one island platform via a staircase.

History: Opened on 2 November 1925 as the terminus of the joint MR/LNER branch which left the main line just north of Moor Park & Sandy Lodge. The line was built in conjunction with the LNER. LNER trains stopped using the branch during the General Strike of May 1926 and services were never recommenced.

Design: Watford is very similar to the station built by the MR only a few years later as the terminus of its Stanmore branch. Designed by Clark, the same 'rural' feel is present at both, especially at street level.

The walls of the ticket hall and staircase down to the platform are adorned with lovely green and mauve mosaics which dates from the building's construction and only survives in any significant quantity at this station and Willesden Green. The platform has a timber and glass canopy with a profile that is unique. Newly refurbished cast iron and timber benches complement the feel of this station perfectly.

Wembley Park

Jub/Met 5.7m 3.9m Surface

Layout: Street level ticket hall leading down to two island and two single platforms via staircases. Also, a secondary ticket hall operational on Wembley event days only.

History: Opened on 12 May 1894, although services on this section of the MR commenced on 2 August 1880 and the platforms were used for special traffic from 14 October 1893. In fact, the station had been substantially completed in April 1891 with two single platforms but the prospect of additional traffic to a proposed nearby leisure/exhibition complex resulted in its reconstruction with one island platform and two singles prior to opening. A modified track layout was introduced in January 1914 following four-tracking from Finchley Road, which involved the conversion of the previously terminus platforms (Nos 1&2) into local 'through' platforms. The street building was reconstructed to coincide with the opening of Wembley Stadium and British Empire Exhibition around 1923, along with the lengthening of platforms at their northern end. The track layout was extensively altered in the early 1930s, including the provision of a new through bay at the back of Platform 4, prior to the inauguration of services on the Stanmore branch line on 10 December 1932. Further modifications took place in preparation for the 1948 Olympic Games, including the construction of a new secondary ticket hall, new platform buildings and canopies, an additional footbridge over the tracks and a subway (later widened) linking the station with the stadium access road.

Design: The low, broad frontage of the street level building has a simple, near symmetrical form which presents a simple yet

Above:
The platforms at Watford. *Hugh Madgin*

Below:
West Acton exterior.

attractive impression. Its only true features are to be found on each of the short chimney stacks and take the form of lettering ('MR' with '23' beneath) on a decorated 'badge'. The ticket hall, accessed by means of three entrances from the street, has been substantially altered in recent years in order to accommodate the UTS ticket office suite and although modernised using high quality materials, its appearance is somewhat sterile. Previously, its layout and finishes resembled those that still survive at Willesden Green. The two island platforms are covered by fairly simple canopies for most of their length, unlike the outer platforms which are generally used on event days only.

Features: In order to accommodate the large crowds expected for the British Empire Exhibition, an additional, temporary platform was added to the eastern side of the road bridge on the north of the existing tracks. It was served by a separate ticket office building on the same side of the road and was also linked to the northern entrance of the exhibition grounds. No remnants of these facilities now remain visible.

Some particularly fine signs may be observed either side of the signal cabin off the end of platforms 2&3, which dates from 3 January 1932 and was built prior to the commencement of services to Stanmore in December of the same year.

West Acton

Central 1.0m Surface

Layout: Street level ticket hall leading down to two single platforms via staircases.

History: Opened by the GWR and used by Central line trains from 5 November 1923, although services on this section of the line had commenced on 3 August 1920. The station was substantially rebuilt in 1948.

Design: The current street level building owes much to the style developed by Lewis & Curtis for the stations on the new West Ruislip extension. Its appearance is dominated by the concrete mullioned window that takes up the entire front elevation and the large canopy that steps out from the main brick facade. The large ticket hall

resembles in scale and form many of Holden's 'box' designs. Cream wall tiling has been extended round the new ticket office frontage in a satisfactory manner but is spoilt by the insensitive location of telephones and other equipment. Staircases from the ticket hall lead down to covered waiting areas, similar to the format developed at Park Royal. Elegant curved timber bench seating and wooden palisade fencing in the open areas are particularly noteworthy features at platform level.

Features: An original 1948 silhouette roundel on the left-hand elevation of the main building retains the words 'Central' and 'Line' above and below the blue bar. Two superb 1940s line diagrams survive on the overbridge.

West Brompton

District 1.2m Surface Grade II (prop.)

Layout: Street level ticket hall leading down to two single platforms via overbridges and staircases.

History: Opened on 12 April 1869 by the DR, the station acted as the terminus for shuttle services from Gloucester Road until the line was extended to Putney Bridge & Fulham on 1 March 1880. An adjacent station on the West London Extension Railway was opened on 1 September 1866 and closed on 21 October 1940.

Design: This small building on the outskirts of central London is perhaps the best preserved example of a DR station and has changed little since it was first built. The attractive facade is set back slightly from the main road and features arches over the windows and doorways in the style of other stations of the same era. Recent refurbishment work has resulted in the removal of the cream paint which had covered the exterior for many years, thereby revealing the yellow brickwork beneath. The wide window to the right of the entrance doorway dates from around the turn of the century and replaces two windows that matched the one surviving to the left of the door. The symmetry of the facade was further lost through the conversion of a further window into a secondary entrance and the outline of the original arch feature can be identified within the brickwork above the collapsible gates. Inside the ticket hall, extensively alterations have taken place over the years and the original layout and finishes survive no more. Nevertheless, newly installed finishes and pendant light fittings have combined to create a most attractive environment. The ticket hall leads directly on to the first of two timber over-bridges which link it to the platforms. They are covered by a high timber overall roof, supported by brick retaining walls. The restoration of the latter, following the removal of paint and advertising hoardings, has turned this area of the station into one of the most impressive on the system.

Features: Some distinctively shaped 1920s signs survive beneath the more westerly staircases and feature rare inter-locking W lettering.

West Finchley

Northern 0.7m Surface Local

Layout: Street level ticket hall leading to two single platforms, which are linked by a footbridge.

History: Opened on 1 March 1933 by the LNER. Services on the Northern Line exten-sion to High Barnet commenced on 14 April 1940.

Design: The station was built in the early 1930s to serve new suburban housing devel-opments in the area. Its street presence is marked by a pole-mounted roundel, with the ticket hall building located almost at platform level in a shallow cutting. The original timber building itself was rebuilt in 1988 and resem-bles a large brick-walled shed, with its grilled gables and metal pitched roof. The appear-ance of the platforms is unlike that of the other stations on this section of line, which is not altogether surprising, bearing in mind their relative youth. However, the lovely lat-ticed footbridge and timber waiting rooms, along with other items of station hardware, were salvaged from other stations on the LNER network, primarily in the north of Eng-land, because of the shortage of funds avail-able. Several attractive turn-of-the-century bench seats are also to be found on each platform.

Features: The footbridge was originally sited at Wintersett & Ryhill station on the Barnsley to Wakefield line, which had closed in 1930.

West Ham

Dist/H&C 2.1m Surface

Layout: Street level ticket hall leading up to one island platform via staircases.

History: Opened on 1 February 1901 by the LTSR. Services on the DR were extended from Whitechapel to Upminster on 2 June 1902 when the station was rebuilt. Known as 'West Ham (Manor Road)' between 11 Febru-ary 1924 and 31 December 1968, Metropoli-tan (now H&C) Line trains first used the station on 30 March 1936 and it transferred to Lon-don Transport Board ownership on 1 January 1969. The ticket hall building was completely rebuilt to coincide with the inauguration of North London Line services to adjacent BR platforms, the interchange link being opened on 14 May 1979.

Design: The external appearance of this station is amongst the most nondescript on the entire Underground network, with the small glazed entrance located in the shadow of the railway viaduct and very prone to vandalism. The new ticket office has been clad with blue glass reinforced plastic panels, which contrast with the yel-low painted girders of the viaduct above. Original glazed brick finishes survive on the upper staircase leading to platform level. The platform itself retains a uniquely crenel-lated valance, distinctive brick paved floor surface in the area under the canopy and the ornate bracketry typical of the rebuilt stations on this section of line.

West Hampstead

Jubilee 4.4m Surface

Layout: Street level ticket hall leading down to one island platform via a staircase.

History: Opened on 30 June 1879 on the M&SJWR extension from Swiss Cottage. It served as the terminus until the line was extended further to Willesden Green on

24 November of the same year. The station originally had two single platforms but from 13 June 1897, trains used both sides of the reconstructed southbound platform in conjunction with the GCR's plans to open a new terminus station at Marylebone and the resultant need for space for additional tracks. The platform was again rebuilt in 1938 in anticipation of the transfer of services to the Bakerloo Line on 20 November the following year, although Metropolitan Line trains continued to use the station's facilities until 7 December 1940. Jubilee Line services commenced on 1 May 1979.

Design: The station consists of an impressive, red brick building which dates from the late 1890s and forms part of the main shopping parade. The entrance is contained within the left-hand of two similar (yet not identical) facades, integrated within distinctively-shaped gables. A comparison of the details between the two windows is particularly interesting. The size and shape of the ticket hall have changed several times over the years, most recently for the creation of the UTS ticket office which ruined the area's symmetry. The platform is very similar to the style and layout of Dollis Hill and Kilburn, which were reconstructed at around the same time. A curved waiting room and rounded concrete canopy at the southern end of the covered area are the most distinctive features of this format.

Features: It is interesting to note that it was the area beneath the right-hand gable that served as the entrance to the ticket hall until the current arrangement was adopted after the commencement of Bakerloo Line services.

West Harrow

Metropolitan 0.8m Surface

Layout: Street level ticket hall leading up to a single London-bound platform via a staircase; separate staircase gives direct access from the street to a single Uxbridge-bound platform.

History: Opened on 17 November 1913 following pressure from local landowners and residents, although services on this section of the MR had commenced on 4 July 1904. The continual slippage of the

platform buildings down the embankment eventually necessitated their comprehensive reconstruction; this work being completed in 1991. A new station building was also provided for UTS.

Design: The original timber platform buildings were somewhat temporary in nature and reflected the station's status as a halt on the main line, although waiting shelters and enlarged canopies were provided during platform lengthening. The new structures are located slightly to the east of the originals and are clad with white vitreous enamel metal panels, in sharp contrast with the brick buildings that comprise the stations elsewhere on the line.

West Kensington

District 3.7m Surface

Layout: Street level ticket hall leading down to two single platforms via staircases.

History: Opened as 'North End (Fulham)' on 9 September 1874 on the DR extension from Earl's Court to Hammersmith. The station was renamed 'West Kensington' on 1 March 1877.

Design: The original station building was similar to that of West Brompton and was rebuilt around 1927. The current entrance has a rather subdued, yet not unattractive, appearance and has remained largely unaltered since the 1920s. Set back slightly from the main building line, it features a low stone wall above canopy level, incorporating a curved panel around a pole-mounted silhouette roundel. The right-hand entrance was blocked-in so as to accommodate the new UTS ticket office and the exterior now consists largely of blue metal panels. Many 1920s finishes survive in the ticket hall and interesting features include a timber roof to the rear of the hall and attractive supporting pillars. Original canopies survive largely intact at platform level, although the painted masonry side walls were not constructed until the 1980s to replace earlier timber screens.

Features: An air raid shelter built during World War 2 is still to be found behind the retaining wall on the eastbound platform. The tracks leading to the former Midland Railway coal depot were removed in August

1966 but their route may still be observed as one approaches the station from the west.

West Ruislip

Central 0.5m Surface

Layout: Street level ticket hall leading down to one island platform via a staircase.

History: Opened as 'Ruislip & Ickenham' on 2 April 1906 by the Great Western & Great Central Joint Committee. The station was renamed 'West Ruislip (for Ickenham)' on 30 June 1947, with the suffix being lost over the years. The platforms were rebuilt in advance of the inauguration of Central Line services on 21 November 1948, although the new street level building was not completed until the early 1960s.

Design: The main station building resembles Curtis's design at Northolt, albeit on a somewhat larger scale. It features a concrete canopy across its full width, with a complete glazed facade above. Extensive use of blue wall tiling is made within the large rectangular ticket hall, which is still lit by early postwar fluorescent light fittings. An overbridge linked to the ticket hall connects the Underground station with the adjacent British Rail staircases and platforms. The Central Line platform is very similar to others on the 1940s extension, with its curved concrete canopy and original sign boxes around the base of the supporting columns, although it is particularly notable for its narrowness.

Westbourne Park

Hammersmith & City 2.9m Surface

Layout: Street level ticket hall leading down to two single platforms via staircases.

History: Opened as 'Westbourne Park & Kensal Green' on 1 February 1866, served by both GWR and MR trains, although this section of line had been opened on 13 June 1864 by the semi-independent H&CR. The original timber buildings were replaced by new structures on an adjacent site on 1 November 1871, from which time the station was renamed 'Westbourne Park'. Ownership transferred to the LTE on 1 January 1970 and British Rail services ceased using the adjacent platforms in 1992.

Design: The current station building dates from 1871 and is the most interesting architecturally – with the exception of Hammersmith – on the entire line from Paddington. The street frontage is amongst the longest of any station on the system, with the plain central portion containing the ticket hall flanked by taller blocks, each housing retail units and displaying a curved parapet wall at high level. Extensive use is made of yellow brickwork, with red bricks to highlight particular features such as window arches. The ticket hall retains few of its original fittings and was substantially modified for UTS installation. Access to the trains is by means of simple, timber staircases and the platforms themselves remain little altered since construction. Their walls, canopies and fluted metalwork have been painted in a white and light grey colour scheme, which creates a bright and pleasant atmosphere, although it is a pity that some of the finer details of the ironmongery could not have been highlighted. Nevertheless, this remains a fine example of mid-Victorian inner London railway architecture.

Westminster

Circ/Dist 8.7m Sub-Surface

Layout: Sub-surface ticket hall leading down to two single platforms via staircases.

History: Opened as 'Westminster Bridge' on 24 December 1868. The station acted as the terminus of the DR until 30 May 1870, when services were extended eastwards to Blackfriars. A pedestrian subway linking the station to the Houses of Parliament was brought into use in the same year, although public access was not allowed until September 1934 when the staircase on the southern side of Bridge Street was opened. The station's name was shortened to 'Westminster' in 1907. On 15 December the previous year, a secondary entrance was opened on the Embankment, mainly to serve LCC Tramways passengers. The main building and ticket hall were reconstructed in 1923-4 and the Embankment entrance was rebuilt to allow the station to remain open in the interim. New canopies were provided in place of the overall roof at around this time.

Design: The station entrance is contained within the ground floor of an impressive stone building, while the entrance lobby and ticket hall are clad with materials common to modernisation projects in the mid-1920s. Large expanses of glazing within both walls and roof give the ticket hall a very airy aspect, although its appearance is marred by the lack of finishes on the ticket office frontage. The platforms retain many of their 1920s finishes and feature a particularly attractive valance along the edge of each canopy. However, the numerous reconstruction projects have left their inevitable marks upon the overall appearance, which seems unco-ordinated.

Features: The secondary entrance has not been in regular passenger use in recent years but is of particular historical interest because the design of the external facade was the first job to be undertaken by Charles Holden for the Underground. The plain, painted frontage is located within St Stephen's Parade on the Victoria Embankment.

canopy level. Pole-mounted roundels are located on the walls on either side, giving the station a very prominent street presence. The ticket hall presents an impressive sight to users, with its high ceiling, dominant supporting columns and overall spaciousness. High quality materials, such as faience tiling and bronzework, have been utilised throughout and fortunately their use was continued when the new ticket office was incorporated in the late 1980s. The platforms are almost entirely under cover, although a large amount of natural light is able to penetrate through large skylights. Four combined roundel/seating units survive on each platform and contribute towards the attractive nature of this interesting station.

Features: The wide bays facing the ticket office once acted as access to a concourse leading to a subway under Wood Lane to the White City stadium. Although partially blocked-in, some original finishes survive, along with a bronze barrier which was once adjacent to one of the three original passimeters. An original lamp standard is located at the southern end of each platform – the only examples of this type that survive other than those in the forecourts at Wanstead and Redbridge. A plaque commemorating the building's Festival of Britain Award for Merit may be found on the facade.

White City

Central 3.7m Surface

Layout: Street level ticket hall leading down to two island platforms serving three tracks, via an overbridge and staircases.

History: Opened on 23 November 1947 to replace the earlier Wood Lane station, located around 300m to the east. The platforms originally served only two through roads, with the other road acting as a reversing bay. The service changed to its current arrangement in July 1948, with all outstanding work to the station buildings being completed at around the same time.

Design: Designed by K. J. Seymour (under T. Bilbow's direction) in the Holden tradition, the main building is a large yellow brick structure, dominated by a large silhouette roundel within the glazing above

Whitechapel

Dist/EL/H&C 6.3m Misc

Layout: Street level ticket hall leading down to two island surface platforms, via an overbridge and staircases, and to two sub-surface platforms (serving the East London Line) via staircases.

History: The original station was opened by the East London Railway on 10 April 1876, although Metropolitan Railway trains did not serve the station until 31 March 1913. It became the main terminus of the East London Line from 19 November 1939 when services to Hammersmith and other Metropolitan Line termini ceased.

The DR platforms were opened as 'Whitechapel (Mile End)' on 6 October 1884 and served as the eastern terminus until

Above:
The street frontage of Charles Clark's building at Willesden Green.

Below:
Great Northern atmosphere intact at Woodside Park.

1 February 1902. It was then closed for exactly four months to allow reconstruction work prior to the extension of services to Upminster. Ticket hall facilities for the two railways were combined from this time. The DR station had been renamed 'Whitechapel' on 13 November the previous year. The trains on the Hammersmith & City section of the MR used the station as a terminus between 3 December 1906 and 30 March 1913, and again as a through service from 30 March 1936. The Hammersmith & City Line assumed its own identity in November 1988.

Design: Most of the upper levels of the station date from its reconstruction at the turn of the century. Two sets of timber entrance doors occupy almost the complete base of an attractive three-storey building, constructed of white glazed brickwork and built to serve passengers using East London Railway platforms. A standard glazed canopy was added by the 1930s and this spoils the facade's appearance by cutting across the decorated keystones of the chequered window arches. The ticket hall is one of the most attractive on the Underground, although its small size renders it inadequate to deal with the station's considerable usage. Its high, fully glazed ceiling is supported by ornate metal brackets. These, along with the timber panelled ticket office frontage, have been highlighted through the use of imaginative paintwork.

Access to the District Line platforms is notable for the many changes of level users are expected to overcome. A high arched interchange area leads on to an overbridge of almost complete timber construction. The platforms themselves are in a substantial cutting and have no features of real interest. The East London Line platforms are accessed from the District Line platforms by means of two subways, constructed in the mid-1930s and clad with the standard faience tiled finishes of the time. The platforms were partially refurbished at the same time as other stations on the line between 1979 and 1982, yet the orange melamine panels do little to relieve the gloomy atmosphere prevalent in these areas.

Features: The remains of the 1880s DR station facade, including the top of the arched windows, may be observed directly to the left of the current entrance.

Willesden Green

Jubilee 5.5m Surface Grade II (prop.)

Layout: Street level ticket hall leading down to one island and two single platforms via staircases.

History: Opened as 'Willesden Green' on 24 November 1879 as the temporary terminus of the M&SJWR extension from West Hampstead. It was renamed 'Willesden Green & Cricklewood' between 1 June 1894 and 1938. Minor rebuilding works were carried out around 1906, including the opening of an extra entrance and construction of a new bay road on the northern side of the station. Reconstruction work, including the provision of new platforms to serve fast trains, was completed in January 1914. The station was later substantially rebuilt at street level, with work being completed in September 1925. Services were transferred to the Bakerloo Line on 20 November 1939, although Metropolitan Line trains continued to use the station until 7 December 1940. The Jubilee Line took over responsibility for the Stanmore branch of the Bakerloo Line on 1 May 1979.

Design: This station's magnificent street building is without doubt the most attractive on the entire line. Designed by C. W. Clark to replace the original brick structure, it is faced entirely with cream terracotta tiling, with gilded lettering at high level. Each of the two entrances is covered by a large cantilevered canopy, with retail units occupying the remainder of the lower frontage. A large diamond-shaped clock – the first example of this distinctive feature of Clark's stations of this period to be installed – is bracketed from the wall at first floor level. The ticket hall retains many of its original finishes and fittings, including an ornate metal gate-line and distinctive green mosaic tiling throughout. It has been further enhanced through the provision of attractive cream floor tiling and a new lighting scheme under a recent refurbishment project. The main island platform is particularly notable for having some of the few tiled surfaces that exist on the open area of a surface station, although the original 1925-vintage tiles have recently been renewed to a similar design.

Features: The rebuilt station of 1925 included the provision of a parcels lift to platform level, although no evidence of this equipment now remains.

Wood Green

Layout: Street level ticket hall leading down to two single platforms via escalators and a low level concourse.

History: Opened on 19 September 1932 on the Piccadilly Line extension from Finsbury Park to Arnos Grove. Some contemporary maps showing the intended route of the new railway referred to this station as 'Lordship Lane'.

Design: The surface building is rather different from any other Holden designed for stations on the Piccadilly Line extensions. Its wide convex frontage is reminiscent of South Wimbledon built six years earlier, although their scale and construction are completely different. A concrete canopy extends across the entire breadth of the facade and covers the three entrances, flanked by a retail unit on either side. Iron balustrades between the entrances incorporate a representation of the stations on the Cockfosters extension in diagrammatic form. The large ticket hall receives considerably less natural light compared with most Holden-designed stations, as most of its glazing is at high level only. The ticket office has been built out from the main building structure, thereby spoiling the space's integrity. However, brown quarry tiles matching the originals have been installed in order to integrate with the overall design. The low level areas of the station are very similar to those of the other tube stations on the eastern extension and distinguished only by the green striped borders around the cream wall tiling. Decorative metal ventilation grilles, designed by Stabler, are to be found within the platform walls.

Woodford

Layout: Two street level ticket halls leading to one island and one single platform, linked by a subway and footbridge.

History: Opened on 22 August 1856 by the ECR. The station was rebuilt by the GER between 1888 and 1892, and further

modifications were carried out in preparation for the commencement of Central Line services on 14 December 1947, with the station acting as the terminus until 21 November the following year.

Design: The ticket hall buildings have been extensively remodelled over the years, the one on the eastbound side having been extended and rebuilt with a new ticket office as recently as the mid-1980s. The westbound ticket hall was added in 1892 but partially rebuilt in the late 1940s and is now reached by means of a covered walkway. Most of the platform buildings date from the main c1890 reconstruction and feature an attractively valanced canopy supported by decorated fluted pillars. The plain brick building to the west of the footbridge on the eastbound platform was added in the late 1940s and contrasts sharply with the lovely timber framed finishes of the original station's waiting room.

Features: Woodford is the only station to retain both its ECR and GER buildings in operational use, although the former no longer serves as a ticket hall.

Woodside Park

Layout: Street level ticket hall leading to two single platforms, which are linked by a footbridge.

History: Opened as 'Torrington Park, Woodside' on 1 April 1872 by the GNR and given its current title on 1 May 1882. Northern Line services were extended to this station from East Finchley on 14 April 1940.

Design: Woodside Park is among the loveliest stations on the entire Underground system and retains the feel of the small, main line station it once was. The main, yellow brick building is fronted by a large forecourt and is spoilt only by the blocking-in of some of the windows for the installation of the UTS ticket office. Some original features of the small ticket hall remain, such as the stone fireplace in the waiting area and the entrance doors. Both platform buildings are constructed from the same yellow brick and retain their valanced canopies and two of their 1940s silhouette roundels. The platforms are linked by a particularly attractive latticed footbridge, which also serves a public right of way over the tracks. The large amount of greenery on either side adds to this station's distinctly rural atmosphere.

Features: The beautifully decorated all-timber signal cabin to the north of the station dates from 1906 and is one of only four remaining on the Underground – the others being found at Ruislip, Chorleywood and Chesham. A still earlier example, albeit with a brick base, survives at the end of the northbound platform and is contemporary with the station's opening. A postbox dating from Queen Victoria's reign is to be found within the main station facade.

Above:
The escalators at Waterloo.

Closed stations on closed lines

Name (on closure)	Line	Opened	Closed	Changes of name
Brill	Metropolitan	1 December 1899	30 November 1935	
Granborough Road	Metropolitan	1 July 1891	4 July 1936	'Grandborough Road' until 5 October 1920
Hammersmith (Grove Road)	Hammersmith & City	1 October 1877	31 December 1907	
Hounslow Town	District	1 May 1883	1 May 1909	also closed between 31 March 1886 and 28 March 1903
Quainton Road*	Metropolitan	1 July 1891	4 July 1936	
South Acton	District	13 June 1905	29 May 1948	
Uxbridge Road*	Metropolitan	1 November 1869	19 October 1940	
Verney Junction*	Metropolitan	1 July 1891	4 July 1936	
Waddesdon	Metropolitan	1 January 1897	4 July 1936	'Waddesdon Manor' until 30 September 1920
Waddesdon Road	Metropolitan	1 December 1899	30 November 1935	'Waddesdon' until 30 September 1920
Westcott	Metropolitan	1 December 1899	30 November 1935	
Winslow Road	Metropolitan	1 July 1891	4 July 1936	
Wood Siding	Metropolitan	1 December 1899	30 November 1935	
Wotton	Metropolitan	1 December 1899	30 November 1935	

*Station on lines still used for BR freight

Closed stations on open Underground lines

Name (on closure)	Line	Opened	Closed	Stations on either side
Blake Hall	Central	18 November 1957	31 October 1981	Ongar/North Weald
Brompton Road	Piccadilly	15 December 1906	29 July 1934	Knightsbridge/South Kensington
City Road	Northern	17 November 1901	8 August 1922	Angel/Old Street
Down Street (Mayfair)	Piccadilly	15 March 1907	21 May 1932	Green Park/Hyde Park Corner
Marlborough Road	Metropolitan	13 April 1968	19 November 1939	Baker Street/Finchley Road
South Kentish Town	Northern	22 June 1907	5 June 1924	Camden Town/Kentish Town
Lord's (St John's Wood Road)	Metropolitan	13 April 1868	19 November 1939	Baker Street/Finchley Road
St Mary's	Metropolitan/District	1 October 1884	30 April 1938	Aldgate East/Whitechapel
Swiss Cottage	Metropolitan	13 April 1868	17 August 1940	Baker Street/Finchley Road
White City (Wood Lane)	Hammersmith & City	1 May 1908	24 October 1959	Latimer Road/Shepherd's Bush
York Road	Piccadilly	15 December 1906	17 September 1932	Caledonian Road/King's Cross St Pancras